# SHAKE SOME ACTION

'Stuart Coupe's passion and love for quality music is infectious. He has chronicled the emergence of generations of Australian artists and influenced both them and those who have followed his writing with respect – and sometimes envy – at his personal connections and observations.'
**Anthony Albanese, PM**

'With extensive music knowledge and a style unlike any other in the industry, I always know when I get the chance to talk music with Stuart Coupe in any capacity that I'm going to get lost down a rabbit hole of unexpected topics and thought-provoking mayhem. This is why he's one of my favourite journalists in Australia.'
**Kasey Chambers**

'Stuart has chaperoned charlatans, tangled with titans and represented reprobates, but ALWAYS with the best soundtrack. There's rarely a delicious music story not blessed with his shadow. About fuckin' time for this book.'
**Tim Rogers**

# SHAKE SOME ACTION

## My Life in Music
## (and other stuff)

# STUART COUPE

PENGUIN BOOKS

PENGUIN BOOKS

UK | USA | Canada | Ireland | Australia
India | New Zealand | South Africa | China

Penguin Books is part of the Penguin Random House group of companies
whose addresses can be found at global.penguinrandomhouse.com

First published by Penguin Books in 2023

Cover photography by Fairfax Media Archives/Paul Wright
Cover design by Josh Durham/Design by Committee
Typeset in 11.5/15.5 pt Adobe Garamond Pro by Midland Typesetters, Australia

Printed and bound in Australia by Griffin Press, an accredited
ISO AS/NZS 14001 Environmental Management Systems printer

 A catalogue record for this
book is available from the
National Library of Australia

ISBN 978 1 76104 636 0

penguin.com.au

We at Penguin Random House Australia acknowledge that Aboriginal and Torres Strait Islander
peoples are the Traditional Custodians and the first storytellers of the lands on which we live
and work. We honour Aboriginal and Torres Strait Islander peoples' continuous connection
to Country, waters, skies and communities. We celebrate Aboriginal and Torres Strait Islander
stories, traditions and living cultures; and we pay our respects to Elders past and present.

*For*
*Susan Lynch*

*And*

*Eddie, Frankie-Rae, Jay, Sara and Hugh*

# CONTENTS

# 1

# BORN TO RUN

'I hear you're from Australia – my name's Bruce too,' laughs the figure sitting at a table covered by glasses, half-finished drinks and pizza boxes; someone who's clearly spent more than a few hours watching the Monty Python sketches on cable TV.

This is Bruce Springsteen. Not yet a global megastar – his *Born In The USA* album is still a few years away – but already one of the most revered and respected rock'n'roll figures on the planet. He's also one of my heroes.

Did I mention that we're in Paris? The one in France. It's 3 am on an extremely chilly morning in April 1981. It's just me and Springsteen sitting at a table backstage after his sell-out show that night at the 5000-capacity Palais des Sports. The previous night was sold out as well. It's Springsteen's first appearance in France.

Towels, guitars and clothing are scattered around the room. The gig ended hours ago but Springsteen is receiving a stream of journalists who've been flown to Paris for these shows. I'm the last to be given an audience.

I'd met him briefly the night before. I'd attended a post-show party at a ritzy nightclub-cum-disco called Captain Video that Springsteen's record label, CBS, had taken over for the evening.

It's like a normal disco but maybe a little classier than most. On the video screen I see clips of Rose Tattoo and some live footage of The Angels. On the way to the gig I'd seen big posters advertising upcoming concerts from the Tatts.

Springsteen and his E Street Band arrive at the party at 3 am. At one point he comes over to the table where I'm sitting. He looks tired and is dressed in the obligatory blue denim jeans and a lumber jacket. His voice is a husky rasp.

'Sorry I can't talk, but why don't you come backstage after the show tomorrow night?'

OK, this is pretty damn weird. Surreal. It hits me just what an out-of-body moment this is. Like seriously, out in the stratosphere of mind-blowing weird.

I'm 25 years of age, on my first overseas trip, have just had my brain explode in New York City, and then had a counterpunch of seeing Springsteen and his band in concert for the first time in Paris and – *hold it right there* – the guy has just invited me to come backstage tomorrow night and – you know, chat. Me and Bruce chat.

This is the kind of thing that's supposed to happen to real deal, established music journalists. It's the conversation you'd expect Springsteen to have with the writers I aspire (in my star-eyed dreams) to be like: people like Nick Kent, Dave Marsh and Lester Bangs. The heavyweights. The legends in their field.

This sorta stuff really doesn't happen to a kid from Launceston, who only just scraped through the equivalent of the HSC and doesn't have a whole lot of writing experience. This kid who can't type with more than one finger, who's never going to win any sort of spelling competition, and who finds all this talk about verbs and adjectives vaguely confusing. Of course, I'm flattered – and more than a little stunned. I'm wondering now if I actually am the real deal or a pretender who's just gotten really, *really* lucky. Am I up to this?

Sure, this kid is an absolute and total music obsessive, who's dreamt for years of being able to convey and share that love and enthusiasm with others in print. But this? Paris. Bruce Springsteen. Tomorrow night.

My head had already exploded once today. Springsteen's three-hour performance had been one of the greatest things I'd ever seen. And I'd watched a lot of it standing next to his manager, Jon Landau, who'd previously been a music writer and a major influence on me. This is the guy who said, back in 1974, 'Tonight I saw rock'n'roll future and its name is Bruce Springsteen.' A line that really did reverberate around the planet.

Even before that, I'd literally gasped after entering my hotel room. Throwing open the curtains, I'd been confronted by the very close and very, very amazing Arc de Triomphe. No shit, Sherlock – I really am in Paris. To see and talk to Bruce Springsteen.

This is the Springsteen that I've been – and I'll use the word deliberately here – obsessively listening to since I heard a song of his, 'Mary, Queen Of Arkansas', from his debut album in 1973. It was played by Chris Winter, the deep-voiced presenter on the *Room To Move* ABC radio show, which I'd managed to pick up on the crystal radio attached to the phone in my parents' bedroom.

A little later, my science teacher, John Woodroffe, returned from a trip to England with a copy of that album, *Greetings From Asbury Park, NJ*, for me. I almost wore it out. I did the same with his next one, *The Wild, The Innocent & The E Street Shuffle*, which I ordered from the CBS Record Club – 'five albums for $1 and then buy one a month'.

Come 1975 and I was moving out of home into my first share household in Launceston and *Born To Run* was the soundtrack to my last summer in Tasmania. I was in Adelaide and about to relocate to Sydney when *Darkness On The Edge Of Town* came out and I reviewed it for *Roadrunner* magazine. I was just starting to think that writing about music was something I could do and I loved writing about Bruce Springsteen – as did every other music writer on the planet. I was reading them all and trying to learn how they conveyed their excitement and passion about him to others. *This* was what I wanted to do.

By the time *The River* came out late in 1980, I was the music writer for *The Sun-Herald*, the biggest-selling newspaper in the country – and I was already known as a Springsteen tragic. I loved an enormous amount of music but *Bruce Springsteen was it*.

This did not escape the attention of the hierarchy of CBS Records, who were – hard as it is to believe now – struggling to break Springsteen in Australia. They reckoned someone needed to see him in concert. They decided that person was me. And that they should send me to Paris to see a few shows and hopefully talk to Springsteen – and soon.

So here I am. I've been eking out a living from writing about music for less than two years and I'm sitting backstage yacking with my idol.

I've been waiting for a few hours, wandering the corridors of the venue, but not ranging too far away in case my turn arrives. Springsteen has come off stage and done what he always does – has a massage. I'm told nothing interrupts that post-show routine. Not even immediate family.

Around 2.30 am the band and most of the touring party leave in a bus for their hotel. Only Landau and a few others are hanging around. There are still about 80 fans shivering outside, waiting to see Springsteen.

Half an hour later and I'm ushered in to see him. The dressing-room reeks of liniment and looks and smells like a football team change room. Springsteen is visibly tired. He's short – shorter than he appears onstage even, dressed again in jeans and an old jacket. His skin bears the marks of adolescent pimples and his jaw juts out. He mumbles and his rambling conversation reminds me of Molly Meldrum on *Countdown*. I'm not allowed to record the conversation. This is not a formal interview, just a chat.

We talk for about an hour and around 4 am Springsteen announces he wants to eat. He signs my concert program, 'To Stuart. It was nice to meet you. See ya in Australia. Bruce Springsteen.'

Then I walk with him outside to the fans who are still waiting. It is seriously freezing. Springsteen signs a few dozen autographs before hopping into a car and heading off. I go back to my hotel and watch the sun come up over Paris as I frantically scribble down everything from the conversation, which will become a 10,000-word cover story for *Roadrunner* and appear in various forms around Australia in numerous publications.

The next day I'll go to London to interview John Lydon, Mike Oldfield, The Psychedelic Furs, and an array of others.

I'm travelling too fast for it all to really sink in. It seems like only a heartbeat since I was wondering if I could get good enough to write about local bands for the Launceston *Examiner*.

Whilst chatting to Springsteen I'd mentioned 'Friday On My Mind' by The Easybeats. Springsteen shook his head in admiration.

'That song . . . forget it . . . it's one of the greatest rock'n'roll records ever . . . and one of the hardest to play. I never could get the chords right to that one. I used to try real hard, but they'd never be exactly right.'

I go back a while with 'Friday On My Mind'. In fact, without that song I mightn't have been sitting with Springsteen. Or writing these pages.

Wanna hear about it?

# 2
# FRIDAY ON MY MIND

There was something about the infectiousness of it coming through my transistor radio that I found irresistible – and still do five decades later and after hearing it hundreds and hundreds of times. It happened again just the other day, after I watched newly unearthed footage of the band performing the song for the BBC cameras in England.

It was the sound of Stevie Wright, Harry Vanda, George Young, Dick Diamonde and Gordon 'Snowy' Fleet, towards the end of 1966, singing a song called 'Friday On My Mind'.

It wasn't the first pop song I'd heard on the radio, but it *was* the one that galvanised all sorts of emotions in me. Of course, I really knew nothing about the working week, beyond it being something my father was engaged in. I had no understanding of that sense of starting the week already yearning for it to end.

'We're gonna have fun in the city.' Hang on, I'm in Launceston, population roughly 30,000, I'm 10 years old, and I'm many years away from the craziness of city life on a weekend. And of despising nothing more than 'working for the rich man'. It would be a stretch to suggest that these words were reaching deep into my political consciousness.

But I loved this song. Craved it. It was, and still is, a near-perfect combination of lyrics and music. Catchy as all get out, and with a seeming simplicity that belies a finely crafted piece of pop music.

In 1967, 'Friday On My Mind' was a big hit record. It was constantly on the radio – on 7EX in Launceston and around the country. I wanted a copy. My own copy. In my mind, I *needed* a copy. My parents told me that if I saved my pocket money, it was up to me what I spent it on. Well, that was the theory, anyway.

My mum and dad owned a large radiogram, which dominated one wall of the living room. They had records. Herb Alpert & The Tijuana Brass records. I recall *South Of The Border*, a Rolf Harris record, *The Black And White Minstrel Show*, and the one with 'Zorba The Greek' on it. There were Burl Ives albums, the soundtrack to *South Pacific*, various *Reader's Digest* collections, the Bing Crosby Christmas album, a Seekers album, and a record by my mother's favourite singer – Jim Nabors, who played Gomer Pyle in the TV show. This wasn't exactly a 1960s hipster household.

I don't recall my father ever putting a record on. If that happened – and it was, believe it or not, a rare occurrence – it was my mother lowering the tone arm. I never really spoke to my dad about music and never observed him listening to it. I didn't speak much to my father at all.

Like his father, my dad was a manager for the English, Scottish & Australian Bank, the ES&A – fondly referred to by my father as the 'Easy, Slow & Awkward'. As a kid, whenever I'd visit the bank to withdraw money (*my* pocket money) he would instruct the tellers not to give it to me if he thought I was overspending.

Being a manager at the Launceston branch of the ES&A was a solid job and by the mid-'60s my parents had bought the house I did most of my growing up in: 19 Walden Street, Newstead. But, what's that saying – never tell the devil your plans? Within weeks of moving in, the bank told my dad that they were transferring him to Hobart. However, moving to Hobart wasn't part of the plan, and, after discussing it with my mum, he decided to turn the role down.

ES&A weren't happy and, from that point on, decided to make my father's life difficult. His new title was Relieving Manager. In other words, whenever a manager at a regional branch was due for holidays, my father would be sent to take over for that period. Consequently, he was away from home a lot, frequently only coming home at weekends if the drive was too long for him to get back each night.

My weekly pocket money was the comparatively new 20-cent coin that had been ushered in on 14 February 1966 – a date I can still remember without looking it up. (There was a massively popular jingle at the time, heralding the arrival of decimal currency. I suspect that nearly every kid of that era can still remember it: 'On the 14th of February, 1966 . . .')

The cost of a single was $1.05, so in effect, with no other outgoing expenditure, I was pretty much there after five weeks. I earnt my pocket money largely from doing a Saturday-night paper round, usually accompanied by my father, as I was scared out of my mind walking down long driveways in the dark to deliver the newspaper, hopeful of getting a small tip.

Nothing wavered. I had enough money for a single and I wanted – no, needed – 'Friday On My Mind'. I was dutifully driven into the centre of town and into Jessups, the furniture shop that doubled as Launceston's only purveyors of vinyl. A tantalising display resided in the left-hand corner at the back of the building, behind the fridges, clothes dryers and other white goods. A quick transaction and 'Friday On My Mind' was inside a brown paper bag, cellotaped closed and on the way to 19 Walden Street with its new owner.

Something important was about to happen in my life. A crucial and early experience of the cultural divide between generations. One that I wasn't really cognisant of. We now reflect on the adage that rock'n'roll is meant to separate parents from their kids. We're always told that your mum and dad are meant to hate it, that it's a marker for your realisation that there's a generation gap – that there's *us* and there's *them*.

This dictum hadn't previously been tested in my home. It would be time and time again in future years, but this was the first occasion I'd waved a red flag at the generational bull. Rock'n'roll was comparatively new and hadn't been a subject for discussion at Walden Street – until now.

And I had no idea of what was ahead. I wanted everyone to love what I did. I still do. It's an attitude that's shaped everything I've done in my writing and radio life. The message is simple: I love this, I think you might too, and this is why. Let's have this experience together. Let's celebrate this song, record or artist.

We arrived home and I insisted that there be a family gathering to hear this – my very first record that I loved so much and assumed the entire world would love as much as I did. My brother, Martin, was only seven, and what he thought wasn't a huge issue. It was my parents whose approval I was desperate for.

I corralled my mother and father into the living-room and positioned them on the couch for maximum exposure to *my record*. I was beyond excited. It was inconceivable that they'd fail to embrace these sounds that had so galvanised me.

After turning the knob to an acceptably loud volume, I'd made sure there were no television sounds from the next room and that the radio Mum listened to in the kitchen was turned off. Did I go so far as to lift the phone handle off the receiver? Almost certainly. I'd put my pocket money on this moment. Nothing was left to chance. I needed two minutes and 43 seconds of undivided attention.

Then I lowered the tone arm on the record player. This was my version of 'Houston, we have ignition'. It was arguably the most important moment of my adolescence, the moment I made a definitive statement about who I was and what I loved.

It didn't go well. It would be the equivalent of an explosion almost immediately after take-off. We were less than 30 seconds in before the look on my father's face made it obvious that, no, we were *not* as one on this. The words 'racket' and 'rubbish' were uttered. My mother remained silent, as my (normally rather subdued) father left no doubt that he couldn't stand this abomination. This was not music. This was *noise*. This was a waste of money. What did I think I was doing?

I wasn't angry. There was no sense of confrontation. No, 11-year-old me was devastated. I burst into tears and ran out of the house. At this stage there was no back fence, just a vacant block of land. I was halfway across it before my father caught up with me, grabbed me and dragged me back home.

Such was my youthful trauma that I seem to have erased what happened next from my memory banks. But I'm sure there was an overriding sense of acute disappointment, coupled with a bewilderment that others – the people closest to me on the planet – weren't embracing something I loved so much. How could someone be so affected by a song – and we're not talking death metal here, we're talking a catchy piece of pop music – that everybody else didn't feel the same way about?

I'd later realise it was a moment that shaped much of what I've done in my chosen career. Sure, there were moments of arrogance in my 20s when I wrote some pretty caustic reviews and commentary. However, even then, it was really me saying variants on, 'There is so much great, great music out there and you're being force-fed a diet by the major record labels.' Or '*You* need to hear this and you need to hear it *now*.' At age 11, I wanted to share my love of songs with others. Nothing's changed.

And whenever a child or younger person in my life expresses delight and excitement about a song or artist that maybe I'm not overly taken with, I'm mindful of never – *ever* – even coming close to suggesting that they're listening to something inferior or uncool. They're listening to music that matters to them – and I'm good with that.

# 3
# I'M A BOY

'I'm A Boy'! I loved that song by The Who. Not as much as 'Friday On My Mind', but it was right up there. It was an articulation – and isn't that what all great songs really are – of who and what I was at the time. A typical boy, very quiet and maybe with early signs of an obsessional personality.

I loved toy soldiers, my Meccano set, and the Cuisenaire blocks I was given when I had my tonsils out. I played Cowboys and Indians around the home, had a collection of Matchbox cars, and later a Scalextric racing track and cars. I loved marbles and was pretty fixated on – but not all that skilled with – the yo-yo. I favoured the Coke one over the Fanta version. And there were family board games. My favourite was Test Cricket. In this game, batters semi-regularly scored five from a delivery. The rarity of this in the real sport seemed a bit of a structural flaw to me. Nonetheless, a wave of nostalgia flooded through me when I found a reasonably priced original game on eBay recently and managed to get it.

And I collected VFL and cricket cards. In those days, not only was there a star on the front of the card, but each one had an image on the back that made up part of a huge jigsaw when you laid them all out on a table or the floor. I was always desperate for the complete set. I'd buy endless – like dozens and dozens – of packets of gum in this pursuit and go to all lengths to trade for the cards I needed in the yard at school. I can still easily conjure up the sugary taste of the bubble gum that accompanied the cards.

But although I was Aussie Rules obsessed, could I play it? No way, I was hopeless. While, more than anything, I loved holding a Sherrin footy, lacing up my boots and running around a field, I was timid, not at all strong and, hey, had absolutely no desire to get hurt. And it seemed as if most of the kids kicking footballs on the oval down the road from our house were much bigger, taller and faster than me. That may not have been the case but perception – and self-protection – is everything. In essence, I was a scaredy cat, which was at complete odds with my love of the game.

The typical Australian kid, I played footy in winter, and tennis and cricket in the summer. I kept scrapbooks in those days, which are fascinating to look back on now. They're mainly full of clippings about tennis – tournaments I was in, local players I knew, and the international tournaments and stars.

I seemed to have a natural aptitude for tennis and cricket, with their smaller and more manageable balls. Tennis was way less scary than footy to play. Whilst I loved cricket, I was no fan of those incredibly hard balls whizzing around my head, particularly when you were expected to catch – or hit – one travelling at some speed.

I'd also talked my parents into getting a subscription to the American magazine *Tennis World*, which arrived surface mail every month. It took about three months to get to Australia, but that did little to diminish my excitement when a new issue arrived. It was partly the magazine itself; partly getting mail from another country. That was a big day.

One scrapbook has a photo of the American star Pancho Gonzales on the front. Inside I found some pics of me at the tennis club, including one with Helen Gourlay, who was a big deal in Launceston. She was a serious player and reached the finals of two Grand Slam tournaments – the French Open in 1971 and the Australian Open in 1977, when she lost to Evonne Goolagong. Her parents lived just up the road from me and had a clay tennis court, which I used to play on often with my dad. In fact, it was the site of my first-ever tennis victory over him. It took him a while to deal with that.

There's also a photo of me with my Launceston junior tennis club team-mates, about to board our Fokker Friendship to go and play in Melbourne. It was my first time on a plane. I thought it would be exciting, but actually I hated flying – and still do. That didn't stop me being obsessed by planes and the pilots who flew them. I still dream of writing a book about airline pilots, but I can't find a publisher who shares my enthusiasm. I suspect there are those who thought a book about what happens in kitchens in New York City was a really silly idea – until *Kitchen Confidential* came along. I am happy to be the Bourdain of the cockpit.

I was an OK tennis player, but one day my world changed when it was raining and my tennis coach suggested we go to the nearby squash centre and hit a few balls around. *Bang*. I took to squash immediately. I loved the precision and the tactics – and I seemed to have an aptitude for it.

I became squash obsessed, played it endlessly, and scored a part-time job at the local centre, where I took bookings and taught the basics to beginners. I'd go in every Sunday armed with my portable record player and a dozen LPs to keep me company. I bought a Rolling Stones tongue logo patch and asked Mum to sew it on one of my squash shirts. Rockin' squash.

Eventually, I became good enough to represent Tasmania in the Australian squash championships in Perth in 1973 and Adelaide a year later.

Stuck in my scrapbooks is also one of the few photos I have of my father. He's smiling and holding his tennis racquet when he was – I'm guessing – about 16 and at the Hutchins school in Hobart. He was sent there as a boarder after his mother died when he was nine years old. I still think how gut-wrenching that must have been for him – to lose his mother so young and then be bundled off to a boarding school far away from where his father lived.

Incidentally, Dad and I didn't do a lot of that father/son stuff – apart from going to the footy together, playing tennis, and watching *Homicide* on TV.

For a while, it was a Thursday-night ritual. My dad loved that show and I still do.

There were so many things to engage with – the instantly recognisable *Homicide* theme music, for starters. I loved the classic cast of Leonard Teale, George Mallaby, Alwyn Kurts and Norman Yemm. My era was the black-and-white, gritty one before the advent of colour television. The crimes were often relatively confrontational for a kid my age. This probably contributed to me being a scaredy cat to this day. Fascinated by crime and mystery fiction and non-fiction but with absolutely no enthusiasm for going near the real thing. The most important thing about these times were that I felt grown up, allowed briefly into my dad's world. That was a big deal.

Back to the scrapbook, and my emerging sense of political awareness is evident in pages of newspaper clippings about demonstrations at Kooyong, the centre of competitive tennis in Melbourne at the time. It was 1971 and I was a fired-up 15-year-old. In big red letters I've written, 'ANTI APARTHEID DEMONSTRATIONS – STOP THE MATCH!'

Another early indicator is a school project that has survived. I'm in class 2A (I think that's Year 8 in today's terminology), it's third term and Mr Murray is my teacher. My topic is 'The 60s'. In it, I've dealt with the landing on the Moon, the Vietnam War, deaths – Martin Luther King, President Kennedy, Malcolm X, My Lai (the massacre of unarmed South Vietnamese civilians by American troops in 1968) – and Pop Art & Music, where I've included a photo 'Bob Dylan on stage at Woodstock'.

(I now know that Dylan didn't appear at Woodstock and the singer with his face obscured by hair looks like – well, it could be Roger Daltrey, or just about anyone really. I was probably bargaining on Mr Murray not being totally down with this stuff.)

There's also a mini-essay on drugs, another on Experiments, which focuses on the first heart transplant, another on the Tasmania bushfires in 1967, two pages on the disappearance of Prime Minister Harold Holt, two more on Woodstock, and a big section on the Manson murders, complete with a colour photo of film director Roman Polanski at the scene, with the word 'PIG' clearly visible in blood on the house door.

What does this add up to? A sport-obsessed kid with a nascent interest in radical politics, true crime, drugs and rock'n'roll. It was all there.

# 4

# GROWIN' UP

When did I first decide that I wanted to spend most of my life writing about music and related bits and pieces? Why did I feel the urge to tell others about my passion? What was the drive? I'd always been a reader and carried ridiculous numbers of books with me in my school bag wherever I went. I even lugged the family Bible with me to church and Sunday school.

Growing up, I'd been fascinated by Enid Blyton's stories of the Famous Five and Secret Seven. I devoured all of my grandmother's Agatha Christie novels and still have the first one I owned myself: *The Mysterious Affair At Styles*. I read the Biggles books – about the fictional fighter pilot and adventurer – and Richard Compton's series about the schoolboy William. I read the classics too, via the Classics Illustrated series of comic books. And I delved into the real thing via a collection of great novels (think Jules Verne, Charles Dickens, Jack London, Alexandre Dumas) that my parents had lined up on the bookshelf, along with the mandatory set of World Book Encyclopedias.

I also read a lot about Australian rules football, and tennis and squash and cricket. Much of my early reading – particularly in the magazine world – suggested that, should I ever try my hand at writing, it would be about sport. And, with tennis, unlike footy, I was playing it, as well as reading endless pages about it.

Naturally, there were piles of music books – lots about Bob Dylan, a *New Musical Express* annual (from the days when magazines would bring out special end-of-year hardbacks), plus Richard Williams' *Out Of His Head: The Sound Of Phil Spector*, Ritchie Yorke's *Van Morrison: Into The Music*, and Hunter Davies' *The Beatles: The Authorised Biography*, which was first published in 1968. Given that I have a hardback, I either bought it very early on, or it was a slow seller in Launceston and copies hung around.

Then, again in a sign of things to come, I have *The Dead Book: A Social History Of The Grateful Dead* by Hank Harrison – not only the first book about a band I love, but written by the father of Courtney Love. And it came with a flexi-disc (which, yes, don't roll your eyes, of course I still have) of Neal Cassady 'rapping' on acid at the Straight Theatre in San Francisco in 1967 with the Grateful Dead doodling in the background.

My future fascinations and loves were clear from this early age. I was fortunate to be growing up in a home where reading was encouraged, particularly by my mother who avidly devoured books. I often looked at a prize she'd won at school – a hardback edition of *The Complete Works Of Shakespeare* – and shared her passion, and *her* mother's, for Agatha Christie mysteries.

Reading and words were in the family bloodline. All that was required was a love of music and what emerged was a young me. Just a kid from the suburbs of Launceston with a head full of dreams.

# 5

# BEHIND BLUE EYES

In day-to-day life, I doubt if many people would list sad or melancholic in descriptions of me. I have rarely been good at showing those feelings, keeping them hidden from even those closest to me. But I've always had a deep sense of melancholia. Was I born with it? Possibly – despite having observed very little sense of that mindset and behaviour in my family. But barely a day goes by that I don't see or hear something that gives me a sensation of deep sadness, isolation and aloneness. Sometimes, there is beauty in it, for sure – but often there is an overwhelming sense of despair.

I've never failed to be moved by a performance of Vaughan Williams' 'Greensleeves', or Henry Mancini's 'Moon River'. More often than not, it's instrumental music that will do it, as it allows free range for my imagination to go for a little run around the paddock. But I'm a sucker – a total sucker – for the sad song, which probably explains why this morning I pulled out the first album by Randy Newman (*Creates Something New Under The Sun*, if you're wondering what to look for), just so I could hear the precisely two minutes of the harrowing and plaintive 'Bet No One Ever Hurt This Bad'.

Sometimes it's the sheer intensity of the vocal delivery, combined with soaring music, that gets me. There are so many reasons why I shouldn't emotionally engage in a powerful, fundamental way with

Elvis Presley's version of 'An American Trilogy' – but when he hits the 'glory, glory, hallelujah, my truth is marching on', I'm a mess.

Although my brother and I never shared any closeness and were not great hombres, he was the source of my first experiences of melancholia. I remember the day he was allowed to walk from the first house we lived at in Tasma Street, East Launceston, to the corner shop by himself to buy a bottle of Fanta. He would have walked there with whatever it cost, stared up at the counter as he paid for it, and then carefully – ever so carefully – clutched it as he walked tentatively back home. Probably a journey of 10 minutes. I remember that he arrived at the front gate, faltered and tripped. The Fanta bottle flew out of his hands and smashed. He was so close. I felt so profoundly sad for him. And all these decades later, it still lingers with me, more than any other memory of that house.

Life was quiet. Because my brother required multiple surgeries for a medical condition, there were periods when my mother and brother were absent. It was probably during those times I remember my father teaching me how to play chess with his classic wooden set. He also loved stamps, which I would surreptitiously pinch from his collection to add to my own. As if he didn't know. I felt terribly guilty, but hey I needed those stamps.

Apart from the usual interaction with my parents and the occasional presence of my brother, I didn't have any close friends or playmates. And this didn't change. But it didn't bother me. I was sorta in my own world, although I wasn't without connection. I remember vividly the days and early evenings when I'd crouch on the floor in my parents' bedroom, with my crystal radio connected to their phone through a single earpiece, listening to the radio. With that tiny little plastic and metal gizmo – whose actual workings I still don't understand – I was plugged into a world of music, and voices talking about that music. Telling me what they liked about it, little snippets of information, and then playing those songs to the sponge at the other end of the line.

# 6
# SCHOOL'S OUT

For most of my school days in Launceston I was at Scotch College, a Presbyterian boys school. All the teachers were male; so were the students. I was told Mum and Dad said I went there because it was my grandfather's wish that I do. I'm not sure whether it was a carry-over from the idea that the first-born male shall ascend to the kingdom – but whereas I went to Scotch, my brother soon elected to jump to the public school Queechy High. I was never sure how my parents managed to scrape together the money for my schooling, because it wasn't cheap.

A large percentage of the students were boarders, kids whose parents owned properties in Northern Tasmania and offloaded the child-rearing side of their lives to the school system. Scotch was big on religion – prayer and a Bible reading before class every morning, and religious studies as a compulsory subject. It was also big on sport and cadets, giving reluctant kids like me a grounding in the military.

It was a typical conservative 1960s school. I wore a blazer and uniform, and any student who failed the hair-length test was sent home for rectification. That test involved a teacher being able to put a ruler between your shirt collar line and the bottom of your hair. If there wasn't a clear gap, you were perceived to be in danger of becoming a long-haired radical and sent home.

The teachers were a weird and wondrous lot. There was a blow-in from San Francisco, Sam Orr, who looked like he hadn't really left flower-power 1960s San Fran. My Economics teacher accused me of promoting communism when I started talking about workers and their rights in one of his classes, while my Maths teacher told me I worried too much. In sync with this, another American teacher, Buck Emberg, once said that I was the only true radical he'd encountered at Scotch. I was flattered, but then again, I realised you didn't need to do that much to earn that accolade. The potential Che Guevaras at Scotch were a little thin on the ground. I liked Emberg's sons too – they carried the flag for Grand Funk Railroad (particularly *E Pluribus Funk* and the live double album) at a time when the band's Tasmania fan club was a little small.

But by far the most influential of my teachers was the guy charged with imparting his knowledge of science. As I recall, I wasn't all that interested in the subject, but I had an affinity with John Woodroffe. He was a hardcore music fan, particularly of the left-field English kind, who was big on Roy Harper, Soft Machine and the like. We hit it off.

As with most teachers, Woodroffe did more than just teach his subject, and was involved in the general development of students. At some point I must have raised the idea of the school having its own magazine and he was particularly supportive of that. So we combined to produce one issue of *Labyrinth*. There was the obligatory school news and sports results and, dotted amongst it – guess what, yours truly writing about music and records. I still have a copy somewhere, which Woodroffe had kept and sent to me.

John Woodroffe was engaging, supportive and pretty darn cool in my eyes. I mean, he knew about Soft Machine *and* Roy Harper. Plus, he loved cricket. His wife, Katie, was an art teacher at Launceston Matric College and they were close friends with Bob McMahon, who was a mountain climber and also the reason I embraced the concept of anarchism. They reflected a life that I aspired to. Smart, erudite, loving books, art and music. I wanted to be like them.

On a trip to London during school holidays, Woodroffe brought me back two albums – *Greetings From Asbury Park, NJ* and John Cale's

*Paris 1919*. I'd heard both on Chris Winter's *Room To Move* ABC program. I was seriously and completely over the moon about these gifts. Records. From London. And two uber-cool releases. This completely cemented an already strong relationship. If only all my teachers were this cool and empathetic with the needs and desires of their students.

On a subsequent trip to London, Woodroffe was walking down a city street, when a pregnant woman attempting to end her life leaped off a building and landed squarely on top of him. He broke her fall, and the woman broke him. She and her baby survived, but poor Woodroffe suffered multiple fractures and still walks with a limp. This strange and bewildering fate makes me think about the consequences of actions. They almost always have an impact someplace else, and that impact can cause a lot of damage.

Despite Woodroffe's help, while I did OK at school I was far from a spectacular student. As my mother so succinctly put it one day, when we talked about my academic progress after a school report card had arrived, 'Darling,' she said, 'You're no Phar Lap.'

For the last two years of my formal high-school education, I left Scotch and went to Launceston Matriculation College. I managed to get my HSC over two years. Not with flying colours, more by the skin of my teeth. But my grades were good enough to gain me entry to a bunch of universities. I was very aware of the line in the folk song about being 'bound for South Australia' – it seemed like that was exactly the destination to which I was headed.

# 7

# INSPIRATION INFORMATION

When conversation turns to great and inspiring music writers, names like Lester Bangs (almost always), Greil Marcus, Robert Christgau, Dave Marsh, Paul Williams, Nick Kent and many others are frequently bandied about. Most of them are blokes, but in more recent years the likes of Australian writer Lillian Roxon, along with Ellen Willis, Lisa Robinson, Val Wilmer and others have received overdue recognition.

I devoured the work of all those figures, but whenever I'm asked about my biggest influence in the world of writing about music, I say Rob Smyth. And unless you're Australian, of a certain age, and a former reader of the weekly newspaper *Nation Review*, the usual response is, 'Who?' But Rob Smyth changed my life in ways that very few other figures have.

Because of him, from the age of 16 I became totally obsessed with communicating my nascent love of music to other people. It was not only the music Smyth wrote about, but the *way* he wrote about it – conversational, insightful, literate, and with the ability to convey a sense that if you heard whatever he was writing about, it really would enrich and change your world. And as much as anything, he taught me that it didn't matter what the music was, if it moved you that was all that mattered.

To that end, I often say that I've always believed there's nothing wrong with loving ABBA and Hank Williams – at the same time. I like to think that I'm not a musical snob, and in fact even less of a one as I get older. There are two types of music for everyone: that which moves you and that which doesn't. And I'm increasingly convinced that there is no such thing as 'bad' music. There's just music that you as an individual aren't moved by.

So, for a long time I've refused to get involved in creating 'Best of the Year' lists, especially in order. I always say that I'll run through the albums or songs that I've personally played the most in the previous year – but I won't rate them beyond that. Who am I to say that one record is better than another? Seriously. I certainly can say that there are albums and music that impacted on my psyche more than others – but does that make them better than those I didn't listen to as much? No, it doesn't.

Hey, I love *Philosophy Of The World*, the album by The Shaggs which is often cited as the world's worst album. If you're in the mood for The Shaggs, their album rocks. People say they can't play? Me – I have no idea. It has always seemed to me that technical proficiency frequently doesn't have much, if anything, to do with the creation of great music. And don't start me on the 'Bob Dylan can't sing' tangent that so many people carry on with. Heck, sometimes I even think that *I* can sing.

That way of thinking about music came from Rob Smyth. In the pages of *Nation Review*, he ranged far and wide with what he wrote about. The only things that albums needed to have for him to extol their virtues were that they moved HIM. And so through his columns, I – as a young kid in Launceston – was turned on to an incredible array of music.

Engaging with the latest issue of *Nation Review* was a ritual of much significance. I'd pretty much sense when the new issue would arrive at the corner shop two blocks from my home. I'd be there. Waiting.

The majority of *Nation Review* was pretty impenetrable to me. I understood the basics – Liberal Party = bad, ALP = good – but that was about it. It was pithy and irreverent and featured the likes of Bob Ellis, Phillip Adams and Mungo MacCullum. It was also where

I first encountered the cartoons of Michael Leunig. Yes, to a kid in Launceston, this was heavy-duty commentary on our life and times. And while I didn't understand a lot of it, boy did I aspire to be across everything these people wrote about and *how* they wrote it.

Really, though, I was buying it for half a page towards the back. I'd have read Smyth's column before I was home – and was devastated if it was an edition in which his ruminations didn't appear. Then I had a singular focus: how to get my hands on what he'd reviewed.

Things had changed in Launceston by now, and there was a dedicated record and cassette shop, Wills & Co, right in the centre of the city. I spent so much time flicking through the racks and buying albums, when I should have been paying rent. Would the Smyth-recommended record be there? If not, would they be able to get it in? How long would that take?

Or maybe Stefan Markovitch would have a copy? If not, how long would it take *him* to get one? I was one step removed from a junkie searching for a fix.

Large, loud and extremely animated, Stefan was my go-to guy for obscure and desirable import records. He had a stall at Salamanca Market in Hobart, which, in itself, was a reason to travel the couple of hours to that city. Stefan also made regular trips to Launceston, armed with crates of albums. He made it very clear that you would be a lesser person if you did not purchase said records then and there.

Stefan and Rob Smyth shared a passion for traditional English, Scottish and Irish folk music, which made it comparatively easy to get records by the Watersons, Martin Carthy, the Dransfields, Steeleye Span, Alan Stivell, Fairport Convention, Shirley Collins and many others.

Then, when the album was finally in my hands, came the almost religious experience listening on the record player at home – straining obsessively, willing myself to hear what Smyth heard, and to be moved like he was. And whilst listening to the latest acquisition, I'd cut out the review and cellotape it into my Smyth scrapbooks to read and reread and memorise. To let his words seep into my consciousness.

Whilst writing this book, I bought a few random issues of *Nation Review,* which no doubt I read at the time. One from March 1974 contained Smyth's rumination on three albums: The Lovin' Spoonful's *Do You Believe In Magic*, and the self-titled albums from The Band and Jesse Winchester.

Smyth reflects that he may have written about them previously, but is listening to them again, because 'I'm still only beginning to understand their depths, and many things that have come after them have taken my attention.' And then the kicker: 'In spite of the quiet space between us, I continue to believe that if it moves me, it will move someone else. Each of these albums is as critical to the essence and magic of rock as any more lately received.'

He concludes that his notes on these albums are brief but, 'if it does nothing more than acknowledge their existence then it'll do, because I trust you to find them somewhere and listen to their story. We mistake friends for strangers, floors for walls and great notions for weary schemes. I imagine no one could mistake the genius of these songs for anything less.'

And here's the other thing – Smyth wrote as if he was talking to *me*. Just me. 'Write like you talk,' another journalist friend would tell me some years later, and of course on radio possibly the most important thing you learn is to talk directly to your listener. There is only one. 'Hello, dear listener,' as Phillip Adams always says, even though tens of thousands of people are tuned in.

Rob Smyth spoke to me. And I listened.

For years, I kept all of the Smyth reviews in scrapbooks and carried them with me to Adelaide, where at some stage amidst a move they disappeared. When I made this discovery, I was devastated. I fossicked through every possession in search of them, and started wondering who might have borrowed – or stolen – them. I still fantasise that they're out there, and one day someone will text me, saying, 'We've found some scrapbooks of yours . . .'

When I started to write about music, all I did was try to mimic Smyth. Others would – more accurately – call it plagiarism. I so wanted to be able to write like he did, to convey my love and emotional responses to music like he did.

It was a bit like Jim Carroll and Frank O'Hara, two of my favourite poets, both chroniclers of New York City. O'Hara's most famous collection is *Lunch Poems*, published in 1964, observations whilst walking the streets of New York during breaks from work at the Museum of Modern Art. Years later, Carroll said that he used to follow O'Hara on his walks, trying to see what he saw and soak it up by osmosis.

I figured if I copied Smyth's writing, listened to the music that moved him and tried to articulate the way he did, maybe I could find a voice that was both respectful to what I'd learnt from him, but my own.

I've never met Smyth. A few people I encountered knew him. Someone told me he was a potato farmer who lived outside of Melbourne. That may not have been true, but I liked the notion of a potato-farming music writer. One certainty was that he used to buy records at the coolest record shop in Melbourne, Archie 'n' Jugheads. I heard this from the owners, two certified music nerds David Pepperell and Keith Glass, both of whom are still friends. Glass would figure prominently later in my story.

Many years ago, Rob Smyth and I somehow made contact. I sent him reams of photocopies of his writing that I had managed to hang on to, which he said he didn't have. At some stage in the 2000s, we talked a couple of times on the phone about Elvis Costello, as well as his plans to do a long review of one of the early volumes of the Bob Dylan bootleg series – but our exchanges petered out. I had the sense that he was faintly embarrassed by his writing from those days, and by my dribbling and gushing fandom for it.

My favourite and most lasting Smyth observation is what he wrote about Martin Carthy, regarding his performance on the *Selections* album with Dave Swarbrick. 'He sings with pity, grace, joy, sadness, love and hate. If these things mean little to you then so will his music. If you see your own life in them, he will elevate your soul.'

I typed those two sentences out and cellotaped them to the top right-hand corner of that album. They're still there and the record has travelled with me over five decades. He may be embarrassed to read this, but the influence of Rob Smyth is – one way or another – in every single word I've ever written. Thanks, Rob.

# 8

# WE GOTTA GET OUT
# OF THIS PLACE

I often think of sitting in the crowd watching Bruce Springsteen doing his keynote speech in Austin, Texas at South By Southwest. By 2012, the annual SXSW was the biggest music conference/event on the planet, with thousands of artists, delegates and music lovers gathering from around the globe. Even so, attracting Springsteen to give a talk was a coup of some magnitude.

In the speech, he explained how he owed just about everything to Eric Burdon and The Animals, and talked about the impact of 'We Gotta Get Out Of This Place', and other songs of theirs, such as 'It's My Life'.

Later that night, I was lucky enough to be at the showcase gig Springsteen and the E Street Band did in front of (for them) an extremely small audience of around 2000 people. There were lots of guests – Joe Ely, Alejandro Escovedo, Jimmy Cliff, members of Arcade Fire, and so forth.

Then Springsteen introduced Burdon, who came out exuding a sense of wonder and confusion – injustice, almost – that it was this Springsteen character and not himself who was the star of the show. But within a few minutes his ravaged and seemingly fragile voice strengthened, his mood appeared to lift, and he embraced the moment and roared alongside Springsteen and the band.

Burdon's songs, as articulated that morning by Springsteen, were – at their core, their very essence – about wanting, feeling, sensing, knowing that there was something better, and that you could get it somehow, but only if you wanted it badly enough.

I listened to these songs a lot, although my favourite album was the more psychedelic *The Twain Shall Meet*, with its songs about the Monterey International Pop Festival and the searing anti-Vietnam track 'Sky Pilot' – with bagpipes, long before AC/DC . . . and Paul McCartney.

But 'We Gotta Get Out Of This Place' was burnt into my psyche, largely because it articulated in just a couple of minutes what I knew in my heart – that I had to get out of Launceston. Even if, as the song goes, it was the last thing I'd ever do. And I didn't believe that bullshit for a second. There was LOTS to do – which was exactly why I wanted to get out.

Don't get me wrong. I loved Launceston – mainly as I really didn't know much else. For some reason I'd never connected with Hobart. The capital city of my island just didn't seem like a place offering the adventures and experiences that I sensed I was looking for. And on top of everything else, it was in the opposite direction, geographically, to where I really wanted to be.

Apart from a too-young-to-take-it-all-in trip to the Gold Coast with my parents as an eight-year-old, I'd only ventured out of the state once, to Melbourne – that week playing tennis in Ringwood. At the time I didn't realise that this was *far* from being the epicentre of the city – roughly 17 miles, actually. It was a bit like a trip to New York in which you only went to Queens.

(OK, there's a photo of me with my aunty at an empty Kooyong tennis stadium, which was a bit closer to the CBD, so I must have briefly gone there. Also, a lifelong claustrophobia reached its zenith on a pirate-themed boat ride at what must have been Luna Park in St Kilda. My stomach still churns writing about it.)

So, the world outside of Launceston was more or less alien to me in terms of personal experience. But I'd read and seen enough to know that there was more. I'd look at Launceston and hear Peggy Lee singing

'Is That All There Is?'. I didn't hate Launceston. Nothing like that. I just wanted more. Lots of more.

First up, I moved out of home, aged about 19. That was a big deal. I took a room in a share house that was far enough away from Walden Street that I felt I had independence – but close enough to take my washing home. The house was a collection of musicians, a travelling backpacker doing seasonal work, and some people my age I knew from around the place. I put posters on the wall of my room overlooking Launceston and moved my records in. People would drop in and out, there were two guys across the road who sold pot in shoeboxes at $30 a box. I never bought from them, but had close encounters around the kitchen table with people who did.

Musicians would arrive after gigs. One night, I sat chatting with the Sydney singer-songwriter Jeannie Lewis, who was in Launceston for a performance. Lewis was an extraordinary singer and performer with a well-honed left-wing political consciousness. She was part of what I considered to be the real-deal, Australian singer-songwriter scene, and, as such, I was more than a little in awe of her, let alone that she was in my room chatting after a performance. I have no recollection of what we talked about, but I suspect I said as little as possible, to avoid seeming totally uncool. That night, Lewis signed the photograph of her foot on my copy of her *Free Fall Through Featherless Flight* album.

That was federal election night, 17 May 1974. We were all hoping that the Labor Party would be returned, so Gough Whitlam could continue as prime minister. In 1972, after 23 years of Liberal–Country Party government, I'd walked the streets in an 'IT'S TIME' t-shirt, and nothing since had shaken my youthful fascination with Whitlam and the ALP.

By now, I'd enrolled at the Launceston university you go to when you're not going to uni, the College Of Advanced Education, with a far-from-committed notion that I'd become an English, Speech and Drama teacher. The campus was dull, and I was about a fortnight into the Drama bit when it became obvious that, as I struggled to be me, I certainly wasn't cut out to adopt multiple personalities and become a stage, or any other sort of, actor. And if I couldn't do it myself, there wasn't much chance of me teaching others.

Before long, though, I met some students who I connected with. Donald Pulford went on to a career in the theatre and Richard Lawrence drove my youthful fascination with Genesis, Family and other English prog-rock groups. Oh, how we pored over the lyrics of those early Genesis albums. There was a lot of heavy shit in *The Lamb Lies Down On Broadway*. Actually, whilst I didn't totally get it then that those early Genesis albums really had something going on, the more immersive true believers were convinced there was more depth than you'd ever get from *The Hobbit* or *Lord Of The Rings* – the two yardsticks of cosmic mind-bending at the time.

For the record I've never read either and can't imagine I ever will. I mean, if you get to 65 and haven't read *Lord Of The Rings*, what are the chances of you changing your mind?

So I bailed from these studies and – gulp – went on the dole. My parents were horrified. Their son relying on the government for support? Dad didn't say much (nothing new there, as he usually kept his thoughts on such things to himself), but my mother told me she was embarrassed to go to the tennis club, in case people asked what I was doing and she had to confront the reality of her dole-bludging son.

But there was a semi-masterplan. I could have gone to university in Hobart at a pinch but where was the mileage in that? Remember, Hobart in 1976 was a slightly bigger Launceston. No MOMA, no influx of cashed-up and sometimes interesting mainlanders. And it was further south. Next stop Antarctica.

No, I needed to get out of Tasmania. Find somewhere I could write, listen to music and read. A place that wasn't Launceston. Where to go? My matric results weren't exactly spectacular, but there were still a lot of universities that would take me. In this pre-internet age, the only way to explore the options was to go to the Launceston public library, where one could find the handbooks for every university in the country. So I sat in there and went through all of them looking for a university that would, firstly, accept me – and also be a place I'd want to be at.

Enter Flinders University. It was a comparatively new institute of learning on the outskirts of Adelaide, and already had a reputation as a radical place after student protests had resulted in the storming of the chancellery. I read through the handbook and noted that the Philosophy department had a heavy leaning towards texts by writers like Karl Marx, Mao Tse-tung, Friedrich Engels and Joseph Stalin. If you're recoiling at some of these names, remember that it was 1975 and I was 19.

As I read on, I realised with blinding clarity that Flinders was my university. This was also a no-fees world, and, incredibly, the government would pay for me to fly back home every holiday. But if that wasn't enough enticement, my friend David Woodhall was already living and working in the city at the ABC radio station. And the decider: my pretty-average matriculation marks were no barrier to Flinders embracing me. I was in.

So it was goodbye, first share house. Goodbye, Launceston. Hello, Adelaide. It was the beginning of 1976. And punk rock was in the air.

# 9

# ADELAIDE

It didn't take long for me to fall in love with Adelaide. In fact, I'm sure I'll never love it as much as I did during the couple of years I was there. These days whenever I go back, there are people I enjoy seeing and hanging out with – but it really feels like a big country town. People who live there like that, I guess.

But for me, when I arrived it was *the* big smoke. This was a city, baby. A big city. With import record shops and a couple of hip book-shops. Just about everything in Adelaide was pretty cool in this era – it was a happening place. For one thing, there was the Premier Don Dunstan, who is still the most impressive orator I've ever experienced. I got chills watching him speak one afternoon near the Festival Centre. He was at one of the focal points of a large progressive community of arty, political and social misfits and activists. I really think 1970s Adelaide was a once-in-a-lifetime occurrence and that I was lucky to stumble into it.

Sure, I was a bit lonely but I had a large room in the house in Collinswood where David Woodhall, his girlfriend and her sister lived. We smoked a lot of super-strong pot, ate mainly vegetarian meals . . . it was pretty good.

David also came from Launceston. I didn't really have close friends growing up – but he was close to being a close friend. His father was my doctor and the family lived within walking distance of my home. David lived in a converted garage with its own entrance. He smoked pot. I smoked pot with him. He had records by the Velvet Underground. In fact, he had all four of their studio albums. That was enough. Through him, I grew to love the Velvets. They were mysterious, decadent and from New York. And a few other things to boot. David also loved Genesis, Family and the like, who were much adored by some other guys we knew. I didn't really know gals who listened to records. It was very much a guy thing.

Another of David's obsessions was Spectrum, and the songwriting of its co-main guy Mike Rudd.

He wrote psychedelic-inspired, literate and wordplay-heavy lyrics, and elongated and musically adventurous compositions. OK, they had a hit with 'I'll Be Gone', but that was the accessible exception, rather than the rule. And there was a lot going on in those lyrics, especially if you were an intelligent Launcestonian teenager, with a head full of pot and an inquisitive mind prone to embracing the tangential.

We listened to Spectrum's double albums *Milesago* and *Terminal Buzz* – recorded live at their final gig. David had been to it, smoked his first joint with Mike Rudd and wrote a lengthy concert review for *Mushroom*, the college paper he'd started and edited. He could have, like me, pursued a career in writing, but chose radio announcing instead.

David had worked at 7LA and moved to Adelaide to be the rock-music announcer on the newly established ABC FM station. From this resulted a scam of some magnitude that still staggers me when I think of it. As part of my relocation, I had – of course – been accompanied by my record collection. Even then, I think I might have had several hundred.

It soon became obvious that the ABC didn't have much of a record library, so David and I concocted a scheme whereby my collection would be housed at the national broadcaster, literally a block and a half from where we lived. The station had someone at the front desk 24 hours a day and only one rock-music presenter, because, aside from David's show and Jim McLeod's jazz program, they played 90 per cent classical music. So it wasn't like there would be dozens of people handling, potentially scratching and 'borrowing' items from my precious collection.

In exchange for this instant library (which they'd hardly use), the ABC paid me $50 a week. This was about half of my weekly living requirements, and if I wanted to hear any of my own records I just had to wander around to the station and sign them out. This was just too perfect a situation and both the ABC and I benefited from the set-up. As far as David and the ABC were concerned, it was a lot cheaper than going out and buying the 1000 albums that Sydney-based presenter and music guru Chris Winter had suggested they needed to get started.

The scam was good – but a number of factors started to impact on David. All-night radio combined with Hunter-esque drug consumption eventually took its toll on him. An unresolved inner conflict between his love for old wave rock and punk exploded in the delusion that Radio Birdman were the same entity as MC5 and out to cause radical political change.

I managed to get David on a plane to Launceston for treatment and he was shocked back into reality. A few months later, he was back compering a season of a music television program, a precursor to *Rock Arena*, which he worked on (as a researcher and eventually producer) in Melbourne in the '80s. A decade more of commercial radio in Sydney and David retired to a quiet life on the east coast of Tasmania with his long-term partner.

Aside from these very real dramas, let us return to the saga of a lonely Launceston boy embarking on a university career in a strange city. Flinders wasn't the most exciting-looking campus. It felt new and purpose-built and was a fair hike to get to from Collinswood. But I seemed to make friends fairly quickly, the bookshop was terrific, and there was a bar – even though I didn't drink much at the time. And the classes were great.

I soon met Murray Bramwell, someone who'd become a lifetime friend. He was one of my English tutors and during our first class he asked if any of us read poetry. I put my hand up and muttered, 'Ginsberg, Corso, Ferlinghetti, Richard Brautigan . . .'

I recall the 'We've got a live one here' look on his face. It turned out Murray was doing a PhD on Ginsberg at the time. We got on. Still do.

Equally fascinating was the Philosophy department, which was unashamedly – proudly, in fact – Marxist–Leninist, with an ancillary component of the Australian Independence Movement thrown in. I really had no idea about this stuff. At school, when I'd argued that the workers knew best what worked for the workers, it was purely instinctual. And when my Economics teacher shut me down with, 'Coupe, you are talking about communism,' he was wrong. I had no idea what communism was. But I learnt pretty fast at Flinders.

The essence of the Flinders Philosophy department was that Marx and Engels were great philosophers and thinkers. Mao Tse-tung was right up there as well, and while Joseph Stalin brought up the rear in the thinking stakes, he was no slouch either and should be paid full attention. Leon Trotsky, on the other hand, was not only a deeply flawed thinker but was a bad man. There were observations about his demise. Little sniggers about ice-picks, a reference to the way he was stabbed to death in 1940.

The cause of this antagonism was that Stalin's brand of communism aligned itself with the Maoist thinkers, and Trotsky thought that thinking flawed. We agreed with Joey Stalin on this. Basically, as far as we were concerned, Trotsky had it coming, and those who took his so-called philosophy seriously – we called them Trots (and not affectionately) – were inheritors of a lower form of intellect and not to be trusted. They were, in fact, more of an enemy of the people than those people who were *real* enemies of the people.

It didn't take long for my bookshelves to be crammed with the collected and/or selected works of all of the above. There was a terrific old-school socialist bookshop where you could buy all these books, which are now collectable and expensive. (Have you searched for them on eBay recently?) I read lots of them and understood much less. The Australian Independence Movement was the dominant group on campus. They hated the Trots and had big issues with the Australian Communist Party.

I recently had to look up exactly what they – or should I say *we* – stood for, and this is what I found. We were following in the footsteps of Maoist communists who, in the 1960s, broke away from the Communist Party of Australia to form the Communist Party of Australia (Marxist-Leninist), who closely followed the directives of the Chinese Communist Party. It was pointed out in what I read that many of its members were students from Monash and LaTrobe universities in Melbourne and . . . wait for it, Flinders University in Adelaide. Members challenged university authority and were very much opposed to Australia's involvement in the Vietnam War.

Then, which is where I come in, the Maoist communists formed the Australian Independence Movement in the mid-1970s, using the Eureka flag as their symbol. We (can I say we?) aimed to persuade members of the national bourgeoisie to join the cause of Australian independence and waged a campaign against what was considered to be the imperialism of the Soviet Union.

I also enrolled in a Feminism course. Along with my friend Mark Burford, we were the only two males. It was a no-brainer for me. I've always been in awe of, and around, strong and intelligent women who are much more capable than me. We did a long essay on feminism, sexism and rock'n'roll for our final assessment. It was Gestetnered, using that most rudimentary of printing machines that were the tools of necessity for small runs of essays, demonstration flyers, newsletters and the like. I still have a copy somewhere.

Flinders, at the time, practised group assessment. This was a process whereby the students in a class collectively decided each other's marks – the lecturer or tutor being just one voice in this process. Mark and I received a grilling over parts of our essay but – of course – we passed. No-one failed.

Like every university, Flinders had a student magazine. *Empire Times* was a typical student/campus publication, edited by an elected group of students and printed by the affable, music-loving, overall-wearing bear of gentle humanity, Andrew McHugh. In my second year at Flinders, I and a group of others (this was the '70s and everything was done as a collective) decided we'd run for the student election to edit

*Empire Times*. Its previous editors had included musician Martin Armiger and Regular Records founder Martin Fabinyi.

My collective, which included Mark Burford, ran on our political agenda. We found a 'KEEP LEFT' street sign and had our photos taken standing under it. We won. I was an editor. This was pretty cool. I still wasn't much of a writer, but I *was* an editor – which is kinda funny, because I'm still not much of an editor and couldn't exist without people who are really good at it.

*Empire Times* became the vehicle for improving my music writing. During that year I did manage to put Johnny Rotten on the cover of an issue. For the Rotten issue, *Empire Times* – abbreviated to *ET*, for those in the know – became *PUNK ET*. And the issue – in my hand-writing – proclaimed that it was 'Presented By The Blank Generation'. I'd somehow managed to turn the university paper into a sort of punk fanzine.

I wrote in the magazine about left-wing political books, reviewed tomes by another significant early inspiration, Melbourne writer Colin Talbot, and one by my friend David N. Pepperell – under the pseud-onym Raphael Alias. There was also a look at photographer Diane Arbus at the time of an exhibition of her work at the Art Gallery of South Australia.

For reasons that completely escape me – but that a scrapbook reminds me – there was an *Alternative Empire Times* published in 1976. I know because I have a copy of some record reviews that I wrote – and they're a reminder that, despite my embracing of punk rock, I was still writing about a broad church of music. OK, I enthused about the first Ramones album (which had been out a bit by now), but also Christy (spelt 'Chrissy') Moore's folk masterpiece *Prosperous* – possibly because I'd just discovered it – along with jazz masters Lester Young and Charlie Parker's *Complete Savoy Sessions* recordings. I also delivered a lengthy review of a new collection of writing on jazz by one of my inspirations, Ralph J. Gleason, a co-founder of *Rolling Stone* magazine.

It's curious that despite Rob Smyth – and the majority of my other music-writing inspirations – never writing about jazz, I was very much drawn to it. I gravitated to the outsider, confrontational, attitude-driven sounds of John Coltrane, Archie Shepp, Ornette Coleman and others – partly because of Trotskyist sympathiser Frank Kofsky and his tome *Black Nationalism And The Revolution In Jazz*. I was prepared to forgive his political sympathies given the subject matter and the fact that there was little else around about these exponents of this confronting and abrasive music.

When I look at the records that have travelled with me since those days, I've never parted with any of the couple of dozen albums released on the groundbreaking free/new jazz label Impulse, the ones with the distinctive orange spines. Lots of Coltrane, some Shepp, Sonny Rollins, Albert Ayler. Those records and the punk rock of the Sex Pistols, The Clash and Patti Smith sat very comfortably alongside each other in my listening world. Still do.

As with most music, things ebb and flow in my listening. Things that I either disdained (on punk or the prevailing trend party-lines), or simply didn't get, have come into focus and meaning with the passing of time – while other things have faded. Despite – or maybe because of – my love for hardcore free and avant-garde jazz, I didn't have a lot of time for Steely Dan when their records first came out. Now I adore them, find them endlessly stimulating and listen to them as much as anything in my sprawling record collection.

Same with Fleetwood Mac. Fuck, we hated them in the punk era. *Rumours? You must be kidding.* They were the enemy. Coke-snorting laidback, no-talents. Oh yeah, we hated the Mac. Why? We thought they were overblown, overproduced and complacent – especially compared to the raw directness of punk. Along with other artists who epitomised the excesses of the early 1970s, Fleetwood Mac were the target we needed to have.

It was also, though, because we weren't listening. Or maybe we simply hadn't had enough life experience to get the nuances that were underneath the sheen of their songs. (Plus, we were also a bit jealous of their lifestyle and couldn't afford their drugs.)

Fleetwood Mac didn't change. I did. I love early Peter Green-era blues Fleetwood Mac. I mean, that was wild. 'Albatross' was a big record when I was growing up and the groovers who were into Hendrix and

Cream also dug the Mac in that era. As for the Los Angeles '70s stuff, I love it to death now. I finally saw the band live a few years ago and was just gobsmacked.

A few years ago, I was chatting to a couple of very style-conscious kids and we got talking about Fleetwood Mac. They were telling me how hip the Mac were, and were stunned when I explained that there was a *long* period of time when the Mac were not 'cool'. And if you listened to them, you certainly didn't tell *anyone*.

I also immersed myself – with great gusto and no-doubt marijuana assisted – in the obligatory reggae records of the day, especially those that appeared in the punk era: semi-early Island Records Bob Marley, Burning Spear, The Mighty Diamonds, Toots and the Maytals, Culture and so forth. I dug Tapper Zukie because Patti Smith did and I wanted to like anything that Patti Smith liked. These days, I'm obsessed and go down long, dark, dangerously expensive rabbit holes of reggae and dub.

Then there are bands like Cold Chisel. It's a go-figure thing. I loved Rose Tattoo, to an extent the late-'70s Angels, The Sports, Mental as Anything, Divinyls, Jo Jo Zep and the Falcons, and the bulk of the other classic Australian pub rock'n'roll bands. But I didn't get Chisel. They knew it too, as I'd never written about them and had been fairly overt in conversations with others about how I didn't understand what the fuss was all about. Opinions seemed to travel fast in those circles, especially as one of the people I mouthed off to was a senior figure in promotions and publicity at their record company.

I remember one day being in the restaurant at the Sebel Town House doing an interview with John Farnham. Someone introduced me to Don Walker and Jimmy Barnes. They didn't say anything, weren't rude, but their body language and deadpan facial expressions spoke volumes. *This prick hates us. Fuck him.*

And that's how it stayed with me and Chisel for some time. That was until years later, when I really started to listen to and engage with their music and songwriting. I've now seen Chisel and the individual band members perform multiple times: at the Sydney Entertainment Centre and outdoors in Tamworth, Don Walker at the Camelot Lounge, Ian

Moss at the Enmore Theatre. I even managed to get into a Barking Spiders (aka Chisel) warm-up gig at the Factory Theatre in Marrickville. There hasn't been a dud show amongst them – and whilst I'm hanging out even more to see The Dirty Three play again, the desire for another Chisel gig isn't too far behind. And the thing is, Cold Chisel haven't changed. I have. I like that.

But back to Adelaide and my time in that city. It was around this time that one of the best-known photographs of me was taken. Thanks to the championing of Ian 'Molly' Meldrum and a crazily infectious song called 'In The Flesh' – not to mention a charismatic and extremely attractive and oozing-New-York-cool chic lead singer named Debbie Harry – Blondie had become a big thing in Australia. They were the first of the punk/new wave brigade to trouble the charts in Australia – mainly because they owed more to classic pop music than the two-chord thrash of many punk bands – and they came from New York, a city that had always had a more artistic, steeped-in-music-history approach to 'punk' rock. Hence a scene that revolved around Patti Smith, Television, Talking Heads, New York Dolls, The Dictators, Mink DeVille – and Blondie.

Blondie were scheduled for an Australian tour but a few months prior to this Debbie Harry came to the country for promotional activities. In other words, to appear on *Countdown* and then do as many other media engagements as possible. She made a pitstop in Adelaide and did a press conference of sorts one morning at a pub on Hindley Street. As one of the editors of *Empire Times*, I had the bona fides and went along. It was a sign of the era that Harry was the only woman at the press conference.

Afterwards, a friend from Launceston who was now also living in Adelaide, Victoria Wilkinson, approached her about taking some photographs. Harry graciously consented. In one of them I'm off to the side, awkwardly resplendent with my beard, a sleeveless vest with a Sex Pistols badge pinned on it – and thongs. All style! Harry appears to be clutching a sack of potatoes – maybe it was a chic bag for her stuff. She looks fantastic in the photo, and then there's the dag photo-bombing it.

Thanks to social media that photograph reappears roughly twice a year, gets hundreds of likes and a barrage of 'Is that really Stuart Coupe?' and 'Look at that beard – and thongs' type comments. I love the photo and never tire of seeing it.

I'm not sure why I grew the gingery beard. I used to joke that I couldn't be bothered shaving and maybe that had something to do with it. Possibly I kept nicking myself, as these were the days of real razors, and my blood phobia made me look for a simple way to avoid it. It wasn't as if beards were the hipster rage of the times – and unlike their appeal today, it never helped me to attract any attention from the girls. On (frequent) reflection, I'm still staggered at the change in my fortunes in that department after the beard was removed. I've never had the slightest desire to grow another one since.

A few months later, Blondie played at the Apollo Stadium. I loved it but it seemed like I was in the minority. 'In The Flesh' was one thing, but live Blondie were a relentless, powerful, take-no-prisoners rock'n'roll band with a dose of pop on the side. This didn't please many who'd come expecting to hear an hour-and-a-half of variations on 'In The Flesh'. Well, they sort of got that – but not at the volume and with the intensity that Blondie delivered it. I remember being mesmerised by Clem Burke's drumming, which came right out of the Keith Moon 'Let's hammer this kit into oblivion' school of playing.

Afterwards I hung around the backstage area and had my first experience of the more sordid side of the rock'n'roll business. Remember, I wasn't long out of Launceston and this stuff was new to me. Outside the backstage door young women were told – presumably by a road-crew member or tour manager – to line up. This they did, maybe 20 or so of them. Then, a band representative pointed to particular women – 'you', 'you', 'you' – and the anointed (in the worst possible sense) were admitted to the backstage area, presumably for the pleasure of the male band members and crew. It was uncomfortable to experience and the thought of it is still a bit disturbing.

Around this time, I met another of my then music heroes – the Celtic harp player Alan Stivell, who hailed from Brittany, in France. I'd been turned on to his music – initially quite traditional harp playing and later very electric rock'n'roll orientated – by both Rob Smyth and Stefan Markovitch. I went to his Festival Theatre concert and was enraptured by an astonishingly spirited and emotional live performance, combined with a bit of old-fashioned showbiz. At one stage, he played Pied Piper as audience members followed him while he danced around the outer perimeters of the venue.

Later, though, I was backstage – maybe the *Empire Times* press credentials again – and found him to be rude and arrogant. An early lesson in 'Don't meet your heroes'. This was my first experience of such behaviour and at the time I was devastated that a musical hero could behave like this. As the years went by, I grew to almost expect it. I noticed the exceptions much more, as there were fewer of them.

In fact, it's easier to remember the nice moments. For instance, some years later, I got a telegram (remember them) delivered to my home in Sydney from the rather legendary blues singer Jimmy Witherspoon, thanking me for a piece I'd written about him in *The Sun-Herald*. Or Julian Cope, who I did a phone interview with in the mid-1990s. He was a super-friendly chap and we chatted about all things, including his recently published *Krautrocksampler* book on German rock'n'roll. 'Give me your address – I'll send you a copy,' he said. I dutifully did and expected that to be the last I'd hear of it. Some weeks later, a large package arrived from one Julian Cope – a pile of his recent records and a copy of the book.

Then there was Tom T. Hall. I was doing a pre-tour phone interview with Tom T. – one of my favourite-ever songwriters. He was friendly and it was a terrific chat, which, at one stage, involved us comparing notes on our favourite American authors from the South. I mentioned how much I love Larry Brown.

'I know Larry,' said Tom T. I did the obligatory 'ohs' and 'aahs' and 'wows' and we moved on.

When Tom T. eventually came to Australia, unfortunately I was overseas so I didn't get to see him perform. Something like six months later, his Australian tour publicist rang me to say that he was sending over a pile of books that Tom T. had brought to Australia for me.

When it arrived, the package was four first-edition Larry Brown novels – all signed to me.

To say that I was gobsmacked would be an understatement. And I was mortified that Tom T. must have thought that I was extremely ungrateful for not thanking him for such an extraordinary gesture. I asked the publicist to try and get a message to Tom T. I wrote a letter to an address that I found but I never knew if it had reached him.

When Tom T. died a few years ago, my first thoughts were that I really hoped he'd received my note thanking him for his extreme kindness.

Instances like that are few and far between. Not that they're expected, of course – far from it – but the simple acts of kindness linger longer than the cog-in-the-publicity-wheel 30-minute interviews.

In 2015, I did a long phone interview with Jackson Browne. We seemed to get on well and the conversation ranged over music and politics and the power of songs in creating change. A month or two later, there was an envelope waiting for me at the radio station. The back said 'From The Office Of Jackson Browne'. Inside there was no note, just a 'With Compliments' card – and a copy of a book about Cuban musician Carlos Varela, *My Havana: The Musical City of Carlos Varela*.

Oh, and that reminds me that, in a rather macabre moment a few months into 1983, I received a Christmas card from Karen Carpenter. Clearly, she had been sat down in the offices of A&M records in Los Angeles, given a list of international media to write cards to, and these had then been posted. Given the notoriously long delay in those days with surface mail, when letters could spend months on ships getting across the world, by the time the card arrived Carpenter had died.

But back to Adelaide days. It was during my sojourn in that city that Hunter S. Thompson had his one visit to Australia. I desperately wanted to see him and contemplated hitchhiking or catching the train to Melbourne to do so; however, for reasons lost in the mists of time the logistics were beyond me.

By this stage I'd moved to a house on South Road, a noisy location but much closer to Flinders. I'd also (finally) been taught to ride a pushbike by photographer John Altree-Williams. Adelaide being so wonderfully flat, I had a newfound mobility, often riding across suburbs at night and by day to go book and record shopping in the city.

The house on South Road was a hotbed of political activity, largely because of the student activist Kim Sattler who ran the house. Still active in politics, Kim was closely associated with the Australian Independence Movement. There were meetings at our place, people who were maybe involved in nefarious activities crashed there and cars were parked across the street on a regular basis. We were pretty sure they belonged to ASIO. One of my housemates – a young photographer called Rosemary – was smoking pot, which sent Kim semi-ballistic and created a lot of tension. As far as Kim was concerned, we didn't need another reason for the cops to kick down the door. They never did – but maybe that was because Rosemary stopped smoking pot in the house.

After South Road, I moved over to Torrensville into a share house with Mark Burford and Alex Ehlert. This was the house that would become 'Roadrunner Central'. But I'm jumping ahead. In love with the idea of fanzines, I'd already put out one issue of *Street Fever*. The only issue, as it turned out.

# 10

# (SHE'S GOT) THE FEVER

I loved fanzines and the punk-rock era was their golden time. They were easy to do and cheap to put out. They were the way for music fans to convey their enthusiasm for music they loved. Write 10 or 15 pages of news, reviews and interviews, stick the copy down with glue (or cellotape) and Gestetner, photocopy or print 50 or 100 copies. Your local record shops would always stock them. It was cool – a badge of honour. There were famous ones – *Sniffin' Glue*, *PUNK*, *Flipside* and *Slash* from overseas – and ones like *Spunk*, *Self Abuse*, *Suicide Alley* and *Pulp* from Australia.

I wanted to do a fanzine, so, with my friend Donald Robertson, I created *Street Fever*. Scottish-born Donald had recently returned from two-and-a-half years living in the UK. He brought with him a very fine selection of punk rock singles. We'd decided we needed to tell the world about our shared passion for this new music.

Issue number one was published in December 1977. I don't have a proper copy, although I do have at least some of the pages stuck in a scrapbook that – not surprisingly – is falling apart. It's been digitalised by the University of Wollongong, if you want to check it out. Donald has a pristine copy. He seems to keep everything, for which I'm glad.

The cover of *Street Fever* (price 50 cents) was a photo of Prime Minister Malcolm Fraser with the words – done in the style of a ransom note – 'WILL THIS MAN LET THE SEX PISTOLS INTO AUSTRALIA?' over his face. Inside, it was proclaimed: 'THIS <u>DEFINITELY</u> AIN'T THE SUMMER OF LOVE.'

Most of the copy was typed, or in some cases handwritten. Contributors to the first issue included a motley assortment of members of local punk bands (although some of the pseudonyms were me and Donald) – Andy Vague, Chuckie Suicide, The Phantom Bantam, and Festering Mick Malicious.

I wrote a piece on a then-obsession, Beserkley Records, home of Jonathan Richman. I pointed out: 'Richman gets included in this monstrous term "new wave" music which would lead people to see blatant connections between his music and that of Radio Birdman, the Pistols, Television, ad infinitum (not a band stupid) – all Jonathan does is illustrate the moronicness of rock'n'roll terminology with simple, funny, understandable – almost acoustic music – the type with choruses you remember = he's about as close to the Sex Pistols as Johnny Rotten is to Annette Funicello – so there!!!'

The issue had an interview with the punk band Moist, 'who are from Elizabeth [a suburb in Adelaide] and have played twice at school socials there'. There were also stories on the Sex Pistols, Stiff Records and the Sydney punk band Psycho-Surgeons.

Modern Love Songs had a full-page ad on page three. The super-cool new record shop was the Mecca for all of us wanting the latest punk rock and new wave singles and albums. This was the shop outside which lines formed the morning the Sex Pistols album *Never Mind The Bollocks* was released. The Modern Love Songs ad was largely hand printed by me – my printing was clunky and basic, but it got the message across.

We added a Wreckless Eric pin-up (go figure) and a full-page drawing of Her Majesty The Queen, festooned with razor blades for a crown and a safety pin through her nose. There was also a pizza restaurant review and some record reviews (I suspect I wrote the uncredited one of the Patti Smith bootleg *Teenage Perversity And Ships In The Night*).

The highlight of the issue, though, was a review of Radio Birdman (supported by Young Modern) at the often-used Adelaide venue Unley

Town Hall on 26 November, written by Chuckie Suicide. It opened with: 'The support band, the Young Moderns, played to an audience of a single drunk swaying on the dance floor in time to the (music). I didn't like them either.' Chuckie loved Radio Birdman, however, and at the conclusion of their performance, wrote, 'I freak into spasmodic fits of bleeding and vomiting while being kicked into a pulp on the floor.'

*Street Fever* was naive, a little self-conscious and very much of its time. It's good there was only one issue – sort of perfect, really. And then I moved on to not one, but two, new publishing ventures.

# 11
# WHAT'S GOING ON

**B**efore the emergence of free music magazines, combined with gig guides which really came into their own in the early-to-mid-1980s, there were many arts/music/culture publications printed up and shoved into corners at cafes, pubs, book and record shops. I was involved with an early one published in Adelaide, *Preview*, the first issue bearing the date March 1978.

I'd left university and was meandering around trying to work out what I was going to do. Could I write for a living? Well, first-up – could I even write? I wasn't really sure. I'd done a few things in the university newspaper, but I had a hand in the decision to publish them. Was I cut out for stringing words and sentences together in a way that other people might decide to publish and actually pay me money for them?

The money side would come later, but in 1978 I found myself hanging out with a bunch of guys who – at least to me – seemed like heavyweights in this writing and journalism caper. They were only a couple of years older but when I was around them it felt like I was the kid allowed into a grown-ups' party. They were world-weary, smart, bitingly sarcastic, and seemed to operate on an intellectual and life-experience level that – well, let's be honest – I desperately wanted to be part of. They were larger than life, swaggering men of letters.

They drank harder, played harder, took harder drugs. And they were paid to write. Oh, I wanted all of that.

Foremost among the gang I wanted so desperately to be part of were the urbane, intelligent and super-cool Dennis Atkins, who wrote about music and politics for the *Sunday Mail*, and the more gregarious, opinionated and older-seeming Terry Plane, a writer for *The Australian*. They'd also both written for *The National Times*, arguably the most credible politics, news and arts publication in the country. This was real journalism.

Also prominent was Kim Krummel, who ran Mother's Book Farm, the hipster bookshop in Coromandel Place in the city. This was where you went to get the latest Whole Earth Catalogue, anything by the Beat generation, Carlos Castaneda, Herman Hesse and so forth. I spent a lot of the little money I had there.

And add into the mix local poet and writer John Kingsmill, who had both layout skills and was a significant player in Adelaide's literary world, editing publications such as the local poetry magazine *Another One For Mary* with his buddy Paul Kelly, who would go on to become quite a well-known singer-songwriter.

One night, someone hatched the idea of a publication dealing with arts and music. More often than not, plans like this among the group came towards the tail end of dinner parties, which usually involved copious quantities of wine and loud conversation that increasingly veered towards the tangential and fanciful. Someone would have said, 'The local arts coverage is shite,' and a chorus of 'We can do better's would have erupted around the table, followed by 'Let's do it! We'll show them how to do an arts newspaper.' With a bit of luck someone would remember the concept the next day. and start to think that maybe it was an idea that had legs.

Most of them were, of course, forgotten, but this one wasn't. Even more remarkably, I was invited onto the 'Editorial Council'. This was serious. Secretly I was delighted, but I kept quiet as I felt very much like an outsider and didn't want my sense of awe to be too obvious. I figured the best way to seem cool and meld with the others was to avoid standing out.

But boy was I nervous when I turned in my first article and review. I knew they were going to be scrutinised by much more talented journalists than I was. I still hadn't found my feet or a real voice, and felt just a bit like a lucky interloper who would, sooner or later, be revealed as a pretender.

Amazingly, my friend David Woodhall had been asked to host a new music show on the ABC, *Rockturnal*. Yes, I was friends with a TV star. Naturally, I wrote about this for the first issue of *Preview*. I also wrote about Sydney's jazz-rock band Crossfire, who were coming to Adelaide.

I tentatively submitted these first articles to the coolest people in the city. Would I pass muster? Fortunately, when Dennis, Terry, Kim and co. got back to me, they didn't throw me out on my ear – and were even quite encouraging. I was in!

Buoyed by this response, I quickly dashed off a review of *Rocket To Russia*, the third album from The Ramones, and articles about Bob Dylan and The Beach Boys – both of whom were due to arrive in Adelaide. The next couple of issues saw me ruminating on Billy Joel (also due in Adelaide), Dave Warner and his From The Suburbs, and reviewing Pere Ubu's *The Modern Dance*, Little River Band's *Sleeper Catcher* album, Lou Reed's *Street Hassle* and the Stiff label's *Live Stiffs Live* album, featuring Elvis Costello, Nick Lowe, Wreckless Eric, Ian Dury and Larry Wallis.

As well, I wrote about the newly formed Mushroom Records offshoot, Suicide Records, and, as I perceived it, their attempt to cash in on the punk/new wave scene in Australia, along with a lengthy opinion piece, 'Punk Off', about the lack of Australian – and particularly Adelaide – media support for the music I was currently obsessed by. Yep, that was punk and new wave.

I always joke that I was born in '56 – just like rock'n'roll; so, obviously, I was too young for the impact of Elvis Presley and the rock'n'roll pioneers. I was only eight when The Beatles came to Australia, so the mid-'70s punk revolution was the first music upheaval I'd experienced first-hand. The first that had impacted directly on me, that I owned and felt part of. I loved it, was committed to it and found it the perfect vehicle for my writing. As well, I could write about it with attitude and passion. It was the right music at the right time for this kid.

Looking back on those *Preview* pieces, I can see that I'd learnt a fair bit about how to write about music since my *Empire Times* and *Street Fever* efforts. Either that, or my more experienced comrades in journalism had done some heavy rewrites on my copy. I was reading a lot in those days and much of it was music writing – but whereas a few years earlier I'd been doing little more than paraphrase Rob Smyth, I was now starting to develop a more distinctive and defined style. I wouldn't say I'd yet found a voice, but I wasn't now in any danger of having charges of plagiarism levelled at me by Mr Smyth.

The piece I'm most proud of from the *Preview* days is my interview with Helen Garner, published in issue 5 in July 1978. It was a lengthy chat about her *Monkey Grip* novel, which had been published late the year before. Garner had become a big deal with the publication of this book, and it allowed me to talk to and write about an author and novel I admired. I was also able to dovetail into the music scene in the inner-Melbourne suburb of Carlton where the book was set and the characters – many playing in bands or on the periphery of that scene – were drawn from. And Garner was a terrific interview subject, so it felt like I was writing something with real substance that wasn't just about music.

It was beginning to get a bit hectic on the music-writing front, and the first few months of 1978 were such a buzz for this raw, but enthusiastic young journalist. My baptism of fire at *Preview* had been terrifying and exciting, but then word came through that I might be able to do some writing for *RAM*. That's right – *RAM*.

This was right up there amongst the things I most aspired to do. Could I juggle all this activity? You bet I could. Pass up the opportunity to write for *RAM* – the number-one music mag in the country, and the absolute business – just because I was flat out with other things? No chance.

One of Australia's finest music journalists, Annie Burton, was on staff at *RAM* – which stood for 'Rock Australia Magazine' – and apparently the editor had decided they needed someone to review bands in Adelaide. She asked an old friend, pedal-steel guitar player Steve James, who was living in South Australia and was part of my group of friends, if he knew anyone.

Steve recommended me. Suddenly, I was going to write gig reviews for the magazine – 'ligging', they called it. According to the jargon, a ligger was someone who went to gigs. And ligging for *RAM* was serious ligging. Top-notch ligging, in fact. I was beyond ecstatic.

I started off writing columns and news stories with an Adelaidian bent – as well as the occasional record review (Adelaidian or otherwise). I remember, in one early issue, I set to dissecting Leonard Cohen's Phil Spector-produced *Death Of A Ladies Man*. I concluded that it was 'a curious album that leaves me a little cold and deeply unimpressed'. (It intrigues me to look back at observations like this. I now adore that Cohen album. The changes in one's tastes are always fascinating. I seem to recall that my initial love of Neil Young (*Harvest*) had moved towards 'fucking old hippie', before he redeemed himself in my eyes when he reconnected with Crazy Horse on records like *Rust Never Sleeps* in 1979. Once again, the change – and my embracing of his acoustic, country sounds – was with me, not Young.)

I also did a review of the Stiff label's *Live Stiffs Live* album. You might recall that I'd already written one for *Preview*. In an early indication that I knew how to milk a story and what 'syndication' meant, I managed to get *RAM* to run pretty much the same piece.

Before long, I was listed as a contributor on the *RAM* masthead – there was 'Chief Demented Scribbler' (Anthony O'Grady), 'Demented Scribblers' (Annie Burton and Andrew McMillan), and then a bunch of 'Scribblers (presumed sane)'. I was one of the 'presumed sane'.

So, I was working for *Preview* and for *RAM* and having a whale of a time. And I had plenty to keep me occupied. But despite the demise of the short-lived *Street Fever* a few months earlier, Donald Robertson and I still had a musical itch to scratch. And, even as the Editorial Council was being assembled at *Preview*, we'd come up with a plan.

# 12

# ROADRUNNER

*Preview* came from the eastern suburbs of Adelaide. *Roadrunner* was from the west. That made sense. The eastern suburbs was more monied and had a rarified air of arts and culture, whereas the western suburbs was more gritty, working class and *rawk*.

*Street Fever* had been fun and Donald and I got on well. So we started to hatch plans for something bigger than a fanzine. A proper music magazine. An Adelaide-based version of *RAM* and Melbourne's *Juke*.

Compared to *Preview*, *Roadrunner* (named after the Jonathan Richman and the Modern Lovers song, not the ultra-fast cartoon bird) would still cling to the punk-rock aesthetic. It initially looked very thrown together, the copy typed and glued down on boards ready for the printers – and the words themselves were maybe a bit classier than those of *Street Fever* – but only just. This was a magazine going for the semi-professional but still streetwise look – maybe a bit like *ZigZag* from London with a touch of *New York Rocker*.

The first issue had a photo of 1960s-era Beach Boys on the cover. They were coming to town and, in fact, I went to Adelaide airport just to stare at a very overweight and bedraggled Brian Wilson getting off the plane. Many years later, Wilson would say that he had a nervous breakdown on the flight from Los Angeles for the tour. He'd already done five shows in Australia before lobbing in Adelaide, and unless there'd been any medical intervention, he would have been in a right state by the time I saw him. Incidentally, if I had my time over I'd have spent just as much time checking out drummer and certified loose cannon Dennis Wilson – but I didn't.

I also went to the airport to try to catch a glimpse of Bob Dylan but failed, leading to a group of us doing our best to weave through traffic and follow his entourage into the city in the hope of getting a look at him. We didn't.

This first issue – dated March/April 1978 – billed itself as 'Adelaide's Music Paper' and sold for 30 cents. I'm not sure why the 20-cent drop from the noticeably less substantial *Street Fever*. It was another low-budget enterprise. Every word had to be typed – and none of us were particularly good at that. We used a lot of whiteout. No-one was paid, we did all the layout ourselves, and we sold what ads we could. And I suspect our friend Andrew McHugh gave us a *very* good deal on the printing; then patiently, optimistically, waited for payment. (Or printed it when no-one at the university was watching.)

I wrote a preview of the Dylan show, noting that 'even the punks arrived to queue 12 hours in order to get front row tickets'. The price was $12.50, which I considered a lot given he was playing an 'atrocious outdoor venue'. I was rather cynical in my punk-rock attitude, citing the English punk band The Stranglers' 'No More Heroes', dismissing the lies of Trotsky and suggesting that if we were being fair we should add Dylan to the Mick Jaggers, Bryan Ferrys, Peter Framptons, Elton Johns and Boz Scaggses of the world, all of whom needed dethroning. I went on to suggest, however, that Dylan would probably never visit Australia again, so this was an opportunity that should be taken.

Obviously, he's been back just a few times since then! File that along with the prediction Glenn A. Baker and I would later make in one of our books that it was hard to imagine Kate Bush being more than a one-hit wonder.

A group of us also interviewed Garry McDonald, aka Norman Gunston, for that first issue. We met up with him at the Hotel Australia, where he appeared clutching a tuna sandwich and a carton of orange juice. The interview was conducted in his slightly tatty room – but we didn't care. McDonald was a bona fide star, and it was fun and a good lark.

In a city that had comparatively little media, the opportunities for us to hang with and interview musicians were much greater than if the magazine was based in Sydney or Melbourne. We were big fish in a small pond and took full advantage of the fact.

We had fun, but we worked hard at it. By issue two in May, we'd assembled a solid team. Under the 'Who To Blame' credits, Robertson and I were editors, and our friend Allan Coop continued as layout and production person – all of which was done in a little shed out the back of the house that I shared with Alex Ehlert and Mark Burford, who also contributed to the magazine. Local booking agent Chris Plimmer was listed as 'Business'. Look out, world – we were getting serious here.

Business was code for 'selling advertising' for us. Plimmer was a highly respected booking agent in Adelaide and his connection with the magazine hugely helped our bona fides. A word from him to venues that we were credible and had reach to potential customers was often enough to secure an ad. This was crucial in helping to sustain the publication.

In the second issue, The Residents were the cover story. The kicker feature, though, was the interview Mark, Alex and I did with Ian 'Molly' Meldrum, whilst he was in Adelaide. Running over five pages, it was my first encounter with Meldrum. On our television screens on *Countdown* every Sunday at 6pm, he sometimes might have appeared to be less than intelligent and thoughtful. But right from the get-go, I realised he was highly intelligent and extremely knowledgeable. I gained enormous respect for him during that interview, and liked him a lot. That respect has only grown every time we've met over the years.

Although I was now a 'scribbler' for *RAM*, I loved the punk spirit of *Roadrunner*. I sent every new issue across to Anthony O'Grady, the founder and editor of *RAM* – usually with some semi-arrogant, semi-sarcastic observation that the new breed was coming and that *Roadrunner* was the future of music journalism in Australia.

*RAM* had started in Sydney in the mid-'70s, and they, along with the Melbourne-based *Juke*, were the two major Australian music publications and well entrenched nationally. So this was the old punk rock versus the establishment carry-on, writ large in the world of music-magazine publishing. Well, that was how it appeared in our eyes at *Roadrunner*, even if most of the planet wasn't paying that much attention.

Working on those first few issues, we believed *Roadrunner* had its finger on the pulse in the way that tired publications like *RAM* and *Juke* used to. I'm sure Anthony just smiled. And secretly we probably wanted to be as successful, polished and revered as they were. We were envious of the big kids and wanted to play in their sandpit.

My one-way banter with the *RAM* editor (who was possibly already tired of my bravado and had other things to occupy his time) continued for maybe four issues. Then one day in July 1978, my phone rang. It was Anthony O'Grady.

'Dear boy,' he began, 'how would you like to come to Sydney and work for a *real* music magazine?'

# 13

# READ ABOUT IT

I realised later that Anthony O'Grady called just about everyone 'dear boy'. Given how momentous it was, I wish I could remember more about that conversation. I hadn't had any indication that O'Grady even liked my writing – he didn't lavish praise easily. I'd noticed that my copy had sometimes undergone significant rewrites and edits, so for all I knew I was simply the only ligger *RAM* could find in Adelaide. When that call came through, I was gobsmacked. I had this heady feeling that my life was about to change – and quickly.

I thought about Anthony's question for seven-and-a-half seconds. Maybe eight. As I've said, *RAM* was the main game – the Australian equivalent of *New Musical Express* and *Melody Maker*. Sydney was too. After Launceston, relocating to Adelaide had been like moving to New York. However, really it was just Philadelphia (in itself a fine city, but . . .), and Manhattan's lights twinkled in the distance. Plus, I'd get paid. To write. About music.

I'd loved working on *Preview* and *Roadrunner*, and I'd learnt so much. I'd miss the friends I'd made there, but this was an opportunity I couldn't turn down. I knew I'd kick myself if I did. It would have been a bit like the Beatles saying no to Brian Epstein and deciding they could manage themselves. Where was the mileage in that thinking?

So I told Anthony I was in. But what about the small matter of moving my clothes, records, books and other worldly possessions across from South Australia? I had no money and no idea how you did things like that. And I didn't really know anyone in Sydney.

Anthony told me not to worry. He made a few calls and I was told to have everything packed up on a particular day and time. Then the road crew for The Angels – who had just done a bunch of gigs in Adelaide – came around, loaded my stuff into the back of the truck, along with the band's PA and other equipment, and set off in the direction of Sydney, albeit via a circuitous route. All I had to do was go to the airport and . . . harbour city, here I come.

By August, I was on the way to Sydney. The *Roadrunner* and *Preview* crews took it in their stride. They were going to be fine. I don't recall even seeing the fifth issue of *Roadrunner*, even though I'm credited as one of the editors. I must have been in transition with a head full of big-city dreams. No offence, Adelaide, it's been great but I gotta get out of this place.

By this stage, the fanzine writer Bruce Milne had become involved in *Roadrunner* and was listed as one of the editors, alongside the very capable Donald Robertson, whilst Cee (later better known as Clinton) Walker was the 'Melbourne editor'. In effect, this meant he wrote for the mag and was based in the Victorian capital. And although he moved to Sydney shortly afterwards, he continued to contribute from there. The poet and counterculture figure Adrian Rawlins was also now listed as a contributor. It definitely wasn't a two-person operation anymore, which made me feel less guilty about leaving. And I was still part of the enterprise, albeit in a greatly reduced role.

I knew I'd always have a soft spot for *Roadrunner*. Not only had it been important to my development as a music writer, it had been the proverbial breath of fresh air amongst the more established magazines. It was breathing some life into the Adelaide scene as well, and providing an outlet for writing about music that was free of the shadow of major record labels and their demands and expectations.

I'd only been to Australia's biggest city twice before – once as an eight-year-old with my parents after we drove to the Gold Coast, then south to Sydney to catch the boat back to Tasmania. All I can remember is going to Taronga Park Zoo in shorts and a light shirt and almost freezing to death. The second time had been when I was 21 and my friend Vicki Wilkinson and I hitchhiked to Sydney from Adelaide so she could visit her boyfriend, Steve James, who was back in Sydney, where he'd originally come from, before moving to Launceston and then on to Adelaide.

We made it, but only after some hair-raising encounters. At one stage, we'd hitched a ride with a freight truck. Later, we rested at a truck stop, where, after Vicki tried to wake the driver up, he raised his fist aggressively as if to punch her, before coming to his senses and realising what he was about to do. Then another suggested the three of us go for a stroll in remote bushland. It was probably a harmless bit of leg-stretching, but it was only years later that I reflected on how vulnerable we were and what could have happened.

On that trip, we were dumped on the outskirts of Sydney, where Steve collected us and took us to the rustic house where members of Uncle Bob's Band hung out. They were a hippie group who played a mixture of country, old-time swing and blues-influenced tunes – what would today be called roots music. That night, Vicki, Steve and I went to see them at the Tin Sheds, the art and music space connected to Sydney University. Another night, we saw the Australian pedal-steel guitar legend Kenny Kitching at a pub near Central Station. Neither act had visited Adelaide, as far as I was aware, and both made my head spin with excitement. It just added to the allure of the city, because I thought, 'Well, if there's artists like this in Sydney, what else is there?'

What I remember most from that trip, though, is Steve taking us on a tour of various parts of the city. I particularly recall a drive one night towards the CBD and the astonishing array of tall buildings and lights. Years later, I'd have a similar experience coming across the Brooklyn and Williamsburg bridges towards Manhattan. It blew my young mind. Dorothy, we weren't in Adelaide anymore. And certainly not in Launceston. Then we drove through Kings Cross. My senses went into overdrive.

When I did finally move to Sydney, I had cause to reflect on what was once said about one of my music journalistic influences, Lester Bangs: that when he moved from Detroit to New York City, he was heading for the big league. And that if you could make it there, you could make it anywhere. Adelaide was my Detroit and, baby, I was moving to Sydney. Eat my dust. Here I come . . . and then here I am.

That was all well and good, but I had no idea how Sydney worked. I spent a couple of nights camped out at Anthony's converted warehouse in inner-suburban Glebe; from memory, though, the return of his girlfriend led to the suggestion that I find somewhere else to go. I didn't have a clue where that might be.

Now I was directionless. Seriously, I had no fucking idea where I was. *RAM*'s office was on Glebe Point Road. That was in Glebe too, right? Of course it was, but this city was just so *big*. And bright. And busy. One night I managed to find my way to a pizza place down Parramatta Road, near Central Station. It was only a kilometre or two from work, but I felt like I'd accomplished the 1978 equivalent of a voyage by Columbus. This was progress.

Nevertheless, as I sat by myself at the table, while I was phenomenally excited to be here in my New York City, I was a bit afraid. Mostly I was really, really lonely.

At this stage the *RAM* office was my home. The two-storey terrace was deserted after usual working hours, and I had a bag of clothes and other essentials. I found a cushion for a pillow. All my other worldly possessions were still in the Angels truck as they wound their way from Adelaide to Melbourne and various other locations.

No-one knew I was staying there. I slept under my desk and made a point of appearing busy until everyone else had left. I then wandered out to Glebe Point Road to get something to eat, let myself back into the building, and then curled up under my desk. I earnt brownie points for always being the first at work. Thankfully, there was a shower.

My fortnight living at the office had its moments. One day the poet Adrian Rawlins was in Sydney and dropped in. I was somewhat in awe of Rawlins – he was as close as Australia had to a Beat Generation figure. He'd hung out with Bob Dylan, been at the early rock festivals at Sunbury, Ourimbah and Wallacia, and, as I was growing up, he'd loomed in my imagination alongside *Oz* magazine's Richard Neville and other iconic counterculture characters.

Adrian and I had dinner together at Rasputin, the – believe it or not – Russian restaurant on Glebe Point Road, just down from the office. After we'd finished dinner, I asked him if he wanted to go to *RAM* headquarters (aka my home) for a coffee. He was enthusiastic about this, so we headed back. As I started to prepare the coffee, though, I felt Rawlins' arms around me. Somewhat taken by surprise, I had to tell him that coffee was all that was on the agenda. He took it well and, after that, we always got on whenever we ran into each other.

The last time I saw Adrian was in Melbourne in 1994, when Bruce Milne and I were on a tram. Adrian hopped on, saw us, engaged in an enthusiastic conversation, and gave us both copies of his latest publication, *Dylan Through The Looking Glass – A Collection Of Writings On Bob Dylan*. I always felt it a shame that Rawlins died on that momentous day, September 11, 2001, as his passing didn't receive anywhere near the attention I felt it deserved at the time. But I'm delighted, as I'm sure he would have been, that there's a statue of him in the Melbourne suburb of Fitzroy. It's a bit of a cliché, but he really was a one of a kind.

During this time, I befriended *RAM* photographer Kathleen O'Brien and briefly moved into a room at her house in Kings Cross. I had no mattress, let alone a bed, and slept on the seagrass matting floor. Never do this. It is not comfortable. In fact, it is torturously hideous. Readers, do whatever you can to get together enough money to buy even the most basic mattress. But I got on well with Kathleen, who was an extremely young, highly accomplished photographer. She had a keen fixation on Sports singer Stephen Cummings, who she'd later marry.

From there, I struck up a friendship with another of the *RAM* writers, and moved into a storage cupboard – literally – in the house in Glebe that she shared with two others. It was tiny and barely fitted a single mattress amongst all manner of household goods. Was it a step up from sleeping under a desk or on seagrass matting? I guess so – but only just. It was dark and claustrophobic, but at least I had my own 'room'.

At *RAM*, I'd taken Andrew McMillan's job. I was never sure how happy he was about that. McMillan had been the resident Lester Bangs meets Hunter S. Thompson figure there. I suspect Anthony had grown tired of his erratic craziness, but whatever the reason for his departure, I was now the new *RAM* staff writer.

McMillan (everyone called him McMillan) liked speed, smoking pot, drinking, staying up late, noisy rock'n'roll, and hammering a succession of manual typewriters into mangled and non-functioning submission. He once described Rose Tattoo as sounding like a 'Mack truck from hell'. He was the gonzo guy.

I think he thought I was a bit of an aesthete and not tough enough for this world. Compared to him, I was shy – a little timid – and he might have reckoned I took this writing caper too seriously. Although he was no longer a *RAM* employee, McMillan was still on good terms with everyone at the office, including me, and was a regular visitor.

McMillan and I would go on to forge a strong friendship. I respected him and most of his taste in music, loved his attitude and take-no-prisoners approach to life. Once he left Sydney in 1988 and moved to Darwin, our contact was sporadic, but I remember him coming to dinner and staying the night on my couch on one of his last visits to the city.

I say he came to dinner, but he didn't actually eat anything – just smoked roll-your-own cigarettes and drank Scotch and beer. This was the McMillan diet of choice – usually combined with a few joints – and was not to be messed with by this stuff called food.

McMillan died in January 2012. He was buried in a remote location in the Northern Territory with his collection of typewriters. That seemed kind of right.

My salary at *RAM* was $90 a week. That wasn't exactly a fortune, but in those days it was a significant living wage for a single guy who didn't need to buy records or pay to go to gigs. If I planned my week carefully, I could spend a lot of it eating and drinking on a record company's dime, given that in those days there was an endless stream of release parties and similar gatherings. Having said that, I recently looked at an online conversion calculator and that 90 bucks would be $377 in today's currency – so maybe it wasn't that great.

At one point I asked *RAM* publisher Phillip Mason if it was at all possible to get a pay rise – to maybe $100. He looked at me and replied, 'Dear boy, I'm afraid not. There's a lot of people on the dole queue who would give anything for your job.'

Anyway, I well and truly managed to get by on the 90 bucks, and for the first time in my life could support myself. I didn't save anything, of course, but hey, I was in Sydney and actually making a living as a journalist. What wasn't to like about that?

By now, I'd moved to Stanmore. It was a nice, respectable, inner-west suburb that felt like a quaint little village, with a small collection of shops, a pleasant park, and a school across the road from the place I rented. The single-storey terrace house was old, rambling, and had three bedrooms, a large living-room, a kitchen you could swing several cats in (and house my two pinball machines) with a nice backyard.

And for a lifelong non-driver, it was great. It was only a short walk to a bus stop or a train station, and not too hideously expensive if I needed to catch a late-night taxi home after a gig in the city, Kings Cross, or, heaven forbid, further out in the suburbs.

Yes, there was a lot to like about my new life. My first real assignment was to go on the road with a band I loved – Graham Parker & The Rumour. This was thrilling for me, partly because of my passion for Parker and his music, but hell, I was *on the road* with an international touring band. Suddenly, I was like Lester Bangs touring the UK with The Clash. On the fucking road, baby. Parker had a terrific dry wit, everyone was super-friendly, the shows were great. This totally rocked. There was only one downside – the tour ended and I had to come back to earth.

I was then sent to Adelaide with KISS. I managed to catch them without make-up when some enthusiastic fan amongst the hundreds of kids hanging outside the Hilton decided it'd be a good idea to phone in a bomb threat, and we had to hastily exit the building.

I'm not sure who was more surprised – KISS, me or their publicist Patti Mostyn, who was accompanying them to the ground floor and presumably to safety. When I hopped into the lift, a look passed between Patti and I which said – in no uncertain terms – *Do not say you are a journalist. I do not know you. And do not even think about pulling out a camera if you have one in your bag.*

I wasn't born with the KISS gene so this wasn't such a big deal, but I could still kinda show off to my Adelaide friends that, yes, I was on the road with a major international rock band. And staying at the Hilton – thank you very much – with KISS and the whole entourage.

I wrote fast for *RAM*. There was a long feature on The Angels, a band I loved at the time. I also had encounters with Talking Heads, Dolly Parton, Bob Marley, Roy Orbison and Midnight Oil (sometimes at press conferences, other times for one-on-one interviews).

As well, I did lots and lots of record reviews and smaller features on everything and everyone, from the newly formed Sydney-based independent label Regular Records (first signing: Mental As Anything) to Chip Monck, the guy who'd done the lighting and many of the stage announcements at Woodstock.

I also spent a day hanging out with notorious rock impresario, and the guy who founded The Runaways, Kim Fowley. Kim came to my home and spent hours reviewing the latest singles for the magazine. He used my living-room as his office for the day as a stream of young talent came to visit him.

The tall and lanky Fowley talked at a million miles an hour, scheming all manner of schemes at a rapid rate. His existence seemed to be a constant performance piece and he clearly thrived on having an audience – any audience. For a few years afterwards, he'd call me at all hours of the day or night from Los Angeles, espousing all sorts of ideas.

He was loud and brash but underneath I detected a loneliness which would come out late at night – and with the time difference he knew people in Australia would be up. Initially, I enjoyed the chats and the wild thoughts: 'Street Talk (a New Zealand band he was obsessed with at the time) are going to be bigger than Springsteen – I need to get them to LA and show these fuckers.' But it got to the point where – this being before the days of caller ID – I'd pick up the phone and my stomach would sink when I heard the words 'Fowley here, Stuart.'

A better experience was when I went to artist Martin Sharp's bohemian and eccentrically furnished house in Bellevue Hill in the well-heeled eastern suburbs to interview Tiny Tim. I was thrilled to meet the singer of 'Tiptoe Through The Tulips', who was every bit as delightful and eccentric as I'd expected. It was one of the few interviews I did that impressed my mother. She was delighted when I presented her with an album signed for her by Tiny.

I also had an unnerving time with Thin Lizzy's Phil Lynott. After the interview, which had gone well, I went to the top of the Boulevard Hotel with Phil for a photo shoot (when I say the top, I mean *the* top). I'm very challenged by heights, and there were absolutely no safety barriers or walls on the roof. I felt like I couldn't chicken out, though, as this was Phil bloody Lynott and the photographer was the rather legendary English snapper Chalkie Davis, who was out here covering the tour. It wasn't until I reached the summit that I realised there weren't any barriers. Silly me. Even thinking about it now makes my palms sweat. But I digress.

During this time, I wrote an article on venue bouncers, an essay on women in rock'n'roll, and saw what seemed like a million gigs and did almost as many interviews. I spoke with everyone from pop star Leif Garrett – who was impossibly blond, bubbly and far too eager to please – to the very austere and serious German filmmaker Werner Herzog, who'd just made the film *Nosferatu*. Our interview, largely done in the back of a taxi as he travelled around Sydney, became my first cover story.

I was totally immersed in this world. This was heaven. It was exactly what I'd dreamt of doing as a kid in Launceston. I was surrounded by music, writing about it, talking to its creators – and getting (sort of) paid for doing so.

One of the more memorable outings was to the international terminal at Sydney airport one afternoon in late 1979 to chat to AC/DC. They were about to depart Australia for an overseas sojourn to Miami for songwriting and rehearsal sessions for a new album. This was before some dates in Japan in the first two weeks of March, then they'd start work on the aforementioned project. Tragically, this wouldn't happen as Bon Scott would die in February.

At the airport the band took over a large portion of an upstairs restaurant/bar area and were in the process of drinking the place dry.

Because only Bon had a correctly-stamped visa, there were departure delays. Instead of going home till the rescheduled departure time the next day, everyone seemed intent on staying right where they were.

I grabbed a few words with Bon, who eyed my female companion up and down, telling her that she should 'look after that great body', before looking me up and down and continuing, 'And if *he* doesn't, let me know and you can have *my* phone number.'

I didn't realise I'd been photographed that day until an image appeared online in 2021 of Bon and his girlfriend Pam Swain. Lurking in the background, leaning against the bar, is a guy who looks suspiciously like me.

It was the best of times – except when it wasn't.

I had a rather terrifying experience early one morning with The Stranglers. They had a reputation for not liking music journalists and recently I'd read that their bass player, Jean-Jacques Burnel, had rendered an English writer almost unconscious with some karate hold he knew. Apparently, he was a black belt who had been training with a Japanese master and running five miles through the snow each morning. As you do.

I wasn't a big fan of The Stranglers and got stuck into them about their perceived sexism, which didn't go down all that well with singer Hugh Cornwell and Burnel. I was nervous and they sensed that. Burnel accused me of being preoccupied with sex – which apparently you were if you asked about sexism. He started writhing on the hotel-lobby couch, in a fashion that seemed like an attempt to simulate a sex act. His motivation was a bit unclear, although seemingly he wanted to belittle my earnest questioning.

Next thing I knew, Burnel got up, stood behind me and grabbed my head. One hand on top, the other under my chin. He started pushing his hands together, then manipulating the nerves in my neck. I was figuring this was his party trick. He was going to leave me unconscious by finding the nerve points in my neck. It was terrifying! Why me . . .

It turned out that Burnel was giving me a rough – apparently necessarily so – Japanese massage. He figured I was too tense, so he relaxed my head, neck, back and hands: the latter with a savage twist that cracked his thumb bone loudly. *Sure, Mr Burnel, I'm relaxed. Anything you say, Mr Burnel.*

The interview lasted for a further, less intense 30 minutes. Cornwell's last observation was that I looked a bit undernourished for an Australian. He was bigger than Burnel, so I was prepared to agree with anything he said too.

Back in the *RAM* office, Anthony O'Grady was a bit less terrifying – sometimes only just so. He was certainly unpredictable, and typewriters were thrown against walls on deadline nights. Anthony was a demanding editor and really tough on his contributors, which I both appreciated and resented at the time. Only in hindsight did I really come to understand what he'd done for me – particularly when I saw what passed for editing at other publications and observed the rudimentary work of other would-be music journalists, who just didn't seem to improve or evolve because they had no direction. What Anthony did was simple. He taught me how to write.

There was no better illustration of that than one night when I was slaving away on a piece about Midnight Oil. By this stage *RAM* had moved to offices near the corner of Crown and Liverpool streets in Darlinghurst, which we shared with various other magazines in the Mason Stewart stable. The Stewart in question was Mason's partner, the affable Barry Stewart, whose main role was advertising sales for the magazines in the stable. There was a fashion magazine and the famous surfing magazine, *Tracks*.

It was always amusing to see the *Tracks* staff appear from the beaches. They'd arrive in a frenzy, throw together a magazine in the time it took to roll several joints and hoover a gram of speed, and then disappear until it was time to do another issue.

This particular evening, I finished my version of the Midnight Oil story and gave the pages to Anthony. I lingered whilst he read what I'd done and observed him scribbling and scribbling . . . and scribbling all over the copy. He handed it back to me with words that basically translated into him thinking it was a heap of shit.

'I can fix it up for you but I'm not going to,' he said. 'You do it – and do it tonight so that I have it tomorrow morning.' Then he left for the night, while I went back to my typewriter and tried to decipher all the handwritten comments in red pen.

I was pretty damn pissed off. Deflated too. I felt I'd done a good job and that he was just picking on my . . . well . . . *everything*: sentence structure, grammar, punctuation, narrative voice, and what felt like every opinion I expressed. To my mind, this neutralised and compromised everything I'd written. It may, in fact, have made it a much better piece, but I wasn't prepared to accept that.

I also thought that maybe he wasn't happy that I wasn't as totally enamoured with everything Midnight Oil as he was. At this point in time, in many people's eyes the Oils could do no wrong, but here I was, suggesting a possible weakness in the vocal department. Although I didn't say it, going through my mind – on repeat – were two words directed at Anthony: 'fuck' and 'you'. But I shut up and did what I was told.

There were many other nights he did the same thing, but I grew to realise how invaluable his instructions and demands were. By insisting that I think about what I'd written, look at his suggestions and then do the rewriting myself, he made me hone what skills I had, and improve on them.

As it happened, this Midnight Oil feature was one that took Peter Garrett several years to forgive me for, because I posited (even after rewriting the entire piece) that they were a great band, let down only by the limitations of the singer. He was an amazing performer – that was a given. As the years have gone by, though, I've become much more a fan of Garrett's distinctive singing style, and its cultural importance for music in Australia and globally, and have maintained a friendship with all of the Oils members.

Of course, all interviews were recorded on cassettes. Everyone in my caper had little cassette recorders that they plonked on the table nearest to the interview subject. There were always the nerves – when was the last time I changed the batteries in this thing? And constant glances at the machine to make sure the wheels were still spinning. Then there was the moment when you walked out of the interview and anxiously checked that the conversation had recorded. That sinking 'I want to die *now*' feeling if for some reason it hadn't.

I remain deeply nervous and suspicious around all recording devices. I was known to run two cassette players in an interview – just to be sure. Digital recorders scare me even more, because I can't see things moving. I'll race from an interview, connect to my laptop and make a safety copy, then immediately transfer that to a back-up hard disc. But, fortunately, then, and now, there have been precious few disasters in that department.

And there were weird times. For some reason – I think it had something to do with advertising and deadlines – Anthony asked me to review an Olivia Newton-John concert in Sydney, but pretend I was at the Melbourne show. That didn't seem a problem, as it was hard to imagine that the performance would change much from city to city. Anyway, my review of the Melbourne gig appeared in print and suddenly the whole world – those who cared, mind you – knew I'd fudged it. I didn't mention the bomb scare in Melbourne that resulted in the show being halted and the venue temporarily cleared, did I? Missed that.

It's interesting (I hope you agree) to look back at my end-of-year round-up in *RAM* for 1978. Here goes:

BEST SINGLES
Young Modern – 'She's Got The Money'
Sports – 'Who Listens To The Radio'
Jo Jo Zep and The Falcons – 'So Young'
Elvis Costello – 'Radio Radio'
Patti Smith – 'Because The Night'

BEST LIVE SHOWS
Graham Parker at Apollo Stadium in Adelaide
Bette Midler in Sydney
Bob Dylan in Adelaide
Young Modern any night of the week
Keith Jarrett at the Opera House
Sports anytime
Dragon . . . sometimes

BEST ALBUMS
David Johansen – *David Johansen*
Brucie – *Darkness On The Edge Of Town*
Elvis Costello – *This Year's Model*
Lou Reed – *Street Hassle*
Flamin' Groovies – *Now*
The Cars – *The Cars*
The Only Ones – *The Only Ones*
The Sports – *Reckless*
The Jam – *All Mod Cons*
Johnny Thunders – *So Alone*
Magazine – *Real Life*
Lou Reed – *Live: Take No Prisoners*
And a million others, depending on the day

REISSUES
Tommy James and The Shondells – *20 Greatest Hits*
The three Big Star albums
Brinsley Schwarz – *The 15 Thoughts Of Brinsley Schwarz*

BEST ROCK'N'ROLL MOVIE
*The Last Waltz*

BEST ROCK'N'ROLL BOOK
Steve Chapple and Reebee Garofalo – *Rock'n'Roll Is Here To Pay*

TIPS FOR THE TOP
Bruce Springsteen for God
Young Modern outside of Adelaide
Sports overseas
The Accountants worldwide
Leif Garrett onstage

The first few months at *RAM* had been great. I often had to pinch myself to realise how things had progressed from my days in

Launceston, dreaming about this. But it wasn't to last. Maybe I became a bit cocky, a bit too sure of myself too early, but by early 1979 things between Anthony and I became a little strained. It wasn't out-and-out warfare – more a smouldering reticence on my part to listen and take on advice. And possibly allowing myself to think that I was a little bit better at this caper than I actually was. I was reluctant to accept that there were still a lot of skills for me to master and for a distinctive Stuart voice to emerge.

Anthony was a hard editor and, as I said, it was only much later I realised what he'd done for me. The fact that I was involved somewhat clandestinely with fellow staffer Annie Burton possibly didn't help matters.

So, Anthony and I locked horns a few times – and then it came to a head. Over bloody Redgum. I mean, seriously, if you're going to have a full-on confrontation with your editor, can it be something huge and life changing? Not a Redgum album. But I guess that was the problem, as I thought the first release from the Adelaide quartet *was* both huge and life changing. Anthony didn't think it was either of these things.

You see, I'd gone to university with the Redgum members, and knew the place they were writing about ('another boring night in Adelaide') and the politics they were immersed in. And they'd become friends. So when their first album came out in 1978, not only did I love it, I thought it was a major landmark in Australian music history and should be treated as such.

Maybe I was overstating its importance and was unduly swayed by knowing the creators of the songs, which was an easy trap to fall into. But I was a real believer in the power of politicised music, especially with Redgum having gone through the same leftie philosophy studies that I had.

I wanted to write a full-page review of the album. Anthony wanted a 150-word capsule review. The tension escalated, so I decided I was out of there. I pulled on my leather jacket, walked over to his desk and told him I quit.

Anthony didn't try to change my mind. He was pleasant, rolled me two joints and wished me luck.

I'd made a brash, impetuous call. I was now out of a regular job and income and could no longer say I was a RAM staffer – something which opened a lot of doors and was a constant source of free albums which (when sold) helped pay the rent each week.

Anthony said he was happy for me to contribute to the magazine, but I had no idea if he was just being nice. How much of my work would actually appear – especially as I'd now be lower in the pecking order than whoever took my job. Was I mad? Maybe? Was this a *huge* mistake? It was an issue to ponder that two joints wouldn't really help evaluate.

The Redgum review was published in *RAM* soon afterwards. The one written by me. It ran about 650 words and was at the top of the reviews page, with a big reproduction of the cover. I felt pretty good about that, but I didn't have a job. Vindicated, sure. Employed full-time? No, siree.

One upside was that I was now free to contribute once again to *Roadrunner*, which I did with great gusto. Along with Double J radio presenter and aspiring journalist Stuart Matchett, I formed the Sydney team for the magazine. I wrote pieces on the likes of Young Modern, Sunnyboys, Jo Jo Zep & The Falcons, Midnight Oil, Mental As Anything and Radio Birdman.

I was pleased too that Anthony was serious about me not being persona non grata at *RAM*, and I continued to contribute regularly. I was feeling the absence of those 90 bucks a week, though. I needed to make my own luck as a freelancer. I had to find a regular gig – and fast.

# 14

# YESTERDAY'S PAPERS

David Dale was probably only a few years older than me, but it seemed like more. He was an old-school journalist and not very rock'n'roll. At the time, he was a respected reporter at *The Sun-Herald*, and would go on to be a highly regarded food and television critic, amongst many other things.

In September 1978, he'd stepped in from his regular gig at the paper to edit *RAM* for a couple of weeks. Anthony was heading overseas and I was deemed (correctly) not to have the degree of experience needed to put the magazine together. I remember that one of the issues he edited commemorated the life of Keith Moon, who'd died earlier that month.

David and I got on well and he had fun moonlighting in the music world. He was quiet, methodical and professional. I'm picturing him wearing a suit, albeit a casual one, to the *RAM* office, but I might just be imagining that. I was a bit in awe of him, though. His by-line was in *The Sun-Herald*. He was a *real* journalist.

These days in the Sunday newspapers, lifestyle rules and it's all about the clicks. In 1979, *The Sun-Herald* was vastly different. For starters, back in the late 1970s and through the 1980s it was the biggest-selling newspaper in the country. It was a big deal. And it was a big paper – running well over 100 pages every Sunday. It was a hard-hitting, news-orientated publication, full of experienced investigative journalists, and it was out to break stories and nail bad people. It was a serious journal of record that was taken very seriously. It scared politicians and dodgy figures from all parts of society.

So, I'd finished up at *RAM* after the Redgum clash and needed other ways to pay the bills. I was officially a freelance journalist now, in an era when – if you were smart and fast – you could make a living from writing. You were never going to buy a house, but you could pay your way.

Sometimes, though, you just need a stroke of luck – for the cards to fall just right. I'd barely finished smoking the two joints that Anthony had given me as a farewell present when I received a call from David. He was pretty matter of fact and straight to the point. There was little preamble. He asked if I was interested in doing the music column for *The Sun-Herald*. Was I ever.

You see, up until this point the motoring writer – a nice enough guy, as I recall – doubled as the music writer. By his own admission, he knew as much about music as I did about cars and how they worked. Ignition keys? Brakes? Out of my league.

David had suggested to the powers that be that it might be a good idea to have the music column written by someone with a working knowledge of, and passionate engagement with, the subject. The other guy could wax lyrical about Holden's latest release and which wheels were best for wet roads – and leave me to ruminate on the latest album from The Clash and whether there might be any longevity in this band called The Ramones.

David told me later that this was a time when *The Sun-Herald* was trying to attract a younger readership. When he'd gone to the newspaper's legendary editor Max Suich, he'd admitted that this new guy couldn't spell and wasn't exactly a master of punctuation. But David added that he could correct the spelling and punctuation – it was the other stuff that was more important.

So, within a week or two of finishing up on staff at *RAM*, I was the music writer for *The Sun-Herald*, with a half-page each week for my column – 'Rock Beat' – and a photo of me next to the heading. Did I mention that it was the biggest-selling newspaper in Australia, with a circulation measured in hundreds of thousands?

It just kept getting better. I was still a freelancer so I didn't have to go to the *Sun-Herald* offices, except to file my copy. And as I wasn't officially on staff, I could write for anybody else who wanted my stories and reviews.

Although I didn't really need to spend more than five minutes a week dropping by the office, on Broadway near Central Station, I loved it there. It was classic old-school journalism in full flight. There were rows and rows of desks, not a computer to be seen, with phones everywhere, connected to the wall by cords that seemed to run in every possible direction – under, over and around desks and chairs. The whole scene looked a little like an explosion in a spaghetti factory. Manual typewriters were clattering, wastepaper baskets overflowing, paper and newspapers everywhere. Ashtrays sat on every second desk, a pall of smoke in the air.

People were yelling and rushing around like their house was on fire. Every journalist's story was the most important thing going down. It was kinda like, 'Do not – I repeat, do not – get in my way. Who are you? The music writer? I know there's a new Talking Heads album, buddy – but there is real shit breaking in Canberra *now*.'

It's a cliché but the atmosphere positively crackled. I used any excuse to go in and hang out. Was I intimidated? Sure. But watching and learning through osmosis.

Copy was delivered to your editor or sub-editor, who marked it up with changes before it was sent to the overall editor for final approval. And then came the bit I loved. Your copy would be rolled up, placed in a small cylinder and dropped into a chute near the editor's desk. There, it was propelled down to the lower floors where typesetters would turn it into pages of text ready to be assembled to look like tomorrow's newspaper, then sent off to the printer.

It was all very rudimentary and without the intrusion of any computers, or any form of the technology that is now taken for granted. In fact, when I started at *The Sun-Herald*, faxes didn't exist yet and people still used telex machines. (Telex machines were a step up from morse code – but only just.) Actually, we were wondering if we'd live to see flying cars. That kind of thing preoccupied us, not ridiculous ideas like a computer on every desk, or phones that weren't connected to a wall by a cord. Get real.

At *The Sun-Herald*, my go-to guy, David, taught me more of the basics of journalism. In those days, each paragraph of a story was typed on a small sheet of paper – about 15 centimetres by six centimetres – and then they were paperclipped together. This made it easy to edit, because it was simple to take out paragraphs or rearrange them.

David instilled in me that the first lines of a story had to grab a reader. It sounds straightforward, but wow, how important is it. 'If you can't get them to read the first paragraph, what makes you think they're going to read the second or third one?' It was good logic. And the conclusion had to relate back to the opening paragraph, tying a bow, if you will, on the yarn you'd just told.

Every single time I've sat down to write in the 40 years since, I remember David's advice. Killer opening par. Don't forget to link the conclusion back to the start. And I've lost count of how many times I've told other aspiring journalists the same things.

They're basic skills, but they're so important. Year after year I've seen kids (i.e. anyone younger than me – which often feels like most people) who've spent a few years writing for the street music papers or their equivalent and who haven't been taught these basics. The only real editing in these publications seems to be to cut the story to fit the advertising. After being paid peanuts, these young writers eventually get fed up and want to contribute to real newspapers and magazines. However, sometimes they come away shocked that their writing isn't deemed to be at a high-enough level for such publications. Why? Because no-one has taken them aside and taught them the basics. Every day I wake up and prepare to write a review, article, press release, or even a basic email – any form of written communication, really – I count my blessings that I had those teachers.

I could never master short-hand and touch typing, though, let alone typing with more than two fingers, and a thumb to hit the space bar. Admittedly, I'm really fast with those fingers: think the cartoon character

Roadrunner. I once timed myself at around 90 words a minute (more if drugs were involved, but the error count was higher), so I could almost have been a professional typist or a secretary. Actually, I'm exaggerating here. I'm super-fast, but super-unreliable when it comes to accuracy.

People marvel at my chicken on speed pecking away at the keyboard, and I'm still pretty average at spelling and grammar and punctuation, having always laughed that I've been on a lifelong mission to keep editors and sub-editors employed. But I like to think I can tell a yarn that keeps a reader's attention. If you've got this far, then maybe I'm right. If I lost you a few chapters back, shit happens. I tried. I really did.

Saturday evening was my favourite time to go to the Fairfax offices. For months I'd head into Broadway at about 5.30 pm to await the first edition rolling off the presses. I'd hang in the loading dock on street level and see it coming down the conveyor belt in bundles, ready to go into trucks that fanned out across the city – and to the airport so that copies would be interstate by the time the sun came up the next day.

I was beyond excited to see my column on newsprint. Sometimes I was glad I'd turned up to check: like the week I did an interview with John Cale. Someone had obviously just grabbed the photo files and assumed there was only one J. Cale, so there was a terrific photo of J. J. Cale illustrating my story on that other guy. But that didn't happen very often.

It was on Saturday evening when things *really* crackled. Especially if there was a big story breaking. The first edition came off the presses at about 6pm. Then there'd be a few hours before the second edition. A lot could happen in that time – especially if there was a major crime incident, unexpected political upheaval or natural disaster. One night I observed editor Max Suich towering over David Dale and others, bellowing instructions and questions as a front-page story was rewritten. He wasn't at all nice about it. There was no time for pleasantries.

The journalists went on strike in 1980. I helped out with the strike paper, which was written, laid out and printed by the striking journalists, as a counterpoint to the daily newspaper being assembled by the Fairfax management. It lasted a few weeks, and my main involvement was getting up super-early (for me, at least) and selling the paper to people as they got on and off buses around Central station and the Fairfax offices on their way to work.

Amongst my favourite people at *The Sun-Herald* were the copy-takers. In the decades before email, if you were away from the office – as I frequently was – you could phone the switchboard and get put through to these delightfully friendly and patient women. I got to know some of them by name, and looked forward to chatting to them whenever I needed to phone my column through. Maybe there were guys doing it too. I suspect not.

Anyway, you'd get on the phone and read your copy to this person – very . . . very . . . slowly – and they'd type it up for you. You'd say 'new par' to indicate – well – a new paragraph. And you had to spell every name so that it didn't appear that weekend as 'Rod Stuart' or 'You Too'. Going through a typical 800-word column would take a good 30 to 40 minutes.

So, those were the logistics of filing a piece and working at a major metropolitan newspaper. Now all I had to do was come up with ideas for the column every week, writing about more or less whatever I wanted, on a subject I was passionate about. What could go wrong?

# 15
# NEWSPAPER PANE

In the early days, my 'Rock Beat' column at *The Sun-Herald* shared a page with the Salami Sisters, who had also been enlisted to 'youthify' the newspaper. The 'sisters' were Kathy Lette and Gabrielle Carey, who went on to write *Puberty Blues*, among many other claims to fame. Kathy and Gabrielle wrote a sort of lifestyle column, and I remember going with them early on to a gig inside Parramatta Jail (for what would become part of the *Canned Rock* compilation album).

Why did we all go? I'm not sure. I'm guessing that the editor suggested we all go – me to cover the rock'n'roll side of things and the Salami Sisters for the lifestyle aspect of the prison experience. Let's face it, how many opportunities would we have to see the inside of a notorious jail, unless we were convicted and sentenced to time there? Despite the tension surrounding the visit, it was an irresistible opportunity.

It turned out to be a frightening afternoon. The guards told us to stick together and demonstrated how easy it would be for a group of prisoners to grab us as they filed past – and that it might take five or 10 minutes for the guards to realise what had happened and to locate us. During this time, they said, 'Anything could happen.' Fortunately, nothing like that did happen and we ate stale sandwiches made by some of the more trusted prisoners before watching Rose Tattoo play to the inmates.

Embedded in my memory is the moment Angry Anderson sang the words, 'Thirty days in the county jail – I'm a bad boy,' with several hundred prisoners leaping to their feet, screaming and punching the air. No-one was assaulted, no-one dragged to a cell, but it was an incredibly nerve-racking experience, and I was glad to hear the final gate slam closed as we left. I've been in and out of jails a little over the years for stories and events and I've never been anything other than terrified.

In my early days at *The Sun-Herald*, I was given a lot of leeway. I unashamedly championed independent and emerging Australian and overseas artists and as such had the perfect vehicle to publicise them. If I wanted to write about a band I loved who could barely draw 50 people to the Southern Cross Hotel on a Wednesday night, then I could and did – in the biggest-selling newspaper in the country. There was no-one looking over my shoulder saying, 'Elton John has a new album out – maybe you should be covering that.'

Of course, some people became jealous – particularly bands who maybe didn't get the attention from me they thought they deserved. I loved a Sydney Mod/R&B band called The Introverts. And my enthusiasm for them clearly got to at least one person, as one night some graffiti appeared on a wall on the corner of Crown and Foveaux Street in Surry Hills. In very big letters it said, 'STUART COUPE FUCKS THE INTROVERTS.' Not long after, someone else grabbed a paint tin and wrote, 'SO WHO'S JEALOUS?' That graffiti stayed on the wall for maybe 20 years and probably did more for my profile and notoriety than most of what I wrote.

On another wall in Darlinghurst appeared more graffiti: 'I WISH I HAD TASTE LIKE STUART COUPE – LIKE SOUP WITHOUT SALT.' Yes, this was an era when people took writing about music and the people who wrote it very seriously.

Ah, the price of infamy! In 1980, the Sydney band The Slugfuckers released an album that came with a sticker with the photo of me from my *Sun-Herald* column in the middle, and the words 'The Stuart Coupe Seal Of Approval' around the outside. Piss-take or praise? Who knows.

A year later, a Wollongong band, the Sunday Painters, released a single called 'Let's Be Moderne'. It included references to Mi-Sex and Space Invaders and a chorus that went 'Oh, how I wish that I was modern – just like . . . Stuart Coupe.' Was it affectionate? Were they having a go? I'm still not sure, but Double J played it a bunch of times.

It was fairly early on that I realised how powerful the column could be. I'd just started there when Marianne Faithfull's *Broken English* album came out very late in 1979. I was incensed that it had been censored in Australia and that certain words had been beeped out. That had always given me the shits, way back to when I bought the *Snoopy Vs. The Bloody Red Baron* EP by the Royal Guardsmen and heard the '*beep* Red Baron'. This was not on.

So I started to wage a written war against Festival Records, who distributed *Broken English* in Australia and had made the decision to censor this still astonishing album. I called them out loudly in my column and it clearly had an impact. I was requested to attend a meeting at Festival, where I sat in an office with Managing Director Alan Healy and General Manager Jim White. They told me in no uncertain terms that they wanted me to stop. And they did it with the air of a headmaster calling in an errant young student for a firm dressing-down.

The grilling reached a crescendo when the very old-school Healy (a lovely man, I must add) asked if I'd be happy if my mother heard this album and the lyrical content. What could I say? I explained that my mother was both unfamiliar with the works of Marianne Faithfull and unlikely ever to fork out $14.99 for one of her records.

There was a stalemate. I was intent on keeping up my campaign and they were equally intent on not releasing an unedited version. In case you're wondering, most of the kerfuffle was over the song 'Why D'Ya Do It'. If you're not familiar with its lyrical content, can I suggest you go to your favourite streaming service or check the lyrics online?

Faithfull definitely wasn't mincing her words. But so what? The way I saw it – and still do – was that it was up to the consumer to decide if they wanted to buy and listen to the album. Maybe – just maybe – do an edit for the few radio stations that might consider playing the song, but after that, buyer beware. Warning sticker on the cover? I'm good with that. But beeping the words. Not on.

This is where it gets interesting. A week or two later, I returned home around 4 pm. There were two glass panels in the front door, and as I looked down the passageway to the living-room and wall where my record collection was, I clearly saw a figure. Not a ragged, snatch 'n' grab junkie, but a suited, well-built guy in his 30s. He looked at me as I opened the door, made sure I saw him, and then bolted out the back. When I got to the rear of the house, I saw that the back gate and door had been super-efficiently kicked in. By the time I reached the street, he was nowhere to be seen.

When I returned inside, I realised nothing was missing. What was intriguing was that a dozen or two records had been partially pulled out of the shelves – just the way I would if I was selecting albums to go back to later and have a listen to. It felt to me very much as though the guy had been killing time and waiting till I came home, so I could see him.

My stressed and semi-feverish brain began to think that he'd come back to reinforce the message – or that if he was actually intending to take a bunch of records, he'd return again when I wasn't around. Maybe with help. Remember that I have a good imagination, am a scaredy cat, and had read a lot of crime fiction. That was enough to have me seriously paranoid and on edge for weeks.

In retrospect, I have no doubt that he wasn't a run-of-the-mill thief. In fact, wasn't a thief at all. Federal Police? Undercover cop? Private investigator? The encounter with the house invader certainly reminded me that having a half-page in *The Sun-Herald* was a vehicle that I should take very seriously. Other people most definitely did.

Having *The Sun-Herald* as my principal outlet gave me a definite cachet with major record labels; hence the trip to Paris to interview Bruce Springsteen in 1981. From there, I flew to London on the CBS tab to interview artists on their books, as well as the Virgin Records label, which, at the time, they distributed in Australia.

I stayed at the Portobello Hotel. It was in Notting Hill Gate, run by women, and hipster before its time. I had a tiny, tiny room, but the Portobello had one big advantage in an era when London closed down not long after the sun set – well, OK at about 10 pm. It had a downstairs bar that seemed to stay open for as long as people wanted to drink. For that reason and its location – which included Virgin Records having their office not far away – the Portobello was a hang. I just looked it up online. It's still going, with a price tag per night that suggests I may never stay there again. But it might have been expensive back then. CBS was paying each time I walked up the stairs.

Because of the relationship between CBS in Australia and Virgin, I spent a number of days sitting in the hotel bar interviewing a seemingly endless stream of Virgin artists – the Psychedelic Furs spring to mind. Some were also conducted at the Virgin offices; in particular, an amusing encounter with post-Sex Pistols Johnny Rotten, now plain and simple John Lydon and with his new band Public Image Limited.

Lydon was witty, smart and extremely entertaining. He was still wearing the wedding ring that was apparently meant to be on his brother's finger, the ceremony having been held the day before, with the singer as best man. To keep the ring safe, John had done the usual thing and slipped it on his own finger – only to be unable to remove it when the time came. Or so he said. If you ever see him, ask if he recalls the incident and how the ring was removed.

Virgin also provided one of the highlights of this trip – ferrying me out of London to Mike Oldfield's home where, yes, I had the opportunity to see and hit his tubular bells. His album from 1974 had saved Virgin Records and kept them solvent until the Sex Pistols, and then Culture Club, came along. It had been huge in my life and – it seemed – that of pretty much everyone I knew. If you wandered around the houses of young people in Launceston in that era, you could reasonably expect that it would be home to a copy of *Tubular Bells*. It was everywhere.

I recall Oldfield being pleasant, but a bit offhand: maybe quiet or maybe arrogant. Or maybe he was simply over talking about *Tubular Bells*. That had been seven years earlier and he'd already moved on to albums like *Hergest Ridge* and *Ommadawn* – which many of us referred to as 'Ommayawn'. But I did get to touch the big-ticket item and was guaranteed of a lifetime of gags about playing with Mike Oldfield's tubular bells. It never gets old. The sniggers and nudge nudges continue to this day. Great record too, which I still listen to often.

Virgin Records was, of course, the brainchild of a young Richard Branson. Seeing as I was in London and doing the rounds of all the key artists on the label, it made sense for me to do an interview with him. It was conducted on the houseboat he lived on, which was moored on the Thames. Branson was animated, amusing, full of exuberance and a great conversationalist. However, most of that chat is lost to time, as he also owned a large cockatoo which was in a cage on the boat and was incredibly noisy and talkative. On my interview cassette, there is a lot of cockatoo and not nearly as much Branson as I'd have liked.

A few years later, he launched himself into the airline business and in 1984 I was back in London and heading to New York. I decided to fly Virgin. They were a cheap, no-frills airline. You took your own food on board with you. As I lined up to check in, there was my old mate John Lydon catching the same flight. He didn't recognise me.

Whilst in London, I was determined to encounter a *real* star of music writing. Nick Kent was the biggest of them all in those days. A star writer at *New Musical Express* and someone who – mythology had it – was capable of making big bands and artists delay their onstage appearance until he'd taken his seat.

Kent was rakishly thin, the result of a constant imbibing of pharmaceuticals like speed and heroin. He was also really tall, pretty much always dressed in leather – reportedly with one worn-out pair of leather pants underneath a new pair. Go figure. Apparently, he never recorded his interviews, simply recreating them from memory. Also, he didn't type – handwriting his copy on scraps of paper, cereal boxes and whatever he could find. But he was good. Very good. And very cool.

He hung around with the serious heavyweight rock stars as an equal. If they were into Class A drugs and in London, they had a friend in Kent. He used to go out with Chrissie Hynde, and he'd been chain-whipped by Sid Vicious at a Sex Pistols gig. He was the real deal.

Via someone at Virgin, I'd gotten him on the phone and we'd set a time for a meeting at the *NME* offices in Carnaby Street. Yep, that Carnaby Street, which, by then, was little more than an endless stream of themed '60s-inspired tourist shops.

When I arrived at *NME* for our 2 pm meeting, the receptionist struggled not to laugh. It was clearly far too early for Kent to make an appearance at the office. I waited for about an hour and sensed that he was a no-show, so I decided to leave. As I walked down Carnaby Street I spotted this figure in leather clutching a plastic shopping bag, walking at a thousand miles an hour.

I caught up to him and introduced myself. We went back to *NME*, where it became evident that he was speeding out of his mind. The words torrented out as his hands shook so badly that he kept missing the cup as he tried to spoon sugar into the coffees he was attempting to make for us.

I told him I'd just come from Paris and interviewing Springsteen. *NME* didn't have an interview with Springsteen. He and I were going to write a piece together. This was a 'Fuck me' moment – Nick Kent and I were going to co-write a piece on Bruce Springsteen for *NME*. This was amazeballs. We made plans to meet up in a few days. He'd call me. We'd do it.

He never rang. I left messages at *NME*. The call never came. We never did the piece. But I did get to hang out with Nick Kent. At *NME*. In London.

# 16
# ROCK AND ROLL ALL NITE

With the exception of smoking pot in Launceston and Adelaide, drugs had never been a big feature of my life until I moved to Sydney. Then they appeared – in particular speed, which was cheap and usually effective. Andrew McMillan at *RAM* loved the stuff, and with my addictive personality I quickly followed suit, never giving any thought to where it might take me. I wasn't a huge fan of the burning sensation in my nose, but I wanted to work. This helped me write and write and write. It also made me much more talkative and more socially at ease. For $25 a gram (or whatever it was), all of this became possible. And it was easy to procure, as it was the drug of choice amongst many musicians and road crew. It was the 'go go go with goey' era.

Anyway, not long after starting at *The Sun-Herald*, I picked up another regular gig that kept things financially ticking over. First came a precursor of the free street press – *Sydney Shout*. They gave me a weekly column to pontificate on whatever independent (or occasionally non-indie) band or artist I wished. The only criteria were that I liked them and that they were either playing in Sydney or based there and had a new record out.

Then there was *TAGG*. That was one hell of a trip. *TAGG* originated in Melbourne and stood for 'The Alternative Gig Guide'. Published by Mick Pacholli, it was a fortnightly, pocket-sized magazine which – at one stage – sold for 40 cents, but, for most of its few years of operation, was free.

Somehow, I became the editor in 1980, and the initial Sydney base was my home in Stanmore. The kitchen, to be specific. The room was huge, and the presence of a large table (and not a lot of cooking utensils) made it perfect for the writing and pasting-up of a magazine that averaged 70–80 pages, each only slightly larger than a cigarette packet.

What I lacked in kitchen utensils (and bedding and furniture), I made up for in the aforementioned pinball machines. The kitchen was easily large enough for the two I'd bought from Anthony O'Grady. One was a classic, based on English football, while the other was a more recent Tarzan and Jane machine. Not surprisingly, everyone who visited headed for the kitchen for endless free pinball.

I wrote a ridiculous amount for *TAGG*. I'd be speeding off my head, hammering out endless small features, record and book reviews – plus palming as much extra work to my friends as I could.

*TAGG* remains an amazing snapshot of early 1980s Sydney, when venues flourished and bands filled suburban and city venues seven nights a week. At the Civic Hotel in Sydney's CBD, you could see the likes of Mental As Anything, Midnight Oil, Flowers, The Saints, and many, many others, playing in the upstairs room to around 200 people, both during the week and at weekends. If you want to know about music in Sydney in that era, track down some *TAGG*s. And if you want to know about Melbourne, find the equivalent editions from that city.

The back end of the operation – the financial and business aspects – always confused me. I do know that my weekly salary was paid in cash from a briefcase that was usually stacked with $50 and $100 notes. The ancillary staff were a ratbag collection of rock'n'roll figures – musicians, roadies, rehearsal studio operators, and at least one individual who I knew to be a middle-range drug dealer. I knew because he was *my* drug dealer.

Other goings on, I turned a blind eye to. One night I was getting a lift home with a couple of the *TAGG* team visiting from Melbourne. They needed to make a stop at a nondescript motel on Parramatta Road, near Five Dock. When we pulled into the parking area, they quickly carried out three or four very large garbage bags and took them inside an open door. I had no idea what was in them but, heck, they smelt like marijuana. In any event, *TAGG* was making a major contribution towards keeping the wolves from my door.

Around this time, I was also writing a book called *The New Music*, with music historian and friend Glenn A. Baker. This was an attempt to create an up-to-date encyclopedia of the contemporary punk and new wave scenes. It was an easy process. We made a big list of all the artists we thought should be included and went to record companies to get biographical information on them. Then we divided the list of artists in half and each wrote the entries about them.

It was 128 pages, full colour, and English ska band Madness featured on the cover. In Australia, it was published by Ring Books, a subsidiary of Bay Books, while St Martin's Press in New York issued a *bright* pink hardback edition. Glenn had done the deal, while my contribution was the co-writing and helping source the photographs. We'd later repeat the process with *The New Rock'n'Roll*, but this time we had enough of an advance to hire a researcher to help us with the writing.

Meanwhile, TAGG wound down. Free street music publications were beginning to appear around the country and many of them seemed better connected with the record labels, promoters, venues and custodians of the advertising dollars. *TAGG* simply couldn't compete.

# 17

# I HOPE THAT I DON'T FALL IN LOVE WITH YOU

The moment I heard Tom Waits, I was hooked. The voice, the songs – the persona. In particular, it was his live double album *Nighthawks At The Diner* that lured me in and held me tight.

I interviewed Waits both times he toured Australia, in 1979 and again in 1981. At the time I revered him and his Charles Bukowski meets Jack Kerouac Beat-Generation persona. So did Andrew McMillan, a fellow music writer, Waits obsessive and the person I'd replaced at *RAM*. We both went to chat with him at the Sebel Town House before his first tour.

Waits looked and acted the part perfectly. He'd embraced every aspect of the beatnik stereotype. He was smoking, dressed in a crumpled suit that looked as though it had never had any relationship with an iron or a dry cleaner. He was hunched, he mumbled, but he was also warm and engaging, and I bought it all. It would be some time before it clicked that maybe Waits was as good at assuming a character as he was writing songs and singing about the underbelly of Los Angeles.

I've always disliked doing interviews in hotel rooms. It's sterile and feels a bit like cornering a chicken in a cage. Best to get them out of that environment. Not that the Sebel was a bad place to hang, mind you. In fact, if you were a visiting artist the Sebel Town House was *the* best place to stay. It was discreet, upmarket funky, and staff were pretty unfazed by most behaviour and kinda knew how to turn a blind eye to all sorts of nefarious activities. The Sebel had a perfect location for its edgy, but chic clientele at the top of Elizabeth Bay, on the cusp of Kings Cross.

I did a lot of cocaine over the years in the hotel bathrooms. To get there, you had to walk past the front desk and wind your way around and around to get to the Men's. I'm pretty sure they knew exactly what I was up to. No-one my age needed to go to the loo that often for any reason other than powdering the old nose.

Pretty much anything that happened within the walls of the Sebel stayed there. And a lot happened. If not in the rooms, then upstairs by the pool, in the front restaurant or the photo-lined bar.

It had a definite air of glamour as well. Some days you'd just have to walk through the door and into the foyer before you did a double take as three or four household names were checking in or out, or just hanging on the couches doing interviews or waiting to be taken somewhere.

Anyway, late in the afternoon, after the interview with Waits, McMillan and I suggested that he might like a stroll up to Kings Cross. He liked the idea. This was before Waits was the revered figure he is today (and one who's never returned to Australia since those first two tours). So this trio of deadbeats – one of whom was Tom Waits – took a stroll down MacLeay Street. Not that we would have stood out in Kings Cross in the late 1970s.

It was dusk and it was noisy. There was a lot of traffic around. By the way, it was highly unusual for a record label and tour promoter to let their artist roam free. They usually kept them on a tight leash, chained to the room or hotel bar doing endless interviews. And, hell, in the hands of McMillan and me, in Kings Cross in that era, it might have been the last anyone heard of him!

As it turned out, we all behaved ourselves. As McMillan and I nattered with Waits about music and books, we were just three desper-adoes going for a walk. Waits was very much an emerging cult artist at the time, and attracted zero attention. It's a bit surreal to think about him strolling around the Cross completely unnoticed.

The second time I interviewed Waits was much less pleasant. If at all possible, I'd always tried to take friends with me to interviews if they were rabid fans, and could cope with being in the presence of their idols without flipping out. I took my buddy Goose (later the singer with Box The Jesuit) to interviews with Todd Rundgren and the Mike Nesmith-less Monkees – both at the Sebel. With Tom Waits, I invited my friend Suzanne Dowling along. I'd met Suzanne at Double J where she was a presenter, and had hung at her place in Newtown – probably the tiniest house I've ever been inside. Later, she became the host of the ABC TV music show, *Rock Arena*. Now, Suzanne absolutely adored Waits, but for some reason hadn't been offered an interview – probably someone else at Double J was covering it.

This time around Waits acted like a complete prick. He appeared to be drunk, even though it was a mid-morning chat. Anything I asked him, it was as if he was engaged in a meeting of great minds with one of the smartest human beings ever to grace the planet. But when Suzanne asked a question – usually more perceptive and interesting than mine – he was dismissive and belittling. She was devastated. I didn't know what to do. In hindsight, we both should have walked out of the interview. But we toughed it out till the allocated time was up, and took our leave, a little shell-shocked.

It took me a long time to be able to listen to Tom Waits albums again, and it still colours my perception of him. Maybe he's less of a dick these days – but who knows? He hasn't returned to Australia, is unlikely to, and rarely does interviews.

Of course, I understand the pressures on touring artists to do endless chats with media, answering the same questions time after time, often clocking up 15 or more interviews in a day. I get it. But if you don't want to do it, tell the promoter or record company you're not going to do it. And if you're going to treat people like shit, then treat everyone like shit – don't pick on the gal for some fucked-up reason of your own.

*

Far more civilised an interviewee was Leonard Cohen. I was probably more in awe of the Canadian poet, novelist and singer than I was Waits. I'd been listening to him since the early 1970s, and his music, poetry and fiction were now deeply imbedded in my psyche.

The first time had been on a trip to Ulverstone on the west coast of Tasmania for a tennis tournament. I was staying with the family of a tennis rival, Stephen Milne. Emanating from the bedroom of his older brother Neville was the album *Songs Of Love And Hate* – which contained 'Joan Of Arc', 'Avalanche', 'Diamonds In The Mine', 'Love Calls You By Your Name' and others. It remains my favourite Cohen album.

At the time it was profound and unlike anything I'd heard before. I was transfixed. It was lyrically dense and evocative, and his voice was deep and mysterious, edgy and just a little bit scary.

Back in Launceston, I found some of Cohen's poetry books at the local bookshop. They've travelled the distance with me from those days. His second novel, *Beautiful Losers*, was still on restricted sale when I discovered it and couldn't be purchased by anyone under the age of 18. But my mother, possibly – or possibly not – unaware of its contents, bought me a hardback copy for $6.50.

I'd continued to listen to Cohen's albums (I'd particularly fallen for his *Live Songs* album) and read his novels and poetry. With hindsight, I had little understanding of what he was on about, but a great desire to be as cool as he was. And carting his books and records around was as close as I was going to get to being that cool.

In March 1980, Cohen was in Australia for his first tour, perform-ing with a large band that included several Greek musicians, when I had the chance to interview him at the Hilton. Was I nervous? Most definitely.

He was globally revered; one of the coolest, most literate figures in music, and someone people talked about in the same breath as Bob Dylan and Joni Mitchell. Could I hold a conversation with him on topics he'd find at all interesting? Yes, I was in awe.

Two years earlier – about six months before I moved to Sydney – there'd been a bombing outside the hotel that killed three people.

It had been attributed to members of a religious group, the Ananda Marga sect.

The band The Thought Criminals, which included my newish friend Roger Grierson, had written a song about it, 'Hilton Bomber'. I was a bit preoccupied that morning by the terrorist attack. It might have lobbed into my mind because of my destination. The Hilton wasn't a typical location for visiting international rock stars, most of them hanging at the Sebel Town House.

It was a late-breakfast interview. After I was greeted by a representative of the record label, Cohen and I went to the hotel café overlooking George Street. From our window, I could see where the bomb must have exploded. Cohen was dressed in a suit. Classy. And he was reserved but friendly.

I must have seemed like a dag in comparison, in my pair of jeans and a band t-shirt. Would I have dressed a bit better if I could? Maybe, but those options weren't in my wardrobe. There was nothing even close to Cohen's dapper style.

We were chatting at the table when Cohen turned over his placemat and took a pen from his jacket pocket. He began sketching. I had no idea what he was doing, but he kept raising his eyes, answering my questions at the same time.

I tried to peek at what he was doing before it became obvious that it was a face. And as Cohen looked up at me and back down to his sketch, I realised (ever the slow learner) that it was *me* he was drawing.

Eventually, the pen strokes revealed the rudimentary outline of a face. My face. And my left hand. Cohen had been taken by the way I was leaning forward, resting my elbow on the table and cradling my face with my extended fingers. It was nothing unusual, but clearly intriguing enough for him to want to record it.

I'd done many interviews prior to this, but no-one had ever drawn me during one – and definitely not Leonard Cohen. He finished his sketch, and we concluded the interview. He got up and went to take the placemat. Naturally, I wanted the drawing. I asked him for it and he politely declined.

'Leonard, it's your sketch,' I said, 'but it's my face.'

After signing my copy of his latest album, *Recent Songs* (with tiny handwriting in a top corner – 'Stuart, All Good Things – Leonard Cohen'), slightly reluctantly he gave the placemat to me.

Now, of course I should have immediately had this framed. But money was tight. And I didn't really think of these kinds of things. I took it home, put it in a pile of stuff, and there it stayed. So no doubt it languished in ever-increasing collections of random objects: concert programs, magazines, newspaper clippings, story drafts. I just assumed the precious sketch was there – somewhere – and it did reappear from time to time.

But during the 1980s, I moved. And I moved often and sometimes quickly. Things went *everywhere*. I'm sure some stuff was tossed out and lots left behind. For years, I didn't really think about the sketch, until one day I did.

Actually, every time I went into a Cohen listening zone it'd come to mind. And one day, decades later, I *really* wanted it. I was emailing Cohen biographer Sylvie Simmons and I told her about the encounter. She wrote back saying she'd love to see the sketch. I had to tell her that, well, regrettably, I didn't have it anymore and hadn't seen it since soon after I met with Cohen.

It was a mystery. Had it been destroyed? Did someone I know have it? Did anyone even realise that that roughly sketched face was the work of Leonard Cohen?

Things come and they go – it's so very random. I don't have the sketch that Cohen did, but I do have the scrap of paper on which Johnny Depp scribbled his phone number at the Regent Hotel, and said I should ask for Dean Moriarty when I called or dropped by. Would I trade that piece of ephemera for my Cohen sketch? You bet. Why does one object travel with you and another disappear?

Yes, I have no proof that I was ever sketched by Leonard Cohen in the café at the Hilton that March morning. None at all. Ah well. So, if anyone happens to come across a sketch of a handsome bloke leaning on his elbow, which looks like it might have been drawn by one of the most important recording artists of the 20th century, could they please let me know? Ta.

# 18
# THE UNGUARDED MOMENT

Inevitably, if you're a journalist you're going to get on the wrong side of people. It might be via an innocent mistake, a misunderstanding or a difference of opinion. And they might let you know through a phone call, letter or (in modern times) a text or email. In the early 1980s, though, it was possible you'd find out when the person in question stuck the boot into you in a live TV interview with Donnie Sutherland.

In an end-of-year episode of *Sound Unlimited*, Donnie was chatting with Ignatius Jones, singer with local rising stars Jimmy and the Boys. He happened to ask the vocalist about his one pet hate for 1980. Immaculately attired – black shirt, tie and shiny PVC(?) trousers – Ignatius paused, then drawled, through theatrically gritted teeth, 'Stuuu-art Coupe.'

This was considered significant enough for *The Sun-Herald* to include it in a quiz early the next year in a summer reading edition. The question was: 'When asked on a national TV show who was his pet hate for 1980, Ignatius Jones from Jimmy and The Boys picked which person?' The possible answers were Prime Minister Malcolm Fraser, Ian Meldrum, advertising guru John Singleton and . . . you guessed it.

How had it come to this? I can't remember. Neither can Ignatius. He did tell me, when I asked him recently, '*Sounds* began filming at some ungodly hour on a Saturday morning, and having performed the Friday night before, Joylene [Ignatius' flamboyant and terrifyingly outspoken bandmate] and I were usually totally shattered. The taxi ride from Kings Cross to wherever-the-f*** *Sounds* was filmed was only made possible by the flagon of Riesling we consumed in the back seat, so we were always a bit of a mess.

'Perhaps you wrote something derogatory about the Boys, and Joylene decided to put you on her hit-list. She was always doing that, someone was always in the crosshairs, and I just followed along because it made good press.'

But a much bigger blow-up was with Steve Kilbey. He of The Church. I loved power pop, The Byrds, Rickenbacker guitars and the like. The Church had all of that and a whole lot more. I'd go see them play as often as I could and became friends with the band. From time to time, Steve would drop by my house in Stanmore to give me a lift to one of their gigs, if it was in that direction.

Late on a Sunday night in early 1981, after the band had finished mixing their debut album, *Of Skins And Heart*, Kilbey and drummer Richard Ploog banged on my door, excited to play me the mixes and see what I thought. One thing led to another and I started writing record-company bios for them. I was a big fan.

Then I was dispatched to Melbourne by *RAM* to watch a show or two and do an interview with Kilbey. One of the shows was in St Kilda. I watched from side of stage and was amused to see their tour manager chopping out lines of white powder for band members to quickly inhale between songs.

After the show I went back to the hotel where the band were staying. I think it was the Diplomat but could have been the Prince of Wales – the Dip and the POW were only 20 or 30 feet from each other. The POW was where you stayed on your first trips to Melbourne, the Dip was where you aspired to when things were on the up and up. Both were pretty dire.

Kilbey was there with his friend Jennifer Keyte, the future television newsreader. We started the interview around midnight. In the case of Kilbey and me, amphetamines were involved. I was holding a couple of grams and Kilbey willingly joined me as I rolled up bank notes and chopped out lines of white powder, with increased frequency as the night went on. We talked and talked – and talked. So much so that, at one stage, I ran out of cassettes to record the conversation. But we kept on talking.

As I've mentioned, one of my journalistic heroes, Nick Kent, reportedly never recorded interviews – he just reconstructed the conversation from memory. Granted, that's an unreliable way to do things – especially when lots of drugs are involved, as they usually were with Kent, and certainly were this night.

At some point, Kilbey and I decided to take a walk and ended up watching the sun come up over the water at St Kilda. I was good at seeing the sun come up in those days. Around the same time, after a show at the Sweetwater Festival in New Zealand, Tim Finn and I had taken some gluggy, brown, sugary-looking speed, climbed a hill overlooking the festival site and nattered about the meaning of life all night, only wandering down as the sun rose, weaving amongst half-sleeping, groggy festival patrons clustered around fires to keep warm. Those who recognised the singer from the previous night's headlining band were amused and surprised to see Finn and me meandering through them.

Kilbey and I covered a lot of terrain during our St Kilda interview, and when the story appeared in *RAM* all hell broke loose. There were two small quotes in the story that inflamed matters. Kilbey had quipped that – in his opinion – the only reason The Church had been on *Countdown* was that Molly Meldrum fancied him. Not only did this imply that Meldrum's choice of show guests was based more on sexuality than musical ability, but at the time Meldrum was so far in the closet that he wasn't aware there was a door to get out. EMI – The Church's record label – in particular were horrified at this.

Then there was Kilbey's utterance that he was the greatest songwriter ever. When I'd challenged him on this ludicrous statement, he retorted, 'Tell me someone who's better.'

This made Kilbey sound like a pretentious egomaniac, which wasn't my intention. I was his friend and I wrote what he said. It didn't occur to me that it might end our friendship. Maybe it was the drugs we were both using in those days. Maybe I was too literal.

Kilbey was furious. He felt I'd betrayed him, that I'd undermined our friendship, and quoted him out of context, or inaccurately. He said that the two quotes that upset him were when I wasn't recording the conversation. Things were strained – to put it mildly.

EMI threatened to pull advertising. They also threatened to stop supplying us with new records, and deny us interviews with other artists on the label. And things didn't calm down quickly. Word kept filtering back from time to time from EMI, The Church's management and other music industry figures that Kilbey was still *definitely* displeased. And not to expect that situation to change any time soon.

Two years later, the new *RAM* editor Greg Taylor, who had taken over from Anthony O'Grady, attempted to make peace. EMI were good advertisers, and hadn't delivered on their earlier threat to stop buying space in the magazine. Taylor had a finely honed instinct for a provocative and potentially engaging story – and this one would have people talking. The Church had a new album coming out, *Seance*, and they wanted publicity. Between Taylor and EMI, the idea was hatched that there should be what he called a 'rematch' – another interview.

Kilbey agreed to it and I headed to his home/studio set-up in Balmain. I decided to write the piece as a pseudo-hardboiled detective yarn, casting myself as the weather-beaten gumshoe on a case. It was billed 'THE BIG KISS OFF – Another Stuart "Little Sleuth" Coupe novel'.

The interview was tense and rather lacking in joviality. Kilbey was clearly doing it under sufferance and I was bemused as to why he'd decided to put himself through it. At the end of the encounter, we were photographed arm wrestling. The photo was included on what was the cover story for *RAM* on 5 August 1983.

Kilbey hated this one too. I was a bad, bad person. Loathsome. Not to be trusted. An enemy of The Church. We wouldn't speak again for years.

# 19

# I LOVE MY LABEL

For a while I'd harboured a desire to have an independent record label. I'd started fanzines (*Street Fever*) and a quasi-magazine-cum-fanzine hybrid (*Roadrunner*), so why not a label? I didn't really know anything about *how* to run a label and what was involved, but it seemed like a bunch of other people who were probably, at best, as smart as me were doing it – so why not? These were the post-punk years and the previous era had spawned dozens of indie labels that I loved. There was Stiff Records in the UK, for a start. And Phantom Records here in Australia. That was actually enough. The others were just add-ons.

So, given that I had no idea about what labels did – apart from releasing records – I figured I should enlist someone who maybe did have a bit of a clue. What about my friend Roger Grierson? He'd had a label, and a booking agency, called Doublethink, and he was about my age. And a bit of a go-getter. He was my guy.

One night, with a head full of speed, I wandered up to his Darlinghurst abode, banged on his door and proceeded to blather away at a thousand miles an hour about starting a record label. Some years later, Roger told me he didn't understand much of what I was on about and thought I was trying to convince him to join forces in starting a new magazine.

We had a few more chats – in daylight and without the input of amphetamines. Roger was a very disciplined, organised and matter-of-fact guy, with seemingly endless energy. He and I both operated at full throttle most of the time, so speed wasn't always essential for animated, dreaming 'n' scheming conversations. We were good at it without drugs too. We decided that a new independent record company was a great idea. Two guys with absolutely no money, one with a little bit of experience in this indie caper, both music lovers. That seemed to be enough.

First up, we needed a name. I was really into calling it Siren, as that was the name of my favourite Roxy Music album, and I knew Roger liked Roxy too. He was keen on 'Green Records', though, citing what Kermit from the Muppets had said: 'It's not easy being green.' Roger also had the idea to make it 'G.R.E.E.N.' like the 'Man From U.N.C.L.E.'. So, G.R.E.E.N. it was.

Roger, who was already very well connected in the independent music scene, knew Warren Fahey at Larrikin Records, the shop in Paddington and a large independent label, specialising in folk, jazz and the like. Warren agreed to distribute our label and pay for the pressing of our records.

So far, so good. We'd worked out that it was a label and not a magazine that we were starting – and had a name. All we needed was records to release – and to find an office. Given the vibrancy of the Sydney music scene, finding bands was never really going to be a problem. Indeed, we had a plethora of options without going too far outside of our immediate contacts and friends.

As for an office, Regular Records was a local label that had formed a couple of years earlier. Among their roster were Mental as Anything and Flowers, who were about to change their name to Icehouse. Both artists were really gaining traction on radio, in music magazines and on *Countdown*. They were selling large quantities of records and playing to ever-increasing audiences. Regular had a house in Woolloomooloo and were looking for people to rent the space downstairs, whilst they ran their business above.

I was keen to move from the Inner West to be closer to the city. 132 Cathedral Street was perfect – a quick stroll across Hyde Park from the CBD. I suggested the place to Roger, who managed to escape from a recently signed lease and he moved in too. It was terrific. It had a sunroom at the front with big glass windows, there was a great pub a block away, the East Sydney Hotel, plus we could eavesdrop on all the Regular Records altercations (of which there seemed to be many), as the raised voices travelled down to us.

Roger was managing, and obsessed by, the edgy post-punk Canberra band Tactics, so we released their magnificent *My Houdini* album in February 1980, after Roger had put their first single out on Doublethink. Also in Roger's management stable were the Sydney ska band The Allniters, so their records were released by G.R.E.E.N. too. The same applied to their offshoot The Igniters, as well as Naughty Rhythms and Stupidity. Superficially, Roger was the ska guy. I was the punk-rock guy. So from my side of things, we released the very first single from Rob Younger's post-Radio Birdman outfit, The New Christs.

Running a record label was no big deal to either Roger or myself and it didn't seem to take up much of our time. The process was pretty straightforward. Someone from a band would hand us a cassette at a gig, mail it to us, or simply do what Tex Perkins did when he first arrived in Sydney – knock on the door, say hi, then ask if we wanted to release a record.

Roger and I would play the cassette and maybe think about it for four or five seconds, before saying 'It's fucking great' or 'Who are they kidding? Next.' If it was the former, we'd have a bit of a chat with the artists, usually at our second office – the beer garden at the East Sydney Hotel. I don't recall us having signed contracts. Maybe we did. Then we'd get the master tapes and the cover art and send the songs off to be manufactured.

Sometimes we'd cough up a bit of money – like the $1000, a few slabs of beer and some grams of speed that were the 'budget' for the recording of the first Beasts Of Bourbon album in 1983 – but if we could avoid that aspect, we would.

Roger and I were a bit like ships in the night – both racing around like maniacs. Our most frequent time together, and when we'd discuss life and business, was late on Saturday or Sunday mornings when we both surfaced from our respective nights out and convened for spicy V8 tomato juice, toast with Vegemite and parsley on top.

I dug having a record label, but didn't allow myself to slow down enough – and nor did Roger – to take in the broader picture of what we were doing. There was no grand G.R.E.E.N. plan. It was a fun hobby, which we weren't really thinking of as a serious commercial venture. Roger and I were enjoying hanging out with the artists, considered most of them friends, and were getting our kicks, not from Route 66 but from being part of the scene and facilitating the release of an array of music that we both personally dug. That was about it.

# 20

# THE MORE YOU IGNORE ME, THE CLOSER I GET

I'd never thought of myself as a publicist. To be honest, I still don't. In fact, someone recently said exactly that – they reckoned I wasn't a publicist in the accepted sense. So, of course, I asked what they thought I was.

'You're more like a lobbyist,' they said.

Hmm. Okay. The word lobbyist had all sorts of connotations and I wasn't sure they were all good ones. On the other hand, I did see myself as a behind-the-scenes agitator for getting what I considered to be excellent music played on the radio, as well as overall exposure for the artists I was working with.

I can't remember exactly how I stumbled into doing publicity. But it was the early 1980s and a few things from that period are – almost inevitably – a bit fuzzy. Maybe it was getting the bug hanging around as part of The Clash entourage and watching established publicists in action. Maybe it was trying to corral Julian Cope and his band The Teardrop Explodes on their Australian tour, with my partner Miranda Jetlag, in our short-lived Behind The Lines publicity business. Maybe it was organising interviews for visiting photographer Dezo Hoffmann upon the publication of a book of his Beatles photographs.

But I'm getting a bit ahead of myself. The Clash came first. Miraculously, I wangled a role on their one and only Australian tour. (That, of course, has been a calling card for the rest of my life. 'So, what publicity work have you done?' 'Well, I worked with The Clash in '82.' I get the gig.) My role on the tour as one of the publicity team was pretty straightforward. I was to hang with their manager, Bernie Rhodes, and keep him away from the members of the band – for as long as possible and as often as possible.

Bernie was colourful, controversial and, if you asked The Clash, a pain in the arse, despite his effectiveness for them. Things between him and the band were rather fractious, so he and I took many trips on the harbour, including a couple of ferry rides to Manly, and generally traversed the city.

I didn't have much to do with the band themselves. I was on nodding and 'hello' terms with them, but hardly their new best friend. They knew what I was doing, though, and were happy that Bernie was being taken care of.

In exchange for being their manager's minder, I was given tickets to every night of their seven-night stand at the Capitol Theatre – concerts that remain amongst the most thrilling I've ever seen. And I clearly did an OK job, as a year or so later I was well received at a Clash gig in Brixton when I was in London, particularly by Joe Strummer.

At the time, I was friendly with a Melbourne woman by the name of Miranda Jetlag, or at least that's the name I knew her by. Somehow we concocted the idea of forming a publicity company – I was partly inspired by my experience with The Clash. As you might have guessed, our chosen name, Behind The Lines, had a double meaning. On one level, it was behind the (head)lines: creating news, providing stories and all that stuff. On another level, it was because Miranda and I had probably never had a conversation in which I didn't have a head full of speed.

The arrangement was very loose, but basically amounted to us pitching for work, with me doing the Sydney end of things and Miranda the same in Melbourne. That covered most of the country's major media outlets and we contracted out work to our contacts in other states.

This arrangement did – I believe – cover the first Australian tour by Teardrop Explodes, a band from Liverpool that I totally loved. They played a series of pub gigs in Australia in March and April, a few weeks after The Clash had departed. But there wasn't a lot to do at their Sydney shows, particularly as their lead singer, Julian Cope, was completely gone for all money to the psychological ravages of LSD. In all honesty, I'm not convinced I talked to him the whole tour. I saw him sing and do great shows, sure – but I recall most of the interviews were done by other band members.

In mid-1982, I came into the orbit of Gary Glitter. I'll be honest here – I totally loved his brand of glam rock. Of course, I had no inkling of what was to be revealed about him years later.

I went to the airport to collect Gary, who was travelling with his band and his 17-year-old son Paul. He was staying at the Gazebo Hotel in Kings Cross, and as soon as we arrived in his room he pulled out a huge bag of gelatine 'vitamin' pills, which he'd somehow managed to get through customs without too much examination. He sat on the bed and started going through them. Half were indeed vitamins, while the other half contained speed.

Glitter had been brought to Australia by promoter Aldo Leonard. These were early days for Leonard and he didn't seem to be thorough when it came to reading contracts. The shows involved Gary coming onstage and appearing at the top of a ramp with a revving motorbike. This required the roof above the stage to be a certain height.

These measurements were clearly outlined in the booking contract. However, in many instances the gigs were cancelled as the appropriate staging couldn't be delivered and Glitter said, 'No show.' So the tour lost a significant sum of money.

When Glitter did do shows, he was simply thrilling – and his gig at Selinas in Coogee Bay was out of this world. It inspired one of the finest pieces of music journalism written by an Australian, in Frank Brunetti's two-page feature review/interview for *RAM*. It magnificently captured both the incredible show and what being a passionate music fan is all about.

One of my other jobs as tour publicist was to organise an 18th birthday bash for Glitter's son. Yep – publicists get asked to do all sorts of things. Making sure there were a dozen red roses backstage at each show for Gary to throw to the audience was just the beginning.

At the time I was occasionally DJ-ing at the super cool'n'hip Stranded Club in the Strand Arcade in the city – plus having a more off than on dalliance with the booker, Helene. So I suggested the venue as a location for the Glitter Jnr birthday party.

I had other interests at heart as well. By now, I'd started getting into artist management, and was representing a young bunch of brash, inner-city, garage-rock influenced kids, the Hoodoo Gurus. They were massive Glitter fans too, and I booked them to play during the party. It was – let me tell you – a very *hot* ticket. Stranded was heaving, everyone had a ball, and the festivities wound up at about 2am on a school night.

At the end Gary walked out of the venue, came over, kissed me on the cheek and said, 'Wonderful party, darling.' I went home, collapsed and slept through media calls for comment from me about the celebration.

I had no problems with Glitter. He seemed to like me and he was a hoot to be around – funny, engaging and very committed to his music and shows. There was tension between him and the promoter, but I kept right away from that side of things. And I know you're going to ask, so let me say that I saw no evidence – or even any suggestion – of what the world was later to find out about Glitter. And if there was anything out of line going on, I suspect I would have seen or known about it.

One of the people hanging around on the tour was a Sydney wine merchant who'd known Gary for some time. This dude was clearly connected, as no sooner had the Glitter tour ended than he invited me to meet what was described as an advance party for the Grateful Dead. Their representatives were in Sydney and staying at the Sebel.

I went to this meeting at the hotel to encounter four Texan dudes in suits, equipped with briefcases and smoking lots of pot (sans tobacco, thank you very much). They looked absolutely nothing like what you'd expect of representatives of the Dead. No tie-dye t-shirts, no long hair, nothing. You'd easily believe they were high-powered bankers.

Apparently, these suited Deadheads were in Australia to canvass interest in the band touring Australia. At the time, the Dead were truly massive drawcards internationally, and I can only imagine their asking price per show – especially with their notoriously massive entourage of partners, technical crew, business associates and general hangers-on.

I could have saved them the trouble of taking whatever meetings they took by telling them there'd be no takers amongst the Australian promoting fraternity. These days it's kinda chic to be a Grateful Dead fan, but then? I think I personally knew every other Deadhead in this country – all four of us. As a result, they're amongst a handful of international superstars (put Aretha Franklin and a few others in there too) never to tour Australia.

By now, I was getting involved in some publicity for books as well. I suspect it was Norm Lurie – who ran the Australian branch of Music Sales/Omnibus Press, the book and music publishers – who first dragged me into this particular part of the publicity world. He'd recently been the publisher for *The New Rock'n'Roll* – the second rock encyclopedia that Glenn A. Baker and I had written together.

I'm not sure we wrote a real lot of that one, come to think about it. As I've said, I think the bulk of it was the work of our researcher, Kent Goddard. We were early franchisers in that respect. Use the Baker and Coupe names and get someone else to do the writing. In case you're wondering, I *am* writing this one.

Music Sales/Omnibus Press had recently published a collection of photographs of the Beatles by Dezo Hoffmann, and he was coming to Australia on a promotional tour. Hoffmann had snapped a lot of other people too: I still have a print he gave me of Marlon Brando and Charlie Chaplin together. It's framed and on my wall. And somewhere I have shots he took of Dusty Springfield.

On one level, organising media appearances for Hoffmann shouldn't have been hard. The other level was not so easy. Hoffmann was Czechoslovakian, and what was a slight problem – OK, a *big* problem – was that he spoke very little English, and what he did speak was not exactly fluid. So he wasn't great talent for television or radio. However, I did manage to get him a few high-profile media appearances – mainly television – where they could show the photos and the presenters could carry the bulk of the conversation. But his lack of English made all of them tough going.

Back to music, and I was happy to take on a few more publicity projects for touring bands. The Dead Kennedys toured in August '83. I wasn't a huge fan – I mean, I liked 'Holiday In Cambodia' and 'Too Drunk To Fuck', and I dug their attitude, but their records weren't regulars on my turntable. I was offered the gig doing their publicity, though, and it turned out that it wasn't a tough one. Lots of people wanted to talk to lead singer Jello Biafra, who had plenty to say on any topic.

A simple 'How are you today, Jello?' would end an hour or two later without the need for you to utter another word. The shows were great; a little scary for a timid dude like me, but they were certainly events. Most of my contact was with Biafra, and it involved listening to him, scouring record and bookshops with him, and watching the piles of stuff he expected me to ship back to America mount up – and up. It felt like he was buying half the second-hand records and books in the country, and putting them in Roger's and my living-room.

Roger was on the road with the band when drummer D. H. Peligro was arrested in Brisbane for drinking alcohol in a public space. Apparently, the can of beer was unopened. These types of arrests were seemingly commonplace in the land of Queensland Premier Joh Bjelke-Petersen (a 'dictator', as Jello would later refer to him).

If anything, Peligro's arrest added to the band's image and credibility. I just focused on doing the publicity and manoeuvring myself around the piles of Biafra acquisitions.

A couple of months later, the Gun Club came to Australia. I got the gig doing their publicity for Melbourne street-press publisher, Rob Furst, who was embarking on his first foray into international tour promoting.

After a mix-up, only the lead singer Jeffrey Lee Pierce and bassist Patricia Morrison arrived in Australia. Roger stepped in and offered drummer Billy Pommer and guitarist Spencer P. Jones from The Johnnys to make up the numbers, before Kid Congo Powers also flew out to be part of the extravaganza. (A founding member of the Gun Club,

Powers had left them to join The Cramps, before rejoining briefly for this tour. He'd play with them again a few years later, before becoming a member of Nick Cave's Bad Seeds.)

On a personal level, there was one unexpected development. I had a brief fling with Patricia, after Roger's and my assistant informed me that she was keen on me. One night after a gig at the Manzil Room – as a strange way of gaining my attention, and in a general mood of on-tour silliness – Patricia managed, without me realising, to tie the shoelaces of my sneakers together. I fell over. We went back to a spare room at my assistant's share house.

The Gun Club shows were great, but maybe not as well attended across the board as everyone had hoped. Patricia called me from Adelaide. She, Jeffrey and Kid were in a panic. They weren't sure they were going to get paid all the money they were due. Could Roger and I help?

It was a weekend and the Gun Club were due back in Sydney on the Monday and flying out the next day. What could we do? Bingo. The Strawberry Hills Hotel, Monday night. It would be a free gig, but publican Ron Audas would pay us $300, which we could give to the band.

I called the Hoodoo Gurus. Wanna open for the Gun Club at the Strawb? No cash, just glory – and beer. They were in. The people who claim they were at the gig now numbers pretty much those who stormed the Sydney Cricket Ground after Buddy Franklin kicked his 1000th goal in AFL football. A lot of people wished they'd been there, and about 150 of them actually were.

Want me to tell you how good it was? I'd be lying, as I don't remember much beyond the elation of pulling it off. And the Gun Club members had $300 in cash that they weren't expecting. I guess it was better than nothing.

Not too long after, I was in Los Angeles. I hung out for a day with Patricia, Kid and Jeffrey Lee. There was some talk of taking acid and going to Disneyland, which didn't happen. I was somewhat in awe of the Gun Club members, so I was pretty taken with the opportunity to hang out with them. And I really dug Patricia, but I was pretty sure that things with her weren't going to go any further. I crashed at Kid's place after a long night with Jeffrey and him. It was the last time I'd see Jeffrey.

I also had a very brief stint being the publicist for the eccentric, but extremely talented and prolific Roy Harper. He'd had Jimmy Page play on one of his early albums and Led Zeppelin had recorded a song called 'Hats Off To (Roy) Harper'. He'd recorded some albums that I adored – my teacher John Woodroffe had turned me on to them – *Lifemask* and the double album *Flashes From The Archives Of Oblivion* (now there's an album title). And Harper had penned one of the great songs about a sport I loved, 'When An Old Cricketer Leaves The Crease'.

Around 1986, Harper had been lured to Australia for his first (and only) visit to these shores – but he didn't get to play a single gig. As I recall it, the promoter, who was clearly new to this caper, hadn't completed all the required work visas and permits to allow Harper to perform in this country.

Only a few hours after his arrival in Australia and a day before his first show in Sydney, a little word was had with the promoter that Mr Harper would not only not be able to perform in Australia, but he'd need to leave the country post-haste. Whilst a frustrated Harper waited for the next available flight back to the UK, he spent an afternoon at the rundown weatherboard house in Bondi that I had bought a year or so before, as a solid base for my partner, Yanni Stumbles, and our two-year-old son, Eddie, and later, our daughter, Frankie-Rae. I didn't mind hanging with Harper at all. The next day, he headed to the international airport, never to return.

He'd been hoping there'd be a last-minute reprieve. I was just a little overawed but tried not to show it. I'm sure I tried not to come across as a gobsmacked, rabid fan, and equally sure I failed.

# 21

# DON'T LET THE RECORD LABEL TAKE YOU OUT TO LUNCH

Golly – we released some weird shit on G.R.E.E.N. Probably nothing beats the soundtrack to the 1982 Sydney University musical/revue, *Dingo Girl*. What were we thinking? Especially because I think the album – yes, a whole bloody album – came out after the production ended. Was it because my girlfriend at the time, Debbie Baer, was involved in the show? Probably.

The concept was good, being based around the Lindy Chamberlain case and the alleged taking of her baby by a dingo. It was topical, irreverent and contained a bunch of fine songs and gags. But did it warrant an album release? Despite it being quite listenable – probably not. Is it ever cited as a nascent work from a now superstar? Well, no.

Roger Grierson and I were also both actively involved in booking bands into the tiny Southern Cross hotel in Devonshire Street near Central Station. It was run by the crusty, no-nonsense Ron Audas, with the assistance of his son Gary. (Of course, Ron would later be responsible for the Gun Club's $300 cash extravaganza at the end of their Australian tour.)

During the early 1980s, the Southern Cross was a mecca for local artists. Some of them even lived in rooms upstairs. Ron and Gary treated the bands well and, in turn, were much respected by everyone who played there. Initially, the room didn't have a stage and bands set up on the carpet. But it oozed atmosphere and hip credentials. If you got a gig at the Southern Cross, you were on your way.

To bolster early-week trade, in 1982 Roger and I proposed a Battle Of The Bands. Three bands a night, short sets, a panel of illustrious local identities – i.e. Roger, me and whichever musician we could rope in with the offer of a few beers. The winning combo would get a release on G.R.E.E.N. The competition ran over three months and featured 64 bands. Ron Audas was – not surprisingly – very keen on this whole idea.

The winners of the hotly contested battle were The Lime Spiders. Their double 7-inch single called '25th Hour' was their first release in June 1983.

Around the same time, we foisted upon an unsuspecting public the wacky '60s hippie/beatnik/psychedelia-inspired Melbourne band North 2 Alaskans, along with early Spy V Spy singles, and the very first 12" EP from Do Re Mi, whose lead singer, of course, was Deborah Conway.

Roger also managed the hard-drinking and partying cowpunk band The Johnnys, so when they needed a label – who you gonna call? From my world came the more '60s-inspired Grooveyard (featuring Jon Schofield, who'd go on to play in Paul Kelly's band) and the inner-city supergroup Super K, featuring various luminaries from the Hoodoo Gurus, as well as others who played at the Strawberry Hills and Sydney Trade Union Club.

For reasons that escape me, G.R.E.E.N. also released a couple of records by the electro-funk outfit Sea Monsters (whose line-up would later include drummer Paul Hester), and the ragged country punk band The Kingswoods. I think that was simply because they knocked on our front door and asked. Or maybe we just liked the idea of their song 'Purty Vacant'. We made decisions based on less logic than that.

The Woolloomooloo house was a hive of activity. More often than not, I'd come home to find a band from interstate camping in the living-room, gear everywhere, eating our food and going through our books and records. The couches always seemed to have a resident guest.

Roger and I went about our respective businesses – for me at the time, it was G.R.E.E.N., *The Sun-Herald*, some freelance journalism and my first excursions into publicity with The Clash and the Teardrops. We often felt like it was a big event when we were both at home for a day or two. There were fun times when we were together. I remember listening to him one day, lying on his bed and doing a series of radio telephone interviews in which he pretended to be one of The Johnnys. They were obviously too hungover or otherwise unavailable themselves.

G.R.E.E.N. also licensed a couple of releases from international artists. One, in 1983, was New York's surf-guitar instrumental band The Raybeats and their *It's Only A Movie* album. As with local releases, it didn't take much to persuade Roger and me to release something. But we didn't venture too far into overseas licensing. There was a huge array of Australian artists knocking on the door – easily enough to keep us busy.

There was even an album that neither Roger nor myself really recall bringing out. For years, I was convinced it didn't exist. I knew it had been mooted in 1984, but because I didn't actually have a copy, I completely forgot we'd released it.

Then, in 2014, someone sent me the *Strawberry Hills Compilation* album. It was a collection of songs by four Sydney bands recorded at the Strawberry Hills hotel. It had the catalogue number SH Ron 1, in recognition of its publican Ron Audas. (In about 1983, the Southern Cross had changed its name.)

If I hadn't seen a copy, I'd still be arguing that it was never released. Hey, Roger and I were involved in a lot of projects, we were doing too many drugs, and, well, there are your two reasons right there.

But the recording we and G.R.E.E.N. are most remembered for is *The Axeman's Jazz* by the Beasts Of Bourbon. The Beasts were an inner-city supergroup featuring Tex Perkins, post-Hoodoo Gurus James Baker, Kim Salmon and Boris Sujdovic from the Scientists, and Spencer P. Jones from The Johnnys.

They'd played a few gigs in 1983 and – much as I'd like to take credit – Roger had the idea of getting them to make an album. Tony Cohen had worked with The Birthday Party and a myriad of other legendary cult/indie bands, as well as engineering Russell Morris's 'The Real Thing', when he was starting out. Tony was approached to produce/engineer the session. By 'session', I mean singular, as only one day was booked in the studio in Sydney's Darlinghurst. Cohen managed to wangle his payment upfront and in cash, and proceeded to hightail it up the road to Kings Cross to score heavy-duty drugs – maybe speed, maybe heroin (sometimes it was hard to tell with Tony, believe it or not) – before returning to the studio.

Aside from the studio time, we provided some grams of speed and cases of Victoria Bitter. The idea was to record an album's worth of songs as fast as possible, then mix them and be done in an eight-hour session. And so it came to be. The band had arrived in various stages of disarray in the early afternoon. Spencer hadn't been to bed after a gig and subsequent partying with The Gun Club, who he was playing and touring with at the time. Somewhere there exists a photo of him passed out on the studio floor whilst the album was being mixed.

*The Axeman's Jazz* became a cult record and copies of the original pressing now change hands for significant sums of money. Some years later, it was rereleased by John Foy's Red Eye Records and sold extremely well, in addition to being licensed around the world.

Originally just a 'Hell, why not' project, its stature has grown over the years. That's largely due to the ongoing careers of all involved and the mythology surrounding the recording of the album. It helps that it's incredibly good. I'd be prepared to bet it's in the record collections of the likes of Jello Biafra, Kid Congo Powers, Henry Rollins, Thurston Moore and many other revered artists.

Overall, G.R.E.E.N.'s body of work was a tidy bunch of vinyl, most of which I don't own. I'm obsessive about a number of things, but I've never obsessively kept copies of every article I've written, or record I've released. But I know they're out there somewhere, if I ever feel a burning desire to own a copy of a specific album. I don't even have a vinyl copy of *The Axeman's Jazz* anymore. But I do have the *Strawberry Hills Compilation*, so I know I didn't dream that.

There was no particular discussion about G.R.E.E.N. winding down. By 1985, both Roger and I had become busy with a host of other things, and on a purely pragmatic note, none of our releases were actually making more than pocket money. And many weren't even achieving that.

We moved out of the Woolloomooloo house, and Roger moved briefly into a place with me and Yanni before finding another abode, so our day-to-day communication lapsed a little.

It would be many years before I ventured back into the indie record label world.

# 22

# WHO DO YOU LOVE

In mid-1982, Roger Grierson and I were happily ensconced at 132 Cathedral Street. We worked in every available space in the house, including the sunroom at the front with the big glass windows. The two of us hammering the phone were obvious to anyone who walked past often enough. A couple of those people who did were connected with a new band known as Le Hoodoo Gurus, particularly their sound guy, Tim Greig, who lived around the corner.

One day, the band's guitarist Kimble Rendall came by and said, 'Hey, Stuart, everyone in the Hoodoo Gurus has had their phone disconnected. You're always on the phone, so could we give you $15 a week to be our phone contact?'

As I've mentioned, when I'd started at *RAM*, which had only been a few years earlier, my salary was $90 a week. Fifteen bucks was a bit more than pocket money. And it didn't seem like there'd be a lot involved in taking messages for a band who couldn't be *that* busy.

Incidentally, this was the era when Telecom regularly disconnected phones. OK, we'd all had accounts in the names of famous people – J. Mitchell and J. Ramone had both apparently lived in my house in Stanmore. When Joni and Joey didn't pay their bills, they got disconnected. Then V. Morrison moved in. Everyone was doing it. But the telecommunications company was wising up and requiring just a bit more background info and security before putting a phone on. B. Dylan now needed a couple of forms of identification.

Roger and I had a phone in our own name and we always managed to pay the bills. We weren't so good with the rent for our hired television, and I remember spending a stressful week trying to avoid the guy who came around to try to repossess it. 'I know you're in there!' he yelled through the mail slot as we ducked for cover. Maybe we shouldn't have suddenly switched the lights off when we heard his van arriving. You live and learn.

I took the money and became Le Hoodoo Gurus' phone contact. (For reasons that escape me, they dispensed with the 'Le' shortly afterwards.) In quick succession, I then assumed the other duties associated with being a manager: talking to booking agents, going to gigs, organising their crew, dealing with intra-band politics, particularly the intensity of their singer and songwriter, Dave Faulkner.

I travelled with them on trips to Melbourne, more often than not sharing a room with the comparatively serious and sedate Faulkner, and leaving the more gregarious party-oriented members to their own devices. Not that I minded a party, but Dave ended up being the odd one out in this. It was a while before we were making enough money to justify separate rooms when on tour.

The popularity of the Gurus quickly went into overdrive, especially around the inner-city scene in Sydney. The band had released some singles on Jules Normington and Dare Jennings' super-hip indie Phantom Records, but were soon snapped up by Big Time Records, a label owned by Fred Bestall and Lance Reynolds, the managers of Air Supply, who were clearly flush with bags of loot. They liked me, as I always took care of them when they came to Sydney, since they both lived in Los Angeles.

I'd been managing the Hoodoo Gurus for less than six months, now under the banner of a company I'd started called Gidget Management. It seemed that everyone in this caper had a company name and I was into the whole '60s surf-culture thing and the character of Gidget. I seem to recall I used an image from one of the Gidget films as our logo.

Guitarist Brad Shepherd nicknamed me 'Boss' – an acknowledgement of both my role in their career at the time and my love of all things Springsteen. That's how I'm referred to on the cover of the band's debut album, the still revered *Stoneage Romeos*, which came out in March 1984.

The album and the band were the right combination for the times. They looked and sounded indie and underground, but Faulkner had the ability to write incredibly memorable and strong songs. Lots of them. 'My Girl' – which was allegedly about love for a greyhound – did surprisingly well on radio, as did a number of other songs from the album. FM radio was hugely powerful in those days and the Gurus were swept along on this wave.

In a short space of time, the band went from playing small inner-city pubs to large suburban beer barns. Suddenly, this management caper became a lot more demanding, time and expertise-wise. I had to learn a lot – and fast.

Of course, the Gurus were now playing across Australia as well. Early in our relationship I'd told the band they needed to drive from Sydney to Perth for their first run of dates there. They kicked and screamed but I explained that, if they did it just once, they'd really appreciate their plane tickets after that. From all reports it was an interesting trip, including people in Kalgoorlie crossing the street with their kids to avoid encountering these strange specimens with large hair.

Then came an American record deal. It was the result of an arrangement between Big Time and A&M Records, the label started by Herb Alpert (the 'A', and that guy from Tijuana Brass) and Jerry Moss – you guessed it – the 'M'. The album was released there in September, and it became a significant success, going to number one on the US college radio charts. Conversations quickly turned to an American tour. This was *way* beyond what I'd signed on for. I was delighted, of course, but far from convinced I had the skill set for dealing with it.

The band themselves were excited about the US record deal, despite an initial hiccup. *Stoneage Romeos* had a memorable cover design – B-movie style artwork that featured a massive dinosaur towering over a terrified damsel. The American version was changed to a blanded-out piece of hideousness, which was so dull you'd forget it the instant you stopped looking at it. It also featured dinosaurs (and no damsel) but incredibly poorly sketched ones and an awful orange background. It was particularly bad when compared to the magnificent – and now iconic – original.

The Gurus were furious, wondering if this was just the beginning of a string of decisions being made without consultation with them – or me. The public reaction to the album after its release defused this a little, but there was still suspicion. A&M, though, had a reputation as an artist-friendly label, and hopefully this would be an aberration in an otherwise good relationship.

I began to travel regularly to Los Angeles, staying with Bestall at his rather classy home on Doheny Drive off Sunset Boulevard, just up the hill from the famous Tower Records. There was a status-symbol Bentley in the garage and his wife ticked me off one morning for picking up my coffee cup and plate and taking them to the kitchen, after we'd break-fasted by the large pool. 'We have the staff for that,' she scolded, as one of the Mexican maids scurried to take over.

When I wasn't at the house, I was given a desk at A&M Records. The company was located on Charlie Chaplin's old film studio lot at the comparatively nearby 1416 North La Brea, near Sunset Boule-vard. There were little offices dotted all over the place, not unlike tiny weatherboard beach houses. My desk was at the back of one housing Bob Garcia.

Garcia was a dry, seemingly uber-cool and world-weary character who had been at the label forever. He never opened the curtains, always had incense burning, and told me great stories of Gram Parsons riding his motorbike onto the lot. He was full of anecdotes about artists I revered – like Phil Ochs, Gene Clark and the Carpenters – who had all recorded for the company and been regular visitors to Garcia's office. I lapped it up.

His secretary was Johnette Napolitano, who at the time was dating Steve Wynn from the Dream Syndicate. She was a tough-talking fun gal who went on to a successful career with Concrete Blonde. Being with these people made me feel like I was part of a pretty cool gang of three – although I suspect to them I was just this naïve kid from Australia.

I remember one day Johnette said, 'Stuart, The Go-Go's have asked me if I'm interested in joining them – do you think I should do it?' What would I know? She didn't join.

Another day, all of the staff just happened to find a reason to be outside their offices as U2's limos drove in for a recording session at the A&M studios. This was one of the things I loved about A&M: the staff were pretty much all unashamed music nerds and fans, just like me. This wasn't a corporate label but a great gathering of music lovers, who worked hard because they loved what they did. It was a great time to be around A&M. Later, it was bought up by bigger interests and lost much of what had made it so wonderful.

And I was learning a bucketload about the industry. Even if I had no real idea what I was doing, and what marketing involved, I'd sit in meetings with Jerry Moss, trying to take in everything that was said. I desperately wanted to be good at this management caper.

My work was full on and I spent extended periods in LA. There were multiple divisions at the label: publicity, marketing, college radio, adult orientated radio, and so forth. I needed to get to know everyone, what they did, and what they needed from me and the band. I met with potential booking agents, tour managers, equipment suppliers, producers – in essence, anyone I thought I should know and who I thought might help my understanding of how it all worked.

So much of it was different. One label person told me that I was going to struggle in his country. I asked why and he said, 'You don't speak American.' I later realised this was his way of saying that Americans were more circumspect about revealing what they thought, whereas I just came right out with it.

It turned out that, at an American label, you didn't say things like 'This deal seems fucked to me – give me whatever clauses those pricks are putting in Sting's contract.' You get my drift. And, yes, I did say that in one meeting in the early days, discussing packaging deductions for CD releases.

Back in Australia, I set about putting together the Gurus' first American tour. It was booked by Frank Riley, a New York-based agent who represented the likes of the Cramps, the Dream Syndicate, the dBs, the Fleshtones etc – all the bands the Gurus loved.

By now, I was using a rudimentary and *very* early portable computer system. It had been pioneered by the music industry and introduced into Australia by the Jands PA and music equipment business. So – dig this – in 1984 I was communicating with people around the globe via electronic mail. Yes, I had an email address – JAND169 – way before fax machines were even invented. Most people were still using telex to communicate.

I used a Tandy Model 100 computer, which retailed for about $1000 and was the size of a chunky laptop. There were only six lines of visible text and the memory wasn't much greater than what now would be five MP3 songs, but it was all that was needed. Data from the Tandy 100 was transported over the phone line to other computers on the system.

Aside from band work, I also managed to suss out how to transmit my *Sun-Herald* music column every week, no matter where I was. My greatest achievement was filing once during a snowstorm from a phone box in Nashville.

Clark Kent-like, I would forever be dashing into these whilst travelling on tour to check my email. Seem weird? It was but it worked and I did my part of setting up an entire Gurus American tour – 42 shows – using it.

In the lead-up to the tour, I had an encounter that impacts on my life to this day. The music industry traditionally operated – and still largely does – on the notion that knowledge is power. That doesn't make it very different from most other industries, I suppose. I was lucky that I came along to the world of writing when people like Anthony O'Grady and David Dale were prepared to share what they knew.

On the management side of things, I had the likes of booking agent Owen Orford, and other music-business figures such as Michael Gudinski, Michael Chugg and Gary Ashley, who took me under their wing and taught me how things worked. They shared secrets, gossip and insight. They wanted me to have the benefit of their experiences to help navigate the world ahead.

Then there was Paul McGuinness, the manager of U2. They toured Australia for the first time in September 1984 and, for reasons that totally escape me now, I was backstage and found myself chatting to him. (Bono, who clearly had time to check the music column in *The Sun-Herald*, smiled as he passed by, and said I looked better in the flesh than in my newspaper photo.)

I mentioned to Paul that I was managing the Hoodoo Gurus, who were about to tour America. He said I should get a pen and paper and sit with him. For the next hour or so – whilst U2 were onstage – he ran through booking agents, publicists, managers and other industry figures I should make contact with in the US. There were serious heavy-weight names on the list. Top of their respective trees.

I was frantically scribbling names and numbers on scraps of paper and in the back pages of my diary. At one point I said, 'This is great, Paul, but when I ring I'll be lucky to get past the secretary's secretary.'

McGuinness looked at me. 'They'll take your calls because I will have called them first to tell them to expect to hear from you.'

And you know what – when I returned to America I called each and every number and, without fail, was told, 'Yes, Paul said you'd be calling. When would you like to come over?'

To this day, if someone needs some advice on how things work in the music industry and I know the answer, well, I tell them. If the manager of U2 could do it for me – literally whilst his band were performing – then I can carry that torch.

Anyway, before we could leave Australia, unfortunately I had to sack the band's drummer, James Baker. This had been on the cards for some time. Dave Faulkner didn't think his playing was up to scratch, plus he drank heavily – not that this made him unique in the Hoodoo Gurus ranks. However, the extremely ambitious and determined Faulkner decided he had to go, and as manager it was my job to do the firing. Which I did at a pub in Surry Hills one afternoon, not long before the band were set to depart for the States.

Baker was gutted and, given that he was clearly the most loved member of the Hoodoo Gurus, the 237 people in the inner-city scene that actually gave a shit suddenly decided that the band were nothing more than calculated, cold and career-orientated. Personally, I really adored Baker, couldn't tell if he was a great or ordinary or terrible drummer and couldn't care less. I still loved the Hoodoo Gurus, but with his departure went a big part of the spirit and soul of what made them great in the first place.

The Baker-less Gurus, with Mark Kingsmill now installed as drummer, headed for Los Angeles. The tour was a disaster waiting to happen. There was a lot of money on the line, we had no real idea how the shows would go, and we were working with all sorts of people – tour managers, equipment suppliers – who we didn't know.

Things started off well enough. The Gurus and their American tour manager, Louis, met up, bonded and headed off on a tour that began with a lunchtime campus performance in Santa Barbara, California, and wound its way around America. It included a show in Chicago opening for The Church, and a sell-out headlining gig at the Ritz in New York. I recall it being something like 42 shows in 44 days.

I didn't go on all the tour. In the days before mobile phones a manager was effectively useless on the road. The Model 100 needed a telephone connection to work, so it was of no help on those eight and nine-hour drives, unless you stopped at a phone booth along the way. The manager was better off staying at a communication hub and sending the band on their way.

This was usually fine, especially if there was a highly competent tour manager, and Louis was a wildcard but a good one. With everyone crammed into a van with their gear, it was tough, relentless touring of the sort that the band probably wouldn't have tolerated at this stage in Australia. But this was America, the crowds were good and the novelty carried them through.

At the University of Nevada in Las Vegas, the Gurus had an opening act called the Red Hot Chili Peppers. The venue itself was dry, but we more than made up for the booze-free gig afterwards, when we hit the casinos and The Strip. We discovered that most casinos provided free beers and food as an inducement to come in and gamble. We consumed the former quickly and easily and did none of the latter.

Someone procured an eight ball of cocaine, so the party was on back at our roadside motel till daybreak ensued. The eight ball vanished, another may have been procured, and much drinking was done. The extremely dishevelled and chemically animated – and still drunk – Gurus left early to head to the next gig. I was driving back to LA with Mark Williams from A&M and his partner.

I was shattered and the drive back through Death Valley was truly hideous. According to Californian law, no booze was allowed in a moving vehicle. Hey, who was going to notice in the middle of the desert, but my companions were sticklers for not taking any risks. And there wasn't exactly a liquor store anywhere around, even if they'd decided differently.

By the time we all hit New York, the partying was taking its toll and everything was starting to fray. The Gurus had friends in New York, chiefly a band they loved, the Fleshtones, who they joined onstage at CBGB before vanishing into the night.

Brad and Dave were due to appear on MTV the following morning. Dave was up and ready to go, but Brad was 17 sheets to the wind and refused to open his hotel-room door. I hammered, I pleaded, I hammered again. And again. I yelled that we had to leave for MTV in five minutes.

'Tell them we'll do it tomorrow!' he yelled.

In the mid-'80s, you did not tell MTV – particularly this late in the piece – that you would 'do it tomorrow'.

Bass player Clyde Bramley was hurriedly roused to go with Dave to the studio. The interview went fine, as far as I could tell, but there was tension between Dave and Brad that took a few days to dissipate. It seemed to me that Dave wanted the career more than the party, while, at that time at least, Brad wanted the opposite.

The tour rolled on. Money was being lost, though, and we had a bunch of unpaid bills – plus we couldn't pay Louis all he was owed. I was learning – quickly – what a thing called a 'contingency' in a budget is for. It's for when the inevitable happens and tours run significantly over and above a manager's back-of-an-envelope projections. I had no contingency plan.

The Gurus and I stumbled back to Australia, exhausted and in the red. But the tour had given them a real taste of what was possible, and they'd begun to realise that they had a future as an international band. They just weren't sure I was the guy to guide them through all that was required.

It was soon clear the Gurus wanted a change, that they needed someone more experienced. Louis had clearly been in the band's ears telling them that their Australian representatives had no idea what they were doing – and he might have had some sort of a point.

Michael McMartin made his move. He worked at Big Time Records, had a background in music publishing, had more experience in the industry than I did, and was more business-like than me. I'd enjoyed being part of the gang, whereas Michael wanted to protect the band and build their careers.

It was a good decision. I don't recall being too upset – maybe just a little – but there was a sense that the move was best for everyone. We parted on good terms.

I've also had time to realise that having an older, more together figure as a manager is frequently what young rock'n'roll bands need. And having a hard-partying, coke-snorting, not particularly organised figure of roughly the same age isn't necessarily the way to go.

Even though I didn't realise it immediately, it quickly came to pass that becoming the former manager of the Hoodoo Gurus had its upside. A few weeks after we parted ways, the phone rang. It was a singer/songwriter from Melbourne, who'd just relocated to Sydney.

# 23

# FROM ST KILDA TO KINGS CROSS

Paul Kelly was at least there in the flesh at the first interview I ever attempted to do with him – which was also the first interview I attempted to do, period. In 1978, I was working at improving my writing skills at *Roadrunner* and *Preview*, mainly by writing a lot, reading as much as I could, and trying to wean myself off being an imitator of the music scribes I loved. So far, though, there was a step I hadn't taken – I'd never had that face-to-face encounter with a musician.

The High Rise Bombers were in town. I was aware of their guitarist Martin Armiger, who was from Adelaide, through having a good idea which character he'd inspired in Helen Garner's *Monkey Grip*. I'd become a fan of his music, first with The Bleeding Hearts and now The High Rise Bombers. Sadly I'd never been to a Hearts gig, but was fortunate enough to see the Bombers at every opportunity possible.

They were a mixture of Lou Reed, Bob Dylan, Television, and just about every other band they loved and listened to. These happened to be the same artists I loved and listened to. And The High Rise Bombers exuded a slightly drug-fucked sense of cool. I liked that too.

Their line-up included a singer by the name of Paul Kelly. I wasn't aware that Paul had grown up in Adelaide and hadn't heard his first bands there, which included the Debutantes. They were later described to me as being a bit like an amalgam of Steely Dan and Bob Dylan, circa the Rolling Thunder Revue.

When I heard that The High Rise Bombers were returning to Kelly's home town for some shows, I thought I'd write a piece about them and try to interview them. Truth be told, I really wanted an excuse to meet Martin Armiger.

Contact was made and one afternoon Martin, Paul and bass player Fred Cass – who was doubling as the band's surrogate manager/ organiser – came to my home. I hate to think what I asked, but I was unbelievably shy and nervous. Did I borrow something to record the chat on? I have no idea, but I do recall that Fred did most of the talking and I can't remember Paul saying anything at all. Not a word.

On a couple of subsequent trips to Melbourne, I again went to see the band. When I interviewed Martin years later, he recalled a show I was at. He said that he and Paul and the rest of the High Rise Bombers had made plans to head out afterwards and probably get up to mischief. However, when I turned up, Paul ditched the others so he could hang with me. Although I was hardly Jan Wenner or Nick Kent at that stage – just a kid from Launceston who did a bit of writing – Martin interpreted this as the first time he'd seen the extent of Paul's ambition.

Paul and I struck up a friendship of sorts. Not exactly close but that easy relationship that musicians have with journalists who, they know, like what they do. When I moved to Sydney I'd always go and see Paul and his band The Dots when they played – usually at the Manzil Room, a notorious late-night venue in Kings Cross. They'd stay at the minus-seven-stars fleapit Burnley Hotel next door. I went to visit one day and Paul looked horrible. Pencil-thin, sweaty, not well. I didn't really know that much about heroin in those days – but I had a fair idea what was going on here.

I recall one of those tours and going to see Paul and the band at the Manzil Room. It was where musicians, road crew and hangers-on gravitated to after their own shows. The first set started around 11.30 pm, the second about 1.30 am and the final one at about 3 am. Patrons – who more often than not had a head full of speed or cocaine, and played backgammon when not watching the band – would stagger out in various states of disarray as the sun came up. I did that often. Probably too often.

This night it must have been the second set and I was standing up near the front with Roger Grierson. We both loved Tom Verlaine and Television and had been excited that Paul and the Dots had played Verlaine's song 'Breakin' In My Heart'.

I looked across to my right and there was the famous artist Brett Whiteley standing there. Paul saw him too and started playing 'Alive And Well'. Whiteley had some well-documented health issues associated with the same recreational drug use that Paul embraced. As he sang the song he walked out into the sparse audience, got on his knees, and, looking up at Whiteley, continued the song, softy intoning the lines 'I'm glad you're alive and well,' before getting up and returning to the stage. It was moving and I've never forgotten it.

Around this time, Paul and I hung out a little at the Mushroom Records 10th anniversary celebrations in Melbourne, which included a concert and then a party at Luna Park. I think we watched Angry Anderson on the dodgem cars. Paul never said much, though. As his current manager remarked to me one day, 'You get used to the silences.'

I wrote glowingly of Paul at any opportunity that presented itself, including an extremely long review of his *Manila* album for *RAM* in 1982. It was the sort of extended discourse you don't get to write these days – maybe 2000 words and taking up three quarters of a page. Small typeface. It was fawning.

That was the extent of our interaction until one day early in 1985, not long after Paul had moved to Sydney from Melbourne. Having recently taken that much mythologised 13-hour bus trip from St Kilda to Kings Cross, he called Gidget Management. In those days, my office was situated above a café in Victoria Street, Darlinghurst. I rented a large room up a winding staircase whilst my friends, entrepreneur and venue booker Tim McLean and transplanted Melbourne musician and cult figure Johnny Topper, ran a café downstairs called Toppers. Johnny lived in one of the other rooms.

Each room in the building had what seemed like an excess of mirrors everywhere, including some on the ceilings. It didn't take long to realise that, prior to us all moving in, it was probably a brothel. But I loved working in the area. I'd do my interviews in the café and roam around the Cross when I felt like it. Plus, my main cocaine dealer lived two short blocks away.

Paul asked if I was free for a beer and a chat – which of course I was. We went to the Green Park hotel (the closest one to my office) and sat for a few hours. I was just on the wrong side of my relationship with the Hoodoo Gurus and hadn't decided whether I'd do any more management. I wasn't sure if Paul knew I was no longer working with the Gurus, or even if there was a plan in his mind when he'd come to the meeting. Many people who know him well insist that there would *have* to have been forward thinking.

As we chatted, I asked what his next moves were. He explained that he'd saved $1500 and was going to record an acoustic single. I posited that this maybe wasn't his best idea and that the world wasn't exactly forming a queue to buy an acoustic single from him. I also suggested he should think about finding some extra money and recording an acoustic album. To me, that would make more sense.

We went back to my home in Bondi and I played him a couple of recent solo acoustic albums from artists traditionally associated with noisy rock'n'roll. Chris Bailey from the Saints had just released his solo acoustic album *Casablanca* on the French New Rose label and Johnny Thunders – he of the New York Dolls and The Heartbreakers – had also recently released a similar-style record in *Hurt Me* on the same label.

At the end of that meeting I was – as far as I could tell – managing Paul Kelly. And he'd clearly listened to my suggestions as he managed to lay his hands on some extra cash and record an album, *Post*. I was pretty happy about this. It was a bit of validation that someone else – particularly an artist I respected so much – thought I had a clue as to what it takes to be a good manager. My confidence about my abilities in this area had taken a bit of a knock.

Still, there was a lot to do with Paul, who was now a solo artist, having left the Dots behind in Melbourne. For one thing, he was effectively without a record deal. Mushroom figured they'd given it their best shot with his two previous albums, *Talk* and *Manila*, and the resulting sales were less than spectacular. There was also Paul's drug use. Whilst he was hardly Robinson Crusoe in that department, it led to people thinking he was unpredictable. Plus, his domestic life was in chaos and he was sharing custody of a young son, Declan. He moved in to a big share house with my friend Irene Kapathakis in Surry Hills and started getting his life back together.

After Paul recorded *Post*, with no real options we'd thought of selling it by mail order. But he still had one major and determined ally at Mushroom. Michelle Higgins, a senior figure in publicity and promotions, loved him and was determined that he wouldn't part company with the label. The label really only wanted Paul as a song-writer churning out songs for other artists, and didn't really think he had much of a voice.

However, Michelle, who was opinionated, highly motivated and well regarded and respected within the ranks, managed to talk Mushroom boss Michael Gudinski into putting *Post* out on the newly established White Records subsidiary. A sort of pseudo-independent offshoot of an already independent label, it was ostensibly formed to release Hunters & Collectors, but soon became a halfway house for the more left-field signings. It was actually kinda cool to be a White Records artist.

Mushroom probably felt vindicated in their initial reluctance to release *Post*. A bunch of critics (all of whom were, of course, given promotional copies for free) loved it, but there wasn't a lot of radio play and no significant sales. I doubt if more than 1000 copies were pressed at the time and they didn't exactly walk out of the shops. To all intents and purposes, Paul Kelly had delivered his third commercial dud.

But Paul was being talked about again. He was playing gigs and had assembled a damn fine band around him.

Then he came up with another of his great ideas. He wanted his next record to be a double album. That would make it one of the few double albums in the history of Australian music. At least he didn't want it to be a triple album. There had only been one of those here – the first release on Mushroom culled from live recordings at the Sunbury Music Festival.

Did I think Paul recording a double set was a good idea? I thought it was complete madness. I mean, you've recorded three albums that have been comparative disasters. Sales wise, at least. Your label only begrudgingly released your last record to keep a much admired and important staff member happy. And it had been recorded for an extremely modest four-and-a-half grand, so no-one was hurt financially. But a double? What planet were we on here?

Paul dispatched me to Melbourne to try to sell Gudinski on the idea. The stakes were high. How many more chances would a company take on an artist who was a consistent non-starter in the charts? What's that saying about three strikes and you're out? We were wanting a fourth chance.

I was terrified. In those days, Michael was a formidable figure who scared the living daylights out of me. He knew it and, I suspect, rather enjoyed it. I wanted him to like and respect me – not think I was a completely deluded idiot. But here I was, about to walk up the spiral staircase to his office at the very top of the Mushroom warehouse conversion in Albert Park and present myself as . . . a completely deluded idiot.

Such was the intensity of trying to do verbal battle with Gudinski, and the stress I was feeling, that the whole encounter is a little bit of a blur. Things happened so fast in Gudinski World that there was no time for reflection or contemplation. You sucked up the verbal barrage as best you could and tried to stay on your feet – metaphorically – for as long as possible.

I managed to get the words 'Paul Kelly' and 'double album' out before he started the barrage. The word 'fuck' was a big part of the conversation, although it's hard to view it as a conversation if the other person is doing all the *very loud* talking. It felt as if he was completely mocking me for wasting his time with this ridiculous request. 'You have got to be fucking joking' was the essence of the Gudinski commentary.

I found it hard to argue, given that I sorta thought it was nuts too. But I'd learnt a valuable lesson early on. A manager works for his or her artist – not the other way around.

After I'd survived the verbal onslaught, remarkably he made an offer. He agreed to give us – well, Paul Kelly – $60,000 as an advance against the publishing income. The key word there being 'advance'. An advance of this sort for a songwriter wasn't spectacularly generous. It also meant that Kelly was tied to Mushroom's publishing company until he or his songs earnt that money back.

So, Paul wasn't going to another company – even if one wanted him – anytime soon. And this was all about Paul Kelly as a songwriter, rather than a recording artist. Gudinski might have ranted about the double-album idea, but in reality he wasn't particularly interested in that side of Kelly's career. He hadn't committed Mushroom to releasing the album – that hadn't even been discussed.

At the time, $60,000 wasn't a huge amount of money. It was an era in which Australian artists were regularly spending $300,000 and more on albums. One Mushroom act was heavily rumoured to have run up bills of over $650,000 on an album that, when eventually released, didn't even trouble the lower echelons of the charts.

As I was being shunted out of the office, feeling hugely relieved and slightly in a state of shock, I managed to get in a request that if we made an album for this 60 grand and *if* it was a double album and *if* Mushroom released it, would Gudinski agree to sell it for the price of a single album?

'Yes,' he said. 'Now get the fuck out of here.'

# 24

# HELLO, *DOLLY*

Around the time that Gudinski was convinced I was a deluded idiot for pitching a double album, there was a vocal minority in Australia who would have agreed with Michael without a second thought. They were the readers of *Dolly* magazine.

For several years, I was a major contributor to the publication whose target audience was teenage girls. And my features and reviews were polarising in the extreme. For a large percentage of *Dolly* readers, I was a long way from winning a popularity contest – but they kept reading. I was the guy they loved to hate. Some just loved me.

By now, my work life was getting quite weird. As well as managing hip, indie and credible artists such as the Hoodoo Gurus and Paul Kelly, I was also dispensing wisdom to hundreds of thousands of readers on a wide range of topics. These included not only good records to buy, but also the concept of romance, including how to kiss. (Yes, I literally wrote an article about that.) But you know what? I never really thought about these parallel worlds as being weird or contradictory.

To that generation, I'll always be 'Stuart Coupe from *Dolly*'. I doubt that I'll ever escape it – but do I mind? Not at all. For decades (and sometimes still), whenever I'd call a publishing company or the like, as soon as I told them my name, there'd be a noticeable pause and then: 'Not *the* Stuart Coupe from *Dolly*?' Never the Stuart Coupe from

*RAM* . . . or *The Sun-Herald* . . . or the guy who wrote that great review of Redgum. Nope. The guy from *Dolly*.

The impact of my time at the magazine occurred to me soon after the advent of Facebook and the rise of social media. As soon as I was visible on these platforms, there was a deluge of 'friend' requests – and they continue to arrive with surprising regularity. It was wonderfully affirming to receive message and notes about how, as 14-year-olds, they'd devour every issue of the magazine, and thanking me for turning them on to The Johnnys / Bruce Springsteen / The Birthday Party / The Go-Betweens. Often with a P.S.: 'You were right about Duran Duran.'

If the *Dolly* phenomenon wasn't part of your upbringing, you have every right to be shaking your head at this stage and asking, 'What the fuck is he talking about.' Let me explain.

In the early 1980s, *Dolly* was an institution. It was *the* magazine for Australian girls aged between 12 and 17 (or thereabouts). It had no competition, and it was huge.

One day in 1983, the all smiling but deceptively business-like Lisa Wilkinson – then editor of the magazine – called up and asked if I'd be interested in writing an article for her. Of course, I was. I'd never read *Dolly* in my life, but I was a freelance gun for hire. I suspect that first piece was on Men At Work. Lisa then kept asking and I kept writing. Pick a (usually) music subject and I was there.

Lisa's stroke of genius, and what turned me from just another contributor into a bona-fide *Dolly* superstar – and I mean *superstar*, baby – was not to let anybody see what I looked like. By this stage, I was around 30. That was old in *Dolly*-land. And while I wasn't the worst-looking guy on the block, maybe I wasn't bedroom-poster material for your average 15-year-old girl. So Lisa decided that her readers could fantasise – they could imagine that I was a Johnny Depp lookalike.

Every time I wrote a story that featured my photo, there was a black strip across my eyes and face. You got an idea of what I looked like, but there was enough left for those with a little imagination to think that I might be God's gift to teenage fantasies.

Lisa also encouraged me to have an opinion, even if it flagrantly flew in the face of the readership. In fact, that was the absolute point and it would be the sealer on my rise to notoriety. Naturally, I was bit disdainful about many of the musical artists the *Dolly* readers held near and dear to their hearts. The most obvious example was Duran Duran.

I just didn't get it. What was all the fuss about? I thought they were dull, and nothing but style over substance. Their records were lousy and they were the epitome of everything that was wrong with music at the time. OK, I was reading a fair bit of Lester Bangs and turning the full force of my Australianised version of his corrosive prose on the unsuspecting *Dolly* readers.

I never referred to the band by their proper name – they were always Yawn Yawn to me. Ask a 50-year-old woman the first two words that come to mind when you say 'Yawn Yawn' and there's a fair chance they'll say Stuart Coupe, or that dick / idiot / goose / fuckwit Stuart Coupe.

And I played it for all it was worth. Any excuse to bait and taunt. Once I was in New York and Yawn Yawn were doing a press conference. I went along and wrote a piece about how the *Dolly* readers had missed nothing; that hanging out with the world's most boring band in New York was a coma-inducing, stultifying dull waste of time.

The hate mail flooded in. How dare he? Who is this idiot? He wouldn't know good music if it bit him in the arse. Sack Stuart Coupe! *I hate him! I hate Stuart Coupe!*

These letters came in their hundreds – every month. Garbage bags full of them. And I'm talking big green ones. I know because I often used to cart them home to read through.

And then Lisa decided to let me write the album reviews. Was I up for this? You bet I was – particularly if I could pick the monthly selections. Albums by artists the *Dolly* readers loved received minus 500 stars. I was breathing disdain for this garbage, while encouraging readers to buy records by all the people I loved and revered.

This was the stuff that (some) people later thanked me for turning them on to – but hated me for at the time. I'd ask: why would you buy a Samantha Fox album when you could be buying Bruce Springsteen? It was a damn good question both then and now. Having said that, not every *Dolly* reader ended up being obsessed with Captain Beefheart's *Trout Mask Replica* – which is what I would have liked.

Picked at random, I noted that Simple Minds' *Street Fighting Years* album was 'pompous and pretentious . . . maybe long-term Simple Minds fans might find the Key To The Universe in this, but personally I find the key to my back door more interesting'.

In 1986, I panned the Rolling Stones' *Dirty Work* album (one star), while also getting the boot into *Hunting High And Low* by A-Ha (two stars) ('there's so many great records around that there just isn't enough hours in the day to waste listening to this stuff'). Meanwhile, I gave five stars to Elvis Costello's *King Of America*, The Triffids' *Born Sandy Devotional* and The Pogues' *Rum Sodomy And The Lash*. I like *Dirty Work* a lot more these days.

I wrote passionately about the artists I cared about, including – OK, cue slight conflict of interest – the Hoodoo Gurus and Paul Kelly. The way I saw it, there was only one *Dolly* and one record reviewer for the magazine. So who else was going to tell readers that *Gossip* was a sprawling masterpiece?

## 25

# SPREADING THE NEWS

As well as managing Paul Kelly and doing a seemingly crazy amount of freelance writing, I'd decided to further augment my income. It was also because I enjoyed it that I started doing some publicity work for Peter Noble. He specialised in touring blues acts, some of which were truly amazing, while others became legends for the course of their Australian tours.

It's a worldwide phenomenon that artists ascend to legendary status by virtue of them being old, often past their prime, and having that 'L' word splashed large across the top of the posters. How many artists had you never heard of until you saw the street posters, 'DIRECT FROM THE USA – THE LEGENDARY . . .'?

Peter promoted other genres apart from the blues, and his tours were economical and tightly budgeted. And unlike a lot of his competitors in that mid-tier of tour promoting, he stayed in business and went on to own Bluesfest, one of the biggest and most respected festivals in the world. Noble loves music and that's reflected in what he does. And he's a businessman.

By the time I arrived in Noble's world in 1985, he was expanding beyond blues (and New Orleans – his other love) artists and presenting some tours that for him seemed positively weird. I worked on those tours.

First up was The Residents. They were a completely wigged-out group from San Francisco, who I'd grown to love since being turned on to them by my friend, fellow music geek, Bruce Milne, in the 1970s. They'd first appeared in 1974 with the album *Meet The Residents*, with a cover that was a parody of the *Meet The Beatles* album. No-one knew who the members of The Residents were – they were represented by large eyeballs and wore masks that obscured their heads. They were an avant-garde musical and art project, and made truly out-there music: no vocals, just whirring sounds and melodies that were unlike anything I'd ever heard before. They're on streaming services, if you want to check them out.

Truth be told, I think I liked the concept of The Residents more than anything. But I was in. Over the years, I had the t-shirts and the albums *Not Available*, *The Third Reich 'n Roll*, *Eskimo* (on white vinyl, natch), *Duck Stab*, *Santa Dog Meets The Residents*: all the stuff from what is considered their classic era leading up to 1980. We'd put them on the cover of a very early *Roadrunner* magazine.

So, of course, I jumped at the idea of doing their tour publicity. And had an (eye)ball doing it. They stayed at the Southern Cross Hotel near Central, which had built a reputation as (cheap) rock-star accommodation, a much more economical alternative to the Sebel Townhouse. We held a press conference for The Residents there. (Ah, writing that gets me all nostalgic for the tour press conferences. Glorious times – drinks, nibblies, 40 minutes with the stars. They rarely seem to happen these days.)

On this tour, at least, The Residents numbered four – two women and two men. One was Hardy Fox, who later identified as the band's co-founder and primary composer. Hardy, who died in 2018, was one hell of a nice guy, as were his fellow Residents. He wasn't smug, not condescending, despite being at the centre of his fabulous globally touring art project. Also on the tour, playing onstage with The Residents and augmenting their sound, was another experimental cult figure, Snakefinger.

The Residents tour was a massive success. A multimedia extravaganza – sort of like a Flaming Lips show, with real weird music and performers cavorting around the stage wearing eyeball costumes. Maybe you needed to be there – but it was the 'Must be seen at' tour of the year, even if you had no love or appreciation for what The Residents were doing. If you didn't see The Residents, you were simply not cool. Not even remotely.

I was equally (maybe even more) excited when Peter called to say that he was bringing the Flamin' Groovies to Australia. I had an intellectual appreciation of, and weird fascination with, The Residents, but I totally loved – in a very immediate, heart and spine sense – the Groovies. They also came from San Francisco and had recorded some very fine R&B records, before evolving into a powerful pop – or power-pop – band. They were the creators of 'Shake Some Action', one of my (to this day) favourite-ever songs. Good title for a book too.

The Hoodoo Gurus revered them. They were stunned when Cyril Jordan from the Groovies turned up unannounced with his guitar to sing and play with them in San Francisco on their first tour of that country. Cyril had heard them on the radio, and friends had told him how great the Gurus were, so he'd wandered down to check them out.

It was fantastic to have one of my favourite bands of the era touring – and to be the publicist. Roy Loney, and the other key figure from the early Groovies, Chris Wilson, weren't in the line-up that came to Australia – but founders Cyril Jordan and George Alexander were. That was enough.

Jordan, Alexander and the two other members were pretty good live. Not as truly awesome as I was hoping, but they played everything I wanted to hear – including 'Shake Some Action'. And I got to hang with them. George was quiet and didn't seem to get what all this Groovies adoration was about. On the other hand, Cyril acted like a rock star, but with an ever-present chip on his shoulder about not being a *bigger* star. To his mind, I think he was as important as an amalgam of Roger McGuinn from the Byrds and any member of the Beatles or Stones.

Cyril and Peter Noble forged a relationship whereby Peter would be the band's global manager and the Groovies would be signed to his AIM Records label. One of the first fruits of this unlikely union was an album recorded in Glebe Studios in Sydney over the course of a single night on 28 July 1986. The band tackled (somewhat averagely) the Hoodoo Gurus' 'Bittersweet' and new versions of some of their better-known songs such as (of course) 'Shake Some Action', 'Slow Death' and others. *One Night Stand* came out the following year and I received a thank you on the cover credits, which I was pretty happy about.

Peter also toured legendary junkie icon – and poster boy for New York rock'n'roll degeneracy – Johnny Thunders. I don't remember much about that tour. And I believe Peter continues to try to erase this one from his memory banks.

The band were heroin sick, and it was completely unpredictable as to whether they could stand up and get through a show without nodding off. They were generally a pain in the proverbial to corral, transport from one city to the next and get onstage for each gig.

I wasn't using heroin, of course, but my own drug intake was escalating, and I was more not there than there. At least, that's how it felt. I have no idea whether my friends noticed, but I suspect they observed that my behaviour was becoming more erratic, my conversation more tangential, and the times when I was missing in action (e.g. sleeping off a big night) were more frequent. I was on a roll – and it wasn't a good one.

I remember getting my payment from Pete in cash advances – usually $200 at a time. It's no coincidence that this was the price of a gram of coke in those days. Needless to say, I went through my publicity fees pretty quickly.

I began not enjoying the publicity work as much, and to be honest my drug and ever-increasing alcohol intake was making me less and less able to deal with the logistics and demands of the job. I wasn't falling-over drunk, but it seemed that if there was a reason to have a drink – hey, it's midday and the sun is shining – I'd take it. And, more and more, I was drinking during the day to try to counter the effects of the night before. It was a vicious cycle that I wasn't doing anything to break. Maybe it was obvious to others, because the phone wasn't ringing as often, asking if I wanted to work on a project.

But before I took a break from tour publicity, I worked on the first Cramps tour of Australia. As I recall, I'd pretty much begged promoter

Michael Coppel to let me do it, as I was such a fan. Somehow, I managed to convince him that I was a better bet than the much more established publicists he would normally have used.

I didn't get to do much with The Cramps. They did the obligatory pre-tour phone chats and, after arriving, went pretty much straight to their first gig – a sell-out at Selinas in Coogee Bay. That night, they were amazing at times, and when they truly exploded, it was off the dial. Intense. Theatrical. Oozing attitude and presence. But throughout a great show, I just had the sense they weren't totally at their finest.

In the dressing-room afterwards, with a head full of coke, I expressed this to singer Lux Interior when he asked me what I'd thought of the gig. Note to self: never tell the artist what you're thinking straight after a show, even if you're doing it with the best of intentions.

Maybe Lux thought it was as good as The Cramps could be and didn't appreciate some upstart they'd never met saying, 'Aahhhhh . . . great but could do better.' It wasn't long before he and his partner, Poison Ivy Rorschach, announced that they weren't doing any more interviews. I had to cancel a very full schedule, whilst the two of them semi-barricaded themselves in their room at the Sebel.

That was it for the tour. No more Cramps interviews. Was it because of what I'd said, or did they decide separately that they weren't talking to the Australian media? I'll never know. Admittedly, I don't stay awake at night thinking about it, but from time to time I wonder if I could have handled Lux's after-show question a little differently.

Around this time, I also worked with another of my musical heroes, Jonathan Richman. That was fun. We ate vegetarian food together in Darlinghurst and, one Sunday, Yanni Stumbles and her mother and I drove him up to Leura in the Blue Mountains. He wanted to look at gardens. Any garden. Nothing big and grand like botanical gardens – just places with plants and flowers and trees in them. And not in the city.

On the way back, the traffic was backed up horrendously and we were crawling down the highway. Jonathan insisted the car stop so he could get out. For the next couple of kilometres, he jogged slowly alongside us, before hopping back in for the rest of the journey.

I often wonder if any of the Sunday drivers realised the nondescript guy in jeans and a jumper slowly running by the side of the road was the founder of the Modern Lovers and the writer and singer of 'Roadrunner', 'Hey There Little Insect' and 'Egyptian Reggae'.

There was no reason for them to know. *I* knew, though, and I grinned at the absurdity of it. I mean, it wasn't as if people regularly jogged alongside cars in traffic jams in Sydney. But Jonathan did.

# 26

# BEFORE TOO LONG

As far as Michael Gudinski was concerned, Paul Kelly had had his stab at recording success with Mushroom. Now, he and Paul were no longer dancing together on the same stage. The company had his publishing rights. That was enough, and what they wanted. If it hadn't been for his publicity guru Michelle Higgins, it would almost certainly have stayed that way.

As Paul went into the studio to record the double album he'd decide to call *Gossip*, nothing about Gudinski's attitude betrayed the slightest enthusiasm for Paul's recorded output. Kelly might have been a potential earner for Mushroom Publishing as a writer of songs for other artists, but that was about it.

I'd introduced Paul to Alan Thorne, who had produced *Stoneage Romeos*. They'd hit it off and decided to work together. Day and night, they grabbed any available studio time to piece together the album.

During these sessions, no-one from Mushroom ever visited the studios. But Martin Fabinyi – who owned Regular Records, and who I'd shared the building in Woolloomooloo with before Roger Grierson and I decamped to the eastern suburbs – dropped in a few times. He was enthusiastic. With no deal in place for releasing the album, Paul and I decided that a new home was a great idea – especially as no other home was being offered.

The album was completed, we negotiated a deal with Regular, and a signing party was organised. It couldn't have been more straight-forward: album on Regular, publishing with Mushroom.

Enter: Michelle Higgins. Gudinski considered Michelle one of his most valuable staff assets. She'd heard the news about Paul signing to Regular and she didn't like it. Not one bit. As I've mentioned, she loved Paul's first three albums, and she believed it was only a matter of time before he broke – and broke big.

Higgins asked for a meeting with me and Paul early one morning at my office in Victoria Street. She walked in, burst into tears and said to Paul, 'You are *not* leaving Mushroom.'

Afterwards, she went to the Sebel Townhouse and called Gudinski, telling him that she was staying at the hotel – on his dime – until a deal with us was sorted. Despite the length of her stay being exaggerated at the time (and in the years since, among so-called industry insiders who care to speculate about such things), Higgins recalls it being a matter of three days. Others had it at two weeks. If anyone less indispensable to Mushroom had made Higgins' move, they would probably have been fired on the spot – if they'd even had the audacity to try such a play on Gudinski in the first place.

Naturally, Paul and I knew we had the upper hand in the nego-tiations as Gudinski's respect (and need) for Higgins was so great. Gudinski and I discussed the basics of a contractual agreement. Even-tually, and with what still appeared to be great reluctance from Michael, a mutually acceptable solution was hammered out. As Higgins recalled it, 'Gudinski bared his bum in Bourke Street for that deal.' Both financially and with regard to Mushroom's obligations to promote the album, we had secured a *very* good outcome.

For Gudinski, as well as being a concession to Higgins, it was a 'Fuck you' to Fabinyi and Regular Records. 'Tell Fabinyi to shove his party pies,' he said on the day we agreed to terms – which was also the day Paul was scheduled to sign to Regular. It was that close to the wire.

*Gossip* was released in September 1986 and Gudinski was true to his word. It retailed for $14.95. It also had an almost hit single on it (number 14 nationally) in the form of 'Before Too Long', plus a string of other songs that the dominant Triple M radio network loved.

Gudinski was suddenly a fan of the singer and the songs. And Kelly and his band, The Coloured Girls, were big business. Previously sparsely-attended gigs were now jam-packed. Kelly's upward trajectory to where he is today was well and truly underway.

Paul and I worked well together during these times. I was keeping my eye pretty firmly on his career, whilst managing to do the usual number of other things on the employment front.

In 1987, I had a meeting with Gudinski and Mushroom's General Manager, the very affable Gary Ashley, to discuss all things Kelly. (Years later, Ashley would explain how he saw my relationship with Gudinski and Mushroom. 'You'd go upstairs and hatch some ridiculous plan with Gudinski and then come down to my office, where we'd work out what was actually practical and doable.')

So, at this meeting, Michael and Gary had a great idea. A really great idea. Remember, it was the music business in the 1980s. They thought Kelly and I should go to America for four to six weeks.

'To do what?' I enquired.

'Just drive, travel around,' they replied.

Whilst the idea sounded attractive enough – both Kelly and I loved many, many things about America – the rationale seemed kind of suspect, not to mention that adventures like this cost money. Money we didn't really have. And if we did, we might want to spend it on things other than a boys' own trip around America. We might decide to make another record, or to pay the Coloured Girls more. There would be lots of options if we actually had the money in the bank. But Paul and I would be unlikely to decide to go for a drive . . . around America.

'Don't worry,' they said. 'We'll pay.'

OK, there was starting to be nothing not to like about this trip.

In retrospect, I realise what they were hoping for – that Kelly would be inspired to write songs about locations other than South Dowling Street and Adelaide. He might therefore increase his marketability as a songwriter when it came to Mushroom shopping his publishing catalogue internationally.

Anyway, Kelly flew to New York. I had gone ahead and we met at the Omni Park Hotel in Midtown where we were staying. This was Kelly's first time in what some people describe as the Capital of the Universe. I asked what he wanted to do.

'Let's walk,' he said.

We stomped 30 or 40 blocks down to Greenwich Village and had dinner. I was enjoying Kelly's wide-eyed examination of New York. I'd visited a lot prior to this and was in love with the city. Still am. Kelly was on his first date.

While in New York, we spent a couple of nights at the Chelsea Hotel. It was an iconic place – Dylan Thomas had been a resident when he died; Brett Whiteley had lived there and a painting from him (offered when he couldn't pay his bills) hung in the foyer; Sid Vicious had allegedly stabbed Nancy Spungen there. Patti Smith used it as a home base at one stage. It's also the hotel where Janis Joplin gave Leonard Cohen head and Bob Dylan stayed up for days, writing 'Sad Eyed Lady Of The Lowlands'. I could go on. It was famous – despite being a hovel. Our room was appropriately filthy, with cockroaches everywhere.

It had a drab sort of view of the back of other buildings, a door that wouldn't lock so we pulled a couch up against it at night, and a guy across the passageway screamed loudly and randomly – usually just when we were hoping he'd stopped for a while. The weather was decidedly grey as well. So much for the romance of the Chelsea.

We had Thanksgiving dinner with the super-friendly, music-geeky *Rolling Stone* journalist David Fricke (who has always looked like the fifth Ramone brother) and his wife, Susan. In later years, Fricke recalled me and Kelly sitting on their couch, poring over a large road atlas like two would-be Jack Kerouacs, planning our examination of the America of our dreams. On someone else's dime. And so we did.

In Nashville we stayed at Shoney's Inn, right in the centre of Music Row. A big black tour bus was parked out front with the words 'Merle Haggard And The Strangers' painted on it. We didn't see any sign of Merle or the Strangers. But, boy, did we keep a lookout.

We heard on the radio playing in our room that George Jones was doing a concert that night for an invited audience. For some years, Kelly had been saying to people that if anyone covered one of his songs, the ultimate would be George Jones. We needed to go to this performance.

Somehow we managed to get in and watch a short set from Jones and his band in front of a couple of hundred people. I was in awe. Arguably the greatest voice in country music history up close. Oh yeah! Jones was in fine form and Paul and I were in heaven.

As the show ended, I lost sight of Kelly. Looking around wondering where he'd gone to, I spotted him over by the side of the stage, near the door where Jones and his band had exited.

Kelly was clutching a cassette he was obviously hoping the security guard would pass on to Jones. He returned without the cassette, so mission accomplished. George Jones never would cover a Paul Kelly song – but it wasn't for want of trying on Kelly's part.

We also spent time in Nashville with Steve Earle and his manager Will Botwin. Will was an enthusiastic, ambitious type who went on to run Columbia Records in New York. At the time he was managing Earle, Rosanne Cash, Rodney Crowell and some other artists in an impressive roster. He was keen to be involved in the North American management of Kelly.

One day we went to the studio where Earle was finishing up work on his *Exit 0* album. Earle and the producer and engineer were mixing the great song 'The Rain Came Down' when we arrived. I decided to hang in the studio and watch the process. Earle wasn't that interested and he and Kelly decided to head off for a few drinks.

They went to a downtown bar that was a favourite hang of Nashville old-timers. The two songwriters settled in for a session that extended until both realised that neither had any money and there was a bar tab to settle. This particular bar had a tradition that if someone couldn't pay their tab, they had to get up and sing three songs. Unfortunately, I missed the Steve Earle/Paul Kelly performance. Kelly loved it, and it was the beginning of a friendship between the two which endures to this day.

In Memphis, Paul and I stayed across the road from the Peabody Hotel. We walked across the road to look at the famous ducks that visit the hotel fountain every afternoon and are a significant tourist attraction. There didn't seem to be a lot else to do.

This was my second time in Memphis and on the previous trip I'd made a pilgrimage to Graceland, which I'd found fascinating. I dragged Kelly along for a visit, but he seemed bored and keen to leave. It wasn't that he didn't like Presley; maybe it was more that the barrage of memorabilia and the commercialisation of the place didn't impress him.

I sensed over the years that Paul wasn't much into 'seeing the sights'. He much preferred to just hang out and observe people and places. Being part of a group shunted through a museum wasn't his thing. And if he wasn't enjoying himself, his body language let you know pretty quickly. Within 10 minutes of arriving at Graceland, I realised he wanted out. Now.

Somehow I had a vague relationship with Tav Falco, an underground cult figure and musician based in Memphis. I had his phone number and called him up. He and his girlfriend collected me and Kelly and took us to what seemed like the middle of nowhere – a classic, now legendary, southern juke joint, The Green Room.

It was everything I'd read about such places. Sawdust on the floor, long tables full of people drinking beer from jugs, a bluesy combo playing at one end. After a few minutes it dawned on me that our quartet were the only white faces in the room. This didn't seem to worry Falco and his girlfriend.

At one point I went to the bathroom, and as I returned to the table I saw Kelly on the dance floor, the slightly built figure clutching for grim death to the hips of one of the largest black women I'd ever seen, as she propelled the hapless Kelly around the area in front of the band.

At the end of the song, he came back and sat down. 'What the fuck happened there?' I asked.

Paul whispered, 'She came up and asked me to dance – I was too scared to say no.'

After six weeks in America, Kelly and I headed home. We'd had a damn fine time in the States. Whether Mushroom – who, remember, had footed the bill – felt it was worthwhile was another matter.

Paul kept writing about South Dowling Street and Adelaide. It would be some years before songs like 'Cities Of Texas' came along.

Paul and I had a good relationship. He was quiet, reserved and single-minded, but that was OK. One way we really connected was that we were both music nutters. Early on, he used to give me a box of C90 cassettes and ask me to make recordings of whatever I was listening to. He told me not to second guess what he may or may not like – just to give him everything and he'd work it out. As each box of cassettes was recorded and handed over, another box of blank tapes would appear and on we'd continue.

We also shared a love of sport, which manifested itself in many ways. We played together in an annual cricket game: Kelly, the band, the crew and myself, up against a team of media figures for the Mushroom Cup, a trophy donated by Gudinski. Then when Kelly wrote and recorded his Bradman song in 1986, he and I sat up all night with cricket historian Jack Egan at his home in Bellevue Hill, watching every existing piece of film and video footage of Bradman, working out how to assemble a seven-minute video to accompany the track.

We mailed the video to Bradman and the Don wrote back, saying that he couldn't really understand the adulation he was subjected to, but that he was flattered by this and other songs. He informed us that he didn't own a video player, but that his daughter did, and when he went around to her place for their regular Sunday-night dinner, he'd watch it.

Generally, I left Paul to his own devices regarding his next career move, his creative development and so forth. He was highly self-motivated and knew exactly what direction he wanted to go in musically. One aspect of things I did get involved in, though, was his interview technique.

Kelly and I would do practice interviews – a trick I'd picked up from Motown Records. Apparently, they used to school their artists in appearance, how to talk to the media, etc. I wasn't going to go near Kelly's looks, but as I'd discovered myself all those years ago in Adelaide he was a noticeably reticent interview subject. For instance, if he was asked about why he wrote and recorded the Bradman song, he'd be more than likely to reply, 'Because I like cricket.'

I suggested that he try to be more expansive. Maybe Kelly could talk about his father knowing Bradman, and that the Don attended his father's funeral. Or about his love of Test cricket, rather than the one-day form of the game. Maybe even mention the games he and the band played against the media.

Paul didn't turn into Mr Verbosity overnight. He clearly listened, though, and started to be more expansive in interviews. Journalists still often described talking with him as being like pulling teeth – but the teeth were just a little looser after these sessions.

It was also during these years that I really began to understand the mechanics, and ethics, of the higher echelons of the music business. Kelly and his band, now known as the Messengers, were doing a run of dates in 1987 – a double-billed tour of the country – with Hunters and Collectors. The night of one of the shows, a figure involved in the gig took me aside before the bands began playing.

'Come and see me after the show,' he said gruffly. 'I'll have something for you.'

I must have looked bemused as he became a little agitated, clearly not used to dealing with naive young managers.

'Look,' he said, 'there's going to be a few extra people in here tonight. See me afterwards.'

I was still a little confused as to what was happening, but dutifully went backstage after the show, where I was ushered into a little room and handed an envelope. A chunky envelope. One that, when I got home and counted every note, contained $18,000 in cash. Then I got it – a lot of extra tickets had been sold that were obviously not going through the books.

I hid the cash in my backyard – literally – for when it was needed for the band's activities. It was only later that I reflected on the obvious: if $18,000 was being handed to me voluntarily, just how much were the people who'd given me the money pocketing for themselves?

Kelly and I did good work together and shared that journey from semi-obscurity to semi-stardom. Sometimes my drug intake got the better of my performance, but not that often. I remember once when I overdid it. I had to spend a couple of days recovering in Los Angeles, instead of accompanying the band to some nearby shows in California. But for the most part, I kept it together.

My relationship with Yanni Stumbles began to unravel and eventually we separated. This was somewhat acrimonious. She and I had been working together with Kelly, but it was now really difficult to continue with that business partnership. I decided to put further distance between Yanni and me, taking a back seat, and slowly drifted out of managing Paul's career. When Kelly and I parted ways at the end of the '80s, it was as friends and without animosity.

# 27

# FREELANCE FIEND

I churned out reams for *Dolly*. Usually with a head full of cocaine and beer and not a lot of thought. I was managing Paul Kelly, writing my weekly column for *The Sun-Herald*, and had a seeming inability to say no to any jobs that were offered.

Declining work is one of the hardest things for a freelancer to learn – and most of us never master it. There's always that niggling voice whispering, 'What if the phone stops ringing?' So you keep saying yes, even when logic and mental wear and tear are telling you to take a break.

As a result, over the years I took on all manner of projects. I pored over the *Guinness Book Of Records* to come up with hundreds of 'twisted facts' for a Twisties campaign – the facts ended up on Twisties packets. I wrote hundreds of artist biographies for record labels; album sleeve notes for the Models, Sunnyboys, Weddings Parties Anything, and many others; and program notes for everything from the first B-52's tour of Australia to Beatles, Led Zeppelin and Joni Mitchell tribute shows at the Opera House.

I did research for musical theatre productions and television shows, produced a magazine to accompany the Hoodoo Gurus' *Kinky* album, did a newspaper for the federal government's Drug Offensive, and an in-house magazine for EMI Records. If it paid, and I had the capabilities, I was in.

There were also interviews, management things to be attended to, band meetings, features to submit. It was a nonstop blur that I was somehow able to negotiate, despite – or because of – my alcohol and drug intake. Some days (I thought) they clearly helped; on others, there was no doubt they were a hindrance.

As my profile increased at *Dolly*, I was asked to write 'lifestyle' pieces, not only for them but for other publications in the stable. When my editor, Lisa Wilkinson, moved on to *Cleo* magazine, one of her first assignments for me was to write a piece on – wait for it – a male strippers' show at a club down near Circular Quay.

Lisa and I got along well, but there's just the one tiny, insignificant thing that I can, well, *never* forgive her for. You see, it was because of this strippers' piece that when Bruce Springsteen jumped onstage with Neil Young at the Sydney Entertainment Centre on 22 March 1985 . . . I was somewhere else altogether.

All sorts of manoeuvring had taken place – between the organisers and the folk at *Cleo* – to enable me to be one of the only males (aside from the talent and the bar staff) inside the venue. Annoyingly, my night with the strippers clashed with my night with Neil Young. I figured I'd try to go to both. Silly me. There was no way it was ever going to work. I *should* have said no to this assignment but lingering in the back of my mind was: 'What if Lisa thinks I'm not committed and gets someone else to do these stories – plus I really need the money.'

So I was at the Neil Young concert with a few friends, totally loving it and working out when was a good time to leave. How quickly could I catch a cab from Chinatown down George Street, race into this club, watch five minutes (I mean, really, how much of the show did I need to see?), and then get a taxi back to the Entertainment Centre? Neil did long shows and I reckoned the round trip could be accomplished in around 30 minutes if I was lucky.

And I *was* lucky. I got to the club, went inside, semi-hid in the darkness, watched the aforementioned preening and prancing accompanied by screams, squeals and lunging hands. Five – maybe 10 minutes – and I was done. Then back in a taxi. Race in, take my seat. Total time taken up – let's call it 35 minutes. Easy.

It was all OK until my friends said, 'You're not going to believe what you just missed!' What I'd missed was Springsteen, who had a night off during his first Australian tour, walking unannounced onto the stage and joining Neil and his band for a quarter-hour version of 'Down By The River'. I was devastated.

So, have I forgiven Lisa Wilkinson? No, not really. I mean, I like her lots and we're friendly on the rare occasions we see each other. But forgiven her for this night? Nope.

Fortunately, not all of these lifestyle pieces ended so tragically. I remember in 1986 *Dolly* sent me out on an assignment to be an extra on the TV soapie *Sons And Daughters*. In case you were wondering (and the episode seems to turn up frequently on early-morning repeats), I was dressed as a hospital orderly and pushed a patient up and down a corridor for what seemed like forever. How hard could it be for them to film my majestic performance?

Another time, I was seconded to 'work' at the Sebel, as *Dolly* wanted me to infiltrate the rock-star hotel. I didn't see any stars but I wore a uniform, delivered some room-service breakfasts, lugged bags into the foyer, and later posed for the obligatory pic – end of a hard day, feet on the table with a bottle of champagne.

That's why there was an issue of the magazine with a cover line that read: 'KISSING – STUART COUPE SHOWS YOU HOW.' There were pearls of wisdom here such as 'Kissing's all about expressing emotion, not how well you can manoeuvre your mouth, teeth and tongue.' Seriously. In retrospect, it was a somewhat creepy idea and it isn't high on my list when I decide to revisit a few of my *Dolly* pieces.

At one stage, I was asked to write a feature on whether romance was dead. In the midst of a drug-fuelled run of gigs, I managed to dash out a piece about the good old days of romance: writing letters, sending flowers and so forth.

The deputy editor, Julie Ogden, received the article. After reading it, she turned to a staff writer, Daphne, and said, 'I'm going to marry Stuart Coupe.' She told that story at our wedding a year or so later.

And there was other crazy stuff. I mean, I got a haircut and did a story about it. Blokes and their approaches to different styles of haircuts.

Riveting. I had no recollection of even writing that, until a few years ago when I decided to compile a collection of all my *Dolly* writing. I keep thinking there could be a book in that stuff – and maybe there is. The world *really* needs to know about that haircut. OK, maybe not.

But I had a ball. Of course, I loved the profile – and for every hundred readers who wanted me sent on a one-way trip to Jupiter, there were at least two or three who thought I was the greatest thing ever. They'd write intense, passionate letters to the magazine about how unfair these other readers were who wanted me dead. Some even embraced my point of view on the Yawn Yawn question.

I knew that a lot of what I was writing wasn't the most brilliant journalism, but I was moving too fast to reflect on that. And I guess the overriding aspect of it was that this quiet, shy and insecure kid from Launceston did want to be recognised and loved. And even if a huge number of the *Dolly* readers didn't exactly love me, they *were* reading me and I'd always craved that large audience. I loved sharing the music and ideas I was enthusiastic about with as many people as possible.

Anyway, after Lisa moved on, Deborah Bibby had a stint in the big chair. Then the editor's role was taken by Julie Ogden. Ever the charmer, I remember my opening gambit to her was, 'Well, I guess I'd better be nice to you now.' I was sort of joking, but a changing of the guard is frequently precarious and I'd become very used to the income from *Dolly* arriving in my bank account every month. It was good money, but aside from the record reviews page I still had to pitch stories every month.

By the time Julie became editor I was a bit of a drawcard for the magazine. Someone suggested that I be put under contract – maybe it was me, or my lawyer. To be honest, I wasn't sure why they agreed to it, as I didn't have anywhere else to go. Maybe they suspected a *Dolly* competitor would emerge and they might try to poach me.

Julie and I went to the Bayswater Brasserie in Kings Cross to negotiate the deal. That was the time when every mover and shaker in the arts/film/music caper went to the Brasserie. It was a mecca for creative hipsters – and a terrific space with good food. And it was only a quick trip up the stairs for a couple of lines in the bathroom if it was that sort of day. And let's face it, if you had the income in the 1980s, most days were that sort of day.

I remember Julie ordered whitebait. She told me later that she hated whitebait. Maybe she was nervous negotiating with *Dolly*'s version of Tom Wolfe meets Lester Bangs. (In my dreams.) We came to an agreement – to my utter astonishment – that I'd be paid a whopping $4000 a month for my contributions to the magazine. This was an outrageous amount of money – both then and now. Julie later admitted she'd been authorised to give me more if I'd asked.

But I was pretty damn happy with four grand an issue. What did I need to do for that? For starters, they expected one long feature story per issue. That was about 1800 words of gibberish on the Models or INXS or Terence Trent D'Arby. Hard going. Not. Then they wanted a short feature – that was about 1200 words. This could be music related, or about kissing . . . or getting a haircut. And the real kicker was that they expected me to write a full page of record reviews every issue. For this, I'd be sent dozens and dozens of free albums by record companies wanting their stuff in the mag.

When you tallied it up, I was being asked to write 4000 words a month for $4000. I figured that would take me less than a day to churn out – so really I was getting four grand a day. There was no exclusivity clause in the deal, and I was still managing Paul Kelly, plus writing for *The Sun-Herald* and anyone else who'd pay me.

At *Dolly* I was also offered the opportunity to talk to all manner of rock'n'roll stars. Many of them I was a big fan of and relished the opportunity. At other times – well, I recognised why the magazine felt they should cover them and why I was being dispatched to do the interviews.

Many of these encounters were part of an endless stream of media commitments for the artists. You'd always pass a journalist or radio personality you knew on the way in or out of the interview and exchange quick observations: 'Idiot has nothing to say' . . . 'Great fun – really good talker' . . . '*Do not mention . . .*'

The cattle-call interviews are gruelling for artists and often not a lot of fun for the journalists – especially if you've been allocated a time near the end of a long day of them. Such was the case when I did my *Dolly* interview with Sting.

I didn't mind The Police, but when they peaked I was in the midst of one of my purist reggae phases and looked down my nose at white boys trying to play the stuff. And I know I'm not alone in considering 'Every Breath You Take' a *really* creepy song about stalking. I can't help but wonder what's going through the heads of couples who have it played at their weddings. A real love song, it ain't. Need wedding-song suggestions? Call me.

By the time of this interview, Sting was solo. It was the tantric-sex period. The I'm-an-intellectual-and-you're-not Sting. The deep-thinking Sting. The boring-as-batshit Sting. My opinion only, mind you.

On this visit he was staying – you guessed it – at the Sebel and when I arrived at 5pm, I realised that I was the last of what I was sure had been a very taxing day for El Tantrico. My interest factor for the interview was closing in on zero, but hell, let's see if we could have some fun here. Maybe we could spice things up. At best, getting thrown out of Sting's hotel room would make for good copy, 'cause I sure as hell wasn't going to start with a question about the new album. Nope, we were going to roll the dice good and proper.

I walked in. Shook hands. Then I sat down and fixed him with that 'Don't fuck with me, I'm from *Dolly*' look.

'Sting . . . what's your favourite colour?'

And fuck me if he didn't laugh, didn't throw me out, but instead spent the next 40 minutes explaining in great detail why it was black. By the end, I wanted to die. He just seemed to go on . . . and on . . . and on. And with no levity at all. But I later realised that I'd actually had a great interview and insight into Sting's character.

There were other times when I was unexpectedly gifted gems. Like the time I spent with a young Kylie Minogue in August 1988. We did this interview in the restaurant at the top of the Boulevard Hotel, although I didn't actually get to ask any questions of my own. The deal here was that readers had been asked to send in the questions they'd most like to ask Kylie – and 'Stu Pot' (another way I was referred to in the magazine) was going to ask them on their behalf.

Kylie and I worked our way through them, starting with 'If you could do anything over again, what would you do?' to 'When's your birthday?' and 'Do you still have any friends from your old school?'. Eventually we reached the one that caused all the trouble. Given the political agenda of the time, it was pretty straightforward.

The question went like this. Read slowly, so there's no confusion.

'What do you think about the situation in South Africa?'

With me so far?

Kylie pondered this for a minute and then said, 'I don't think they should be shooting the rhinos.'

I'm completely with her on this – still am. However, I don't know about you, but it's not the first thing I'd think of if asked that question. I didn't reflect too much on it, though. I wrote up her responses and they were duly published in the next issue.

Of course, that was the one answer all the media homed in on. And Kylie was hugely embarrassed. To this day I understand that whenever she's reminded of it, she says she never gave that answer and that the journalist made it up. In this case, I still have my transcript of the interview. I'm really not sure why I'd concoct her response. I didn't have an issue with Kylie – then or now.

But I can see why she'd want to distance herself from her rhino comment. With one quick answer to a question posed by a reader of *Dolly*, she suddenly had a reputation for being politically naïve – which may well have not been the case. And I suspect she became very tired of niggling, snide references to rhinos in subsequent articles about her.

Anyway, these things happen. I'm sure I've given some pretty crazy answers to questions from time to time and I haven't been interviewed a 10th as many times as Kylie.

So, a completely innocuous, thoroughly forgettable interview became one of the more memorable ones of my career. And speaking of memorable interviews . . .

# 28

# CAN'T FEEL MY FACE

'You're driving back to the hotel with me tonight,' Michael Gudinski told me in a gruff, don't argue, tone as we stood together outside the Auckland Showground.

'Any reason?' I asked.

'You're interviewing Dylan tonight.'

This was clearly not a question or a discussion. Gudinski had just told me that, within a few hours, I was to be talking with the artist who had most shaped my life, the figure who – as we spoke – was onstage performing with Tom Petty & The Heartbreakers.

It was 1986 and, as with so many things in my life, I'd stumbled upon the idea that I could syndicate my stories and interviews. I'd been reading a book by a Chicago-based writer I liked a lot named Bob Greene, and noticed on the back cover that it said his weekly column appeared in over 300 publications.

One column paid for by a few hundred outlets. I could work with that concept. Years later, I'd find out that Charles M. Schulz had the same caper going with his 'Peanuts' cartoons – except his syndication was measured in thousands of newspapers.

OK, I was never that great at maths, but I know there weren't 300 outlets for what I did. However, in those days there were street-music publications in pretty much every capital city, and daily newspapers did their own editorial deals. So I could write one piece and sell it to all the individual takers, who all paid a pittance (but 10 × pittance added up to something), and to *The Age*, *The Sydney Morning Herald*, *The West Australian* and so forth.

If I placed the same piece, or variants on it, around the country I could pick up a nice pay packet, and become the go-to guy for promoters and record labels. They'd get the big international stars to do one Australian interview – with me – and I'd take care of the rest. Which is why I was on the New Zealand leg of the Dylan/Tom Petty tour, which was happening prior to the Australian dates.

Until this moment, there'd been no mention of me interviewing Dylan. The voice of a generation wasn't talking to the Australian or New Zealand media. I was just going to the shows – on Gudinski and his Frontier Touring's dime – to write reviews of the concerts and phone in reports to a number of radio stations around Australia. 'Build up the vibe,' as Gudinski put it.

But I wasn't complaining. Not one bit. I was 30 years of age and doing something that was beyond any dream I'd ever had, something I'd never really allowed myself to imagine was possible. Playing squash for Australia had – I dreamt – been a possibility, but this? No way.

I was on tour with *Bob Dylan*. This was better than going to Paris to interview Springsteen. Much better. I was actually on the tour, part of the entourage – not just flying in for a chat and a couple of shows. This meant I could observe the machinations of a big-level international tour. An added bonus was that Dylan was touring with Tom Petty and the Heartbreakers, who I also adored.

For a kid who'd grown up listening obsessively to early Dylan records and devoured every word he could find about him, who'd searched out and savoured mail-order bootlegs, drawn sketches of him with that famous '60s head of hair and sunglasses, fantasised about *being* Bob Dylan, this was it.

Three shows in and here I was, staying in the same hotels as Dylan, hanging around and taking it all in. I was witnessing the interaction between the musicians and the crew, hanging at soundchecks, seeing Dylan and Petty and the band playing around with songs. It was heaven.

I looked on in awe (albeit from a distance, as I didn't want to intrude too much – well, I did, but figured I should hang back and be cool) at Elliot Roberts and Gudinski deep in conversation. Roberts was only the bloke who had guided the careers of Neil Young, Joni Mitchell, Dylan, Petty and so many others – another legend to be in awe of.

At one point, I saw Roberts and Gudinski emerge from a backstage caravan. They were rubbing their noses and talking more animatedly than they had been 10 minutes earlier. I accidentally found myself closer to them than I'd realised and, in a rash moment, made some quip to Elliot about what I perceived was their drug use.

Roberts looked at me and paused. 'Stuart, my artists are onstage. It's my turn to have some fun.' So, Elliot Roberts knew my name. That took a while to sink in.

Earlier in the day, I'd been wandering around backstage during soundcheck. A limousine pulled up and I could see Stevie Nicks sitting in the back seat. Nicks was on the tour but not performing. She was somewhat close with Tom Petty and travelling semi-incognito with him.

I was trying not to stare as the driver opened the door for her. She almost fell out of the back seat and I watched her totter towards the back of the stage. There were three steps she needed to navigate to get to where Dylan, Petty and the band were running through a bunch of cover versions. I remember a Buddy Holly tune being amongst them.

Nicks managed two of the three steps. Just. A fall seemed imminent and then her brain and feet connected briefly, and she realised the impossibility of the last step, abandoned all efforts, and managed to make her way back to the ground and to the back seat of the limousine.

There was a lot of cocaine on this tour. A real lot.

New Zealand's customs service was notorious for its vigilance and, years earlier, an officer who was much younger than me had delivered a stern lecture when he found Serepax in my bags as I entered the country with Split Enz. I told him they helped me sleep. His view was that at my age I shouldn't need help sleeping. I pointed out that they weren't an illegal substance, and I had a prescription. He let me through. Begrudgingly, I felt.

But Serepax wasn't the drug of choice on this tour. I spent a bunch of time wondering how cocaine had made its way into New Zealand. I was much more naive then about the workings of organised crime and the connections that major concert tour promoters might need to make to satisfy the requirements of the artists they brought to the Southern Hemisphere.

Gudinski and I drive back to the hotel in Auckland. I'm more than a little stunned. Excited, of course. And terrified. This is Bob Dylan we're talking about. I've now interviewed hundreds and hundreds of rock'n'roll stars. But there are rock'n'roll stars and there's Bob Dylan.

I've watched and read enough to know that Dylan doesn't particularly like interviews. He can be playful with them. And he can be nasty. And I have no real time to prepare.

I've spent my life listening to Dylan but what do you ask him? I'm told it's a chat and that it will be up to him how long it goes for. Gudinski has explained that ticket sales in Australia have been a little slower than he'd have liked, so via Elliot Roberts, Dylan has been leaned on to do one . . . chat. With me.

This already puts me on edge. Just being told that Dylan has been pressured to do this. Does anyone actually tell Dylan to do anything? Clearly, he and Roberts have a relationship where this can happen. I have no idea what form this 'chat' will take and how long it might go for. So I start scribbling – as I've always done – little crib notes of subjects to keep the conversation going. I've always tried to establish early on in interviews that I know what I'm talking about and can be relied on – I hope – to provide an interesting conversation.

For Dylan, I've written words like 'Lenny Bruce', 'Ginsberg', 'Hank Williams', 'country music history' and so forth. Once we're up and running – as I hope we will be – I'll just rely on my wits and knowledge (and natural curiosity about all things Dylan) to carry us through.

Arriving back at the hotel, Gudinski informs me that Dylan has already gone to his room. He likes to call his kids each night, which

I think is kinda cool. How long will he be? No-one knows. Gudinski tells me to come up to his suite and wait. We'll get a call.

Did I mention there was a lot of cocaine on this tour? Gudinski's door is barely closed before he's chopping out a line . . . and another . . . and another. We're talking shit. I'm nervous. I can't sit down. Cocaine is probably the worst thing to be indulging in at a time like this. But I like drugs and I like cocaine a lot. And cocaine makes you like cocaine even more. And Gudinski has good cocaine. Both of us are circling the room. I'm occasionally scribbling a note about something else to ask Dylan. We do more cocaine. It's now well after 1 am. Maybe 2 am. We've been waiting since around midnight when we got back to the hotel. Who cares? I'm flying high and about to interview Bob Dylan.

The phone rings. Elliot Roberts says to come down to the hotel bar. After a quick chat with Roberts, Gudinski makes himself scarce. The bar is now closed to everyone except Roberts and me. And Bob Dylan.

Roberts and I sit at a table, clearly visible through glass to all the other journalists and media people on the tour. Word has gotten around that Dylan is doing an interview tonight. With me. I can feel their eyes zeroing in. Their collective thought is: 'Why that prick and not me?'

Dylan walks in. He's even shorter than I imagined. I figured he wasn't a tall guy, but I wasn't prepared for the fact that he's about five foot five. Roberts introduces me. Dylan puts out his hand – it's clammy. He doesn't move his arm. I find myself moving it up and down in an uncomfortable version of a handshake. There is a clear air that he doesn't want to be here. But I'm as high as several kites. And, shit, I'm suddenly really, really terrified.

I am not relaxed. I am not cool. The zenith of my life as a journalist, music lover, fan is now happening. I am sitting at a table in a bar with Bob Dylan.

I start asking him questions. Probably more animatedly than I realise. Things get off to a bad start when I suggest that his association with The Heartbreakers was good for him, bringing out performances the likes of which he hasn't given for a long time. In hindsight, it wasn't the best opening gambit.

'Since when?' Dylan taunted. 'Come on, tell me when I last gave good shows. You tell me when I last gave spirited shows.'

Sensing I'm on shaky ground, and with a sinking feeling in my stomach, I suddenly find myself changing tack. I ask Dylan about his politics. He stares at me from behind his sunglasses.

'Well, I never had any politics. I'm still searching for some. Maybe one of these days I'll run into some that make sense, but at the moment I don't even know what politics are, to tell you the truth.'

Dylan keeps talking and opens up about the crisis for farmers in America, but displays no real engagement with anything I ask. I try to draw him on Lenny Bruce, who he's written a song about, his friendship with Allen Ginsberg, the writing of Jack Kerouac. He doesn't shut me down – but he's not expansive either.

I'm drowning. But still trying to think of something to connect with him. I'm coming across as an obsessive fan, something I'll later learn is the worst way to approach talking to Dylan. Especially a Dylan who agreed to the conversation only under sufferance.

I'm still sinking and once again I change tack. I ask Dylan about a response to Irish writer Brendan Behan's comment that anyone who hates America hates the human race.

'That's kinda putting it a bit strongly,' he says, 'but it's hard not to love America – don't you love America? It's the kind of country where if you don't like where you're living, then you can always move on someplace else.'

In hindsight I wish I'd followed with a question about whether that was why he was spending so much time on tour. But I was flustered, grabbing at any straws.

For a brief moment I think we might have lift off, but Dylan doesn't continue. He takes a sip of his drink. Sits there. His body language says, 'You got anything else, kid? Otherwise we're done here.'

And, yes, I'm sensing we're done. Roberts is muttering something that sounds like: 'This isn't happening.' In what I sense may be my last chance at a connection, I bring up a recent interview Dylan has done with an American magazine, in which he was asked who he'd most like to interview. He replied that most people on his list were already dead and cited Apollinaire, Joseph (from the Bible), Marilyn Monroe, Mohammad, Paul the Apostle, John F. Kennedy and Hank Williams.

Dylan had said in another interview that there was a time in his life when he listened to nothing but records by the country singer, and that one of his most famous songs, 'Like A Rolling Stone', was directly inspired by Williams' 'Lost Highway'.

So I ask Dylan, if Williams was sitting at our table what would he most like to ask him. He looks up and straight at me for what seems like minutes, but in reality is probably only seconds. He knows what's been going on. He knows what state I'm in.

'I'd probably ask him where he gets his drugs,' he replies, laughing for the only time in the interview. 'What else would I ask him? I think that would be enough. I always liked his clothes and I probably would have wanted to know where he got those.'

With that, Roberts, whose presence I've found extremely discon-certing; as if I've needed to impress them both – mutters that time is up, and that Dylan needs to finish. He makes it clear he and Dylan are staying and it's time for me to leave.


It wasn't the greatest interview I'd ever done. Not by a long shot. But I'd done something the kid sitting at home in Launceston, listening to all those dozens of Dylan songs and records, would never have thought imaginable.

The article I wrote appeared in many publications in Australia and in *Spin* magazine in America. The initial piece was relatively short – maybe 1200 words – but for Spin it was much longer, as it included an interview I did with Tom Petty the next day. Despite my addled state at the time, I thought the piece turned out OK.

Dylan read it (even hearing that was pretty cool) and apparently didn't like that I described his hands as clammy. He was also upset with Gudinski for telling me he'd gone to his room to call his kids. I thought it was an admirable thing to do, but clearly it was a personal detail that Dylan didn't appreciate Gudinski passing on to me.

And I'd learnt a valuable lesson. Never snort half of the gross national product of Bolivia before you interview Bob Dylan. Just. Don't. Do. It.

# 29

# HOTEL ROOM SERVICE

So I've interviewed Dylan, chatted with three Rolling Stones – Bill Wyman, Mick Jagger and Keith Richards – but never a Beatle. *Almost* a Beatle.

War stories. In my line of work and fun, you end up with a few, and of course you're expected to trot them out at dinner parties and other gatherings. Did I ever interview a Beatle? Well, it was 1983, I think, when EMI dangled the idea of a chat with Paul McCartney.

You might imagine I'd be jumping out of my skin at the opportunity. However, the fact is that I was a Rolling Stones kid – and that meant not being a Beatles one. That was just the way it was. Growing up, I knew all the Beatles songs (no kid of my generation could fail to), but I wanted to be like the Rolling Stones, or Cream, or the Jimi Hendrix Experience – not the Beatles. And I think Paul was my least favourite Beatle.

I remember watching an Opera House tribute to the White Album years later. I remarked to a well-known manager that I thought Josh Pyke's performance was really sappy and he looked at me and quipped, 'Well, someone has to be Paul.'

But still, a Beatle was a Beatle, so I was in, and so was *The Sun-Herald*. The only sticking point was that, apparently, McCartney's management wanted complete veto of what was printed – and demanded to see the full story before it appeared in the newspaper. In effect, this meant I'd be writing advertorial for McCartney and his people. They just wouldn't be coughing up any loot, which is usually how advertorial works.

My editor, Tony Stephens, wanted the interview but wasn't having a bar of this. He dashed off a reply, saying that 'even the Australian Prime Minister doesn't insist on such requirements'.

Back came a masterful response. 'Prime Ministers come and go – there is only one Paul McCartney.'

I didn't get to talk to McCartney.

In fact, the closest I ever came to interviewing a Beatle was a phone conversation with Yoko Ono a decade or two later. During that perfectly pleasant chat, I happened to mention that I'd been in Central Park in 1985 for the opening of the Strawberry Fields memorial to John Lennon.

'Oh,' she gushed, 'you should have come and said hello.'

Of course, Yoko was being polite, in the way well-meaning stars often are. But could you imagine it? The love of her life, John Lennon, had been shot a few years earlier and an unknown bozo pushes through the crowd at this event, yelling out, 'YOKO! YOKO!' That would never have ended well.

But back to the Rolling Stones. I interviewed Bill Wyman when he came to Australia in 1982 – and he signed my copy of *Between The Buttons*. I spoke to Keith on the telephone and what a delightful and fun conversationalist he was. It was back in the '90s and there were lots of chuckles as I imagined him sitting there on the other end of the line with a huge spliff in his hand.

And when, in 1987, Mick Jagger released his solo album *Primitive Cool*, I received a call from a record company publicity person asking if I wanted to interview Mick. I said yes – very loudly and quickly – and asked which day the call was scheduled for. Mick bloody Jagger? Now we're talking.

There was a condescending sniff at the other end of the line. 'Oh, it won't be a phone interview. Mick is doing a day of international press in Paris, so you'll need to get yourself there. And before you ask – no, we're not paying.'

I explained this to Tony Stephens, who was excited. He asked the date, then picked up the phone, chatted to someone, and said, 'OK, I've got you a business class ticket to Paris via London on Qantas.'

Incredulously, I asked how he'd managed to do that – and so quickly.

'Don't worry,' he said, 'we'll run some stuff about them in the future.' Next subject.

As it happened, I'd just returned home after a stint in America with Paul Kelly and the band. Things were going well in that department, but it was incredibly time-consuming dealing with their day-to-day activities, the US label, overseeing the booking of tours and all the other logistics of record promotion and publicity. Paul's life on the road also needed to be dealt with, and of course I still had all my writing commitments. Back to the airport for another long flight.

In those days, I travelled comfortably. Very comfortably. Most people would say that my definition of comfort was raiding the bins outside Vinnies, and OK, my favourite pink windcheater did have a few holes, and maybe I should patch those jeans. Anyway, I arrived at check-in for my flight and asked about a pass for the Qantas Lounge. The person who'd checked me in said, 'Unfortunately, sir, that won't be possible, given your appearance.'

Admittedly, I looked slightly more ragged than usual, probably hadn't brushed my hair that year, and may have had a few drinks. I contested his position, at which point another Qantas staffer came over. I enquired as to which aspect of my appearance was causing consternation, as I would look to rectify that part.

The staffer looked me up and down and said, 'Well, to be perfectly honest, sir, all of it.'

There was no Qantas Lounge for me.

En route to Paris, I flew in to London, where I had a meeting at Heathrow with Hunters and Collectors' manager Michael Roberts. We argued – in a semi-friendly fashion (just) – about which of our bands should headline a mooted double-billed Australian tour. In case you're wondering, he got his way.

After a night in London, I arrived in Paris the following morning. I wandered around the city before heading to the prestigious and ultra-expensive George Cinq hotel, where the interviews were being conducted. I discovered that Jagger was flying in for the day from England, which begged the question as to why the interviews couldn't have been conducted there. This was particularly pertinent because I was also told that Jagger had a bad back and his flight had been delayed while he was having it looked at.

Then I found out I was nearly the final interview of the day. So . . . more wandering around Paris. By mid-afternoon I was back at the hotel. In the bar. Jetlagged and waiting for Jagger.

Eventually, I was ushered in to the Presidential Suite, where Mick was holding court. A slightly overeager PR person plonked me into an armchair opposite an affable but bored-looking Rolling Stone. His back looked OK to me, although maybe it was causing him grief. Or maybe the painkillers had kicked in. But it all felt very business-like.

I asked a few perfunctory questions about his new album – what it was like being produced by Dave Stewart from Eurythmics – which he answered with a lack of enthusiasm that suggested this was his 10th interview of the day. Which it probably was.

It must be said that Jagger is not the most exciting of interview subjects. He's a political animal – very guarded – and only wants to talk about the stuff that interests him: in this case, his new album. The trouble was that I wasn't interested in talking about that at all.

I was getting just a little frustrated at Jagger's seeming lack of engagement. Within 20 minutes we were talking about cricket, but I couldn't even get much out of him on that, despite it being one of his passions. At the end of my 40 minutes, it dawned on me that I'd just talked to one of the most famous humans on the planet and I'd come away very underwhelmed. Jagger was, frankly, fairly dull. Or maybe I asked shit questions.

I now needed to get a photo with Mick, partly for the Qantas in-flight magazine story I'd been informed I was writing as part of the payback for my business class ticket. So we went out on the balcony outside the room that was Jagger Central.

But there was a slight problem. I'm not exactly super-tall – just a smidgeon under six feet in the old calculations. And Jagger, a bit over four feet (actually, he claims five feet eight), didn't want to have his photo taken next to me: at least until the hotel brought him a foot stool to eliminate the disparity. When the stool was eventually procured, the photograph was taken, and my mission was accomplished. Check the photos of us together. Voila! The same height!

That was almost the end of Mick's day and he announced that he was – as expected – heading back to London. I was flying to New York early the next morning to meet up with the Paul Kelly entourage, who were in the middle of a lengthy run of dates in the US. I needed a place to stay, so I asked Julian Shapiro, from the Sony-owned Columbia Records (who had the rights to Jagger's album in America), if he could recommend a cheap hotel nearby. In my semi-zombie state – and not exactly knowing my way around Paris – I'd filed it in the too-hard basket until it needed to come out of there and be dealt with.

Julian, who I knew from my various trips to New York to do interviews with artists on his label, told me that they'd paid for Jagger's room for the night, so I might as well stay there. Amazing. Room after room full of antiques, a spectacular view of Paris and a fridge full of expensive champagne. Bring it on!

Feeling quite dazed, and having no real idea of what day it was, I settled in on the couch, poured myself the first of many, many glasses of Moet, pulled out my phone book and called just about anyone across the planet who I knew for a chat.

'Yes, I'm in Mick's suite. It feels like it's about 14 rooms. No, he's gone back to London. He's kinda dull. Yes, the fridge seems to only have Moet in it. Have another glass? OK, if you insist. Cheers. To you and me and Mick . . . and Sony/Columbia – whichever is picking up the tab.'

At around 6 am, I walked out and caught a taxi to the airport. I guess the staff at George Cinq knew that Jagger had left the previous day, and that somehow countless quantities of Moet had still been consumed, and hours' worth of international phone calls made. But the bill? Well, I never heard a word about it.

# 30

# EDGE OF REALITY

It was late 1987, and life at *Dolly* had stopped being fun. The money was still great, but by now I'd probably written about as many stories about kissing techniques, a trip to the barber and getting the boot into Yawn Yawn as I was capable of. There was one other negative factor too – and it was a big one. Kerry Packer.

From the beginning *Dolly* had been published by Fairfax, which also published *The Sun-Herald*. For someone like yours truly, it was all pretty cosy. Then, Australian Consolidated Press bought the mag and in came its boss. Life wouldn't be cosy under Kerry.

The relaxed atmosphere we'd all enjoyed for years was suddenly not so casual. The magazine stable that included *Dolly* moved into Park Street, over the road from Hyde Park – the headquarters of Packer's empire. Keeping traditions alive, the staff who'd been brought over went for their customary long lunch. Most days, this consisted of three hours of drinking, chatter and some food.

One day, soon after the Park Street move, one of the editors arrived back in the office to find Packer sitting in her chair, his feet on her desk. He was making it clear that ACP was a very different place to Fairfax. In his world (unless it was him and his cronies), lunch *didn't* start at midday and extend through the better part of the afternoon.

Now, there were endless meetings, demands, expectations. *Dolly* was a hugely important part of the Packer purchase, because at the time it was doing incredibly well. It was selling around 280,000 copies per issue, and with a pass-on factor (that's magazine and advertising talk for how many people cast their eyes over each printed issue) of 5–1, that was about 1.5 million readers every month.

This was pretty remarkable, but Packer's expectation was that *Dolly* could do even better. What would that mean for me, though? Would there still be a place for Stu Pot if things changed? After the new over-lords had completed their overhaul, would my style fit in?

With all these pressures, editor Julie Ogden's patience with ACP was waning. So she and I started thinking about a hair-brained idea. And the more we talked about it, the less crazy it seemed. Mind you, drugs were usually involved in my side of these discussions. The sort of drugs that can make the most off-the-wall schemes seem totally doable.

You see, at *Dolly* we got a lot of letters from guys. Or gals mentioning that their boyfriend had read something in the latest issue. We realised that there were a lot more non-gal readers of the magazine than people assumed. We probably convinced ourselves that half the *Dolly* readership was male. Did I mention that drugs were involved?

Then we moved to next-level conceptualising. Girls had *Dolly*. What did guys have? They had surfing magazines and music magazines and football magazines and skateboarding magazines, and women-with-very-few-clothes-on magazines. But they didn't have a 'lifestyle' magazine – a publication that combined all the interests that an Australian guy presumably had. Hell, they *needed* one. And we were going to give it to them. Oh yes, we were.

So we quit *Dolly*. The potential for this new venture looked so rosy that I don't think we spent much time reflecting on what we were doing. We were just out of there.

Julie had maintained contact with four of the old Fairfax publishing group who'd broken away from the mothership and decided to start their own magazine-publishing venture. They had a little money, a lot of experience and they also dug the idea. No drugs were involved with them, although they did, I must say, have lunch pretty much every day from midday till 4 pm and kept the Australian red-wine industry alive in the process. They were excited and bought the idea completely. A deal that – on paper – was extremely generous to Julie and me was worked out.

Not only would we receive a generous salary (Julie as editor, me as associate editor), we'd also get a car (hello, red jeep with a removable canvas roof). However, there was even more of a kicker than the 'Edgemobile', as we called our new vehicle. We were also offered potentially a very lucrative share of any profits the magazine made. And, of course, we knew we were going to be rolling in money. Now that I think about it, there's a repeated pattern in my life. Foolproof business plans that can't possibly fail . . .

We decided to call the fledgling magazine *The Edge*. It was on the edge, had an edge, and, we thought and hoped, would have the edge over what we believed was our closest competitor – the Australian edition of *Rolling Stone*. So, offices were rented in Commonwealth Street in Surry Hills (198, to be precise, if this book ever becomes the basis for a walking tour) and we set about hiring a small but cool staff. A couple of them were lured over from *Dolly* and we set about putting together the first issue.

I had the top office. You could only reach it via a rather narrow spiral staircase – it was perfect for me to get up to no good in. There was a real feeling as well that we were creating something innovative and exciting.

For the first issue, we wanted someone that screamed 'BUY ME' on the cover. It had to be someone recognisable, popular and blokesy, without being alienating to those of the female persuasion who we also hoped were potential readers of this new magazine. Who you gonna call? Mushroom Records.

So we spoke to Mushroom and, guess what, Jimmy Barnes had a new album out and, yes, he'd be available for an interview and cover shoot. I flew to Coffs Harbour to hang out with Barnes on his Barnestorming tour.

We were backstage at one point and there was a youngish boy hanging around who didn't seem that comfortable, and not part of the scene. I asked someone who he was and was told in a whisper – which strongly implied, 'Don't you dare write about this' – that he was Jimmy's son, David, from an earlier relationship. Father and son were in the process of really getting to know each other.

The night of the show it was bucketing down. There was mud everywhere. Everyone – including Michael Gudinski – headed back to the rather luxurious Aanuka Resort. There was a lot of cocaine involved. I went and hung with Barnes and Gudinski. At some point in the night Gudinski came to my room chatting away, going a million miles an hour. His shoes were caked with mud, and with each lap the carpet got muddier and muddier. I was terrified I'd be blamed. But thankfully, it didn't come to that. This was the Jimmy Barnes tour and there was bound to be a contingency for such activities and damages.

Actually – a bit of a digression, while I think of it. I'd had other experiences like this with a slightly, shall we say, heightened, Gudinski. A couple of years earlier, in 1986, I was expanding my management activities and had stumbled upon a Sydney band called The Chosen Few, who I liked a lot. I started pursuing Michael to check them out.

Eventually, his office nominated a Monday when he was going to be in Sydney. Not wanting to leave anything to chance, I said I'd pick him up. My partner and I drove out to the airport and a dishevelled Michael jumped in. The plan was to go straight to the Hopetoun Hotel as I'd pulled a favour and organised for the band to play that night.

Michael had other ideas. 'We have to go via the eastern suburbs. I need to pick something up.' Something was a number of grams of cocaine (three for him and one for me, as it transpired) from the home of someone well-known in the industry, who obviously moonlighted as a cocaine supplier. This wasn't exactly on the way – the airport and the Hopetoun being in a fairly direct line.

Anyway, we raced to the eastern suburbs, Michael grabbed what he needed, and off we headed to see The Chosen Few. Soon after we arrived at the Hopetoun, he yelled in my ear, 'Should I tour Bros?' I yelled back that I thought it wasn't a bad idea, as they were on the rise, but that I'd do it quickly as I wasn't sure their popularity would last. A few weeks later, Frontier Touring announced a Bros tour.

Michael watched a few songs of The Chosen Few, before muttering, 'OK, let's do it,' and added that he needed to be somewhere. Before I knew it, he was gone.

A contract was negotiated and then it was time for signing. Again, Gudinski was in Sydney, midway through a tour with Sting. A signing was organised at Mushroom's offices, which were then situated on William Street on the main drag up to Kings Cross. The inking of contracts was set for 2 pm.

The band and I were there on time, as were the Mushroom staffers. No sign of Gudinski. By 2.30, he still hadn't arrived. I knew he was staying across the road at the Boulevard Hotel, which I could see from the window.

After a while, I rang him. When I was put through to his room, it was clear it had been a very long night – or maybe it was still a very long night going into day. He mumbled something about being there shortly.

It was an unseasonably warm early April afternoon and I watched with amusement as Gudinski – in bare feet with his shirt hanging out – dodged between cars as he crossed William Street and emerged out of the lift.

Seeing me, Gudinski said, 'Come with me!' and dragged me into an empty office, where I asked what the fuck he wanted. He was already nearly an hour late.

'What's the name of the band again?' he asked.

I informed him that it was The Chosen Few and that he loved them. He nodded, then walked out of that room and into the one where everyone was waiting.

'Chosen Few – welcome to Mushroom. I love you guys.'

In the early 2000s, when I decided to tell that story in a book, the lawyers said it had to be deleted – as there was the potential for Gudinski to take legal action. Incredulous, I asked why. They informed me I was stating that Michael Gudinski had done business when not in full control of his facilities.

'Tell me something I don't know – everyone knows that,' I countered.

Back came the reply. 'You may know it. Everyone – whoever they are – may know it. But you can't say it – at least without his permission.'

I really wanted it in the book so I contacted Gudinski who asked to see the page of the manuscript. Initially, he was reluctant, muttering something about having kids, whilst I was thinking, 'Do they really not know you take drugs?' Eventually he sent a note giving his approval for it to be in the book.

But back to *The Edge*, and the first issue in 1988 looked great. Barnes was on the cover sitting in a red sports car. The other cover lines were: 'Ecstasy: The Perfect Drug?' 'Why Get A Tattoo'. 'How Sex Sells Music'.

After the magazine hit the newsstands, we copped it from John Laws. Big time. He was on the radio railing against this filth that we'd created. Apparently, the world was going to hell in a handbasket and it was all because of this vile publication called *The Edge*. We got a recording of his comments, typed them up, and stuck them on the wall in the foyer. Bring it on, Johnny Boy.

The trouble was that we'd made a miscalculation with *The Edge*. And it was a big one. Boys hadn't been brought up to embrace this thing called 'lifestyle'. They had a lifestyle – of course, they did – but we hadn't realised that they were much more specific about these leanings than women were. If a bloke was into surfing, he bought surfing magazines. *Tracks* was his Bible. If he was into whatever code of football, he'd buy the magazine that was devoted to that code. He wasn't interested in reading widely, apart from footy. Why would a rugby bloke embrace an Australian rules footy magazine?

As for music, for starters we were now entering the world of the free music newspapers, so a lot of that was available freely anywhere. It was similar to the current streaming-services era: why buy a record or CD? The hardcore music nerds bought – you guessed it – magazines directed at hardcore music nerds. If they were into sex and girls – well, that's what *Playboy* and *Penthouse* were for, surely.

And the twain did not meet. We were a few years ahead of the so-called lads magazines that came largely from England. A little later, a bunch of disenfranchised former *Rolling Stone* folk would start a magazine called *Juice* and pretty much replicate what we'd tried with *The Edge* – but do it better, given they'd been able to observe where we screwed up. And, of course, the times had changed.

*The Edge* battled on from issue to issue as we tried to get the content mix to gell with whatever readership was actually out there. Cricketer Merv Hughes was on one cover, boxer Jeff Harding on another. The Guns N' Roses logo adorned another. One had an image of a woman of the night and a cover line, 'PROSTITUTES: THEY WORK HARD FOR THE MONEY'.

Work/time pressures were increasing as well. Julie and I had just had our first child, our daughter, Jay.

It was becoming clear that the magazine wasn't going to fly. Dreams of mega-fortunes were vanishing. We moved to offices in Rushcutters Bay, where the publishers were building a stable of magazines, all trying to replicate existing titles – but not as well. If you bought *Women's Weekly* and *Woman's Day*, were you going to add a third magazine to your reading list? Probably not.

But we had fun. It was a friendly and talented bunch of ratbags running the show and we carried on with a good-natured, but ferocious sense of 'us and them'. And we kept searching for ways to increase the readership. After discussions with the publishers and looking at the fairly depressing sales figures, Julie and I started to reposition *The Edge* to try to bring in female readers as well. And maybe they'd buy it and show it to their boyfriends. It didn't work.

Then, to keep the budgets looking acceptable, we – in most cases, I – began churning out a seemingly endless array of one-shot publications under the banner of *The Edge*. It was simple: pick a big band (try U2, Guns N' Roses, etc), get a big poster image, a bunch of good (and ideally free from the record label) photos, and put minimal text around it – usually rewritten from record company bios. I did one on the up-and-coming Johnny Diesel & the Injectors, another on Jason Donovan, an authorised Craig McLachlan one. I even churned out one on Poison.

Yep, it had come to that. When you're doing one-offs about Poison, the end can't be far away. And it wasn't.

## 31

# WRITING'S ON THE WALL

**I**'d been at *The Sun-Herald* for a while now, doing my weekly column, as well as the occasional feature for the front of the newspaper. After a few years, Kathy Lette and Gabrielle Carey – the Salami Sisters – moved on, and I shared the page with another contributor. For the longest time it was TV personality Donnie Sutherland, who presented the Saturday morning music show, *Sounds*.

I had a remarkably trouble-free run at the paper. In those days they had fine sub-editors and copy was scrutinised within an inch of its life for possible defamation. Only once did I, and they, screw up. And we did it fairly spectacularly.

In 1983, I was writing one of those end-of-year round-up columns. I'd heard some idle gossip that a few concert promoters had experienced tough times and were sailing a little close to the wind. My 'source' almost certainly didn't have any idea of the reality of the situation when he suggested to me that Michael Coppel had suffered some heavy losses and, as such, might be on his way out of the concert-promoting business, or at least having trouble matching it with the other big-league promoters.

Without really thinking, I included a paragraph in my column saying as much. My warning lights should definitely have been on about a claim as flimsy and unsubstantiated as this. And, to be honest, the sub-editors should have seen pulsating red flashing lights as well. But it went to print.

Coppel – also a lawyer – took action, arguing that not only was his business *not* in trouble, he was currently negotiating to bring Whitney Houston to Australia. He claimed that this suggestion of mine had seriously undermined his reputation and likelihood of securing that tour. Fair call. I believe the Fairfax payout for this little slip may have been around $10,000 (roughly two years' *Sun-Herald* salary for me at the time) – and Coppel did get the tour.

Of course, I was mortified when I realised the mistake. First-up, I thought that might be the end of my tenure at the paper, and there were moments of blind panic when I thought I might be personally liable for the payout. Things were sorted out between Fairfax and Coppel without me having much involvement. I didn't speak with or interact with him.

Strangely, we've continued to have a reasonable amount to do with each other over the years – including that Cramps tour – but the 1983 incident has never been raised. On one occasion, when we met to do an interview for a book I was writing, he got me to pay for lunch. It did cross my mind that after what I'd inadvertently handballed him, he could have picked up the tab!

The incident with Coppel was a valuable lesson about sources, repeating gossip and pub talk and the consequences. Ever since, I've been *extremely* careful about putting the 'Mate, this is 101 per cent on the money' assurances in print.

The other great advice on that front came from one of my book publishers when he instilled in me the need to look carefully at every fine legal detail.

'Stuart,' he said firmly, 'the big names are less likely to sue. It's the people who are in the footnotes in a book who call their lawyers, because they're upset that their role wasn't more prominent. It's the little asides you need to watch.'

Legal dramas aside, my dream run at *The Sun-Herald* couldn't last. In fact, it lasted much longer than I'd ever expected. The newspaper started to change, as the publicity departments of record and touring companies began to flex their muscles. There was a new breed of journalist who was very comfortable getting into bed and cuddling with them. This wasn't my style at all.

Towards the end of my tenure, in the latter part of the '80s, a particularly annoying figure was appointed arts editor, with a brief that included overseeing the contemporary music content in the paper. He started to look at my column and ask, 'Who are the Laughing Clowns?' and 'Is it important that we cover this Do Re Mi?' I thought he was an idiot and I suspect he cared even less for me – either way, he took the fun out of doing the column.

Along with that increasing emphasis on being populist in our music coverage, there was also a softening of the hard-nosed journalism that had been the hallmark of the paper. The dreaded Murdoch publication *The Sunday Telegraph* started winning the circulation battle with their lame, tabloid approach to everything – so the knives were out at *The Sun-Herald*.

Pretty much the last straw for me came in 1992, when I interviewed Bob Dylan for the second time. In marked contrast to our first in-the-flesh encounter (which he didn't refer to), Dylan was in a good mood and extremely chatty. Maybe I'd learnt my lesson too and didn't come across as an obsessive fan. He opened up about poets he was re-reading: Shelley and Keats from memory.

At one point Dylan asked if I knew Brett Whiteley. I told him that I had a passing acquaintance with Brett. 'Well, if you're talking to him,' said Bob, 'tell him those drawings he gave me last time still look good to me.'

Once I'd hung up, I did what you knew I was going to do. You only get to have this sort of conversation once.

'Hi, Brett, Stuart Coupe here. I was just having a chat with Bob Dylan and he said to tell you . . .'

We had a terrific conversation and, once I'd spoken to Whiteley, I moved on to the matter of letting *The Sun-Herald* know that I had this interview. Why I hadn't pre-empted the possibility with them is anyone's guess. I suppose I thought I'd wait till the interview had actually happened, and worked on the assumption that it would be a no-brainer as a feature story for the paper.

Excitedly, I called the aforementioned arts editor, telling him we had this scoop – a new interview with Bob. To my amazement, he told me he wasn't interested. He didn't think the *Sun-Herald* readership really cared about Dylan and that I should take the piece somewhere else. This guy really was a complete fool. I was furious.

I drank far too much that night and typed a vitriolic letter to the editor – the very wonderful investigative journalist David Hickie. It was one of those times when, having hit 'send' on the fax machine, you go to bed and wake up the next morning with your stomach churning and your brain going, 'Oh God, I hope I've just dreamt that I wrote – and sent – that.' But there it was, on the floor next to the fax machine.

I'd given Hickie a piece of my mind, explaining in great detail how fucked *The Sun-Herald* was and why it was obvious to anyone why *The Sunday Telegraph* was killing us in the sales department. Sober and in daylight, nothing had changed about my thoughts, but I would have expressed them much more diplomatically and not made it seem such a personal attack on Hickie's editorship. It wasn't really his fault that the arts editor was an idiot.

I consider myself beyond fortunate to have been part of the golden days in the early 1980s of *The Sun-Herald* and Fairfax. Every time I go past that building on Broadway, I have the same sentimental pangs about the work we did in that nondescript structure. I can still easily conjure up standing in the expansive foyer – with no security checks or anything – waiting for those big lift doors to open and transport me to this amazing world of newsprint and smoke and characters. Golly, I miss it.

# 32

# GUMSHOE

**W**hen I arrived at Flinders Uni in 1975, the campus bookshop was run by an opinionated, extremely well-read guy called John Scott. He was big on John D. MacDonald and his Florida-based crime novels, and because I wanted to embrace what the people I looked up to were into, I read John D. MacDonald. A *lot* of John D. MacDonald.

From there, John pushed me in the direction of the other heavy-weights of hardboiled American crime fiction: Dashiell Hammett, Ross Macdonald and that Raymond Chandler guy. I adored them all. Chandler, in particular – I was moved by the sheer poetic beauty of his writing. It fuelled my fascination with Los Angeles that lay dormant for some time and then exploded one afternoon on Sunset Boulevard. Previously, I'd visited the city a number of times and found it confounding and unattractive. I'll get to that. Hammett's novels were also gripping and I loved the deep family intrigue and buried secrecy at the core of Macdonald's books. Years later, I'd get to discuss his writing with Warren Zevon, who was a huge fan.

I dreamt of being a crime writer and it occasionally dovetailed into my music writing. As I've mentioned, after my initial falling-out with Steve Kilbey, I wrote up an interview with him for *RAM* as a gumshoe/ private investigator-styled encounter. The cover photo of me and Kilbey arm-wrestling was an image straight out of a hardboiled comic/graphic novel.

So I continued reading these novels; not obsessively, but I kept up with what was coming out. The most successful Australian crime-fiction writer was Alan G. Yates, who wrote as Carter Brown. He hammered out over 300 novels and was hugely popular around the world. But Yates never mentioned Australia in any of the books – well, maybe in one – and could have been located anywhere.

Local crime fiction was considered old fashioned and irrelevant. Things changed in 1980, though, with the publication of *The Dying Trade* by Peter Corris. After dozens of rejections, Corris found a sympathetic ear in James Hall (later the literary editor at *The Australian*), who published his first novel. It featured the weather-beaten private investigator Cliff Hardy, who had his office in St Peters Lane in Darlinghurst, drove a battered Falcon (before it gave up the ghost), and meandered around Sydney and its environs solving crimes. This was great. Suddenly, there was a home-grown detective story with its protagonist treading our own mean streets. I devoured all the early Cliff Hardy novels.

Then came Marele Day. Her novels featured sassy feminist Claudia Valentine, so we had tough guys and gals to read about. In their wake came a whole slew of new Australian crime-fiction voices.

Yes, I was a massive fan of crime fiction. And I let everyone know about it. Fortunately, one or two of those people I'd earbashed on the topic over the years worked at *The Sydney Morning Herald*. When the paper's crime-fiction reviewer Stephen Knight stepped down from the role in 1990, word about me must have passed swiftly down the line. Before I could blink, I'd been offered the job.

Now, as well as being inundated with records and CDs, I could add the delivery of mountains of books as another reason for the postman to come and visit. I was beyond happy about this new gig. I'd really wanted to expand from just writing about music, and books were my other great love. I sometimes felt that if the unthinkable happened and I lost touch with contemporary music, I could always keep doing these reviews.

I was also on a mini-crusade. I'd never bought into crime fiction being considered genre fiction – a poor first or second cousin to real writing. And I really hated the fact that my reviews appeared under the banner 'Crime Fiction'.

My criterion for writing about books was the same as about music. Was it as good as the big league? And I'd always thought that crime fiction at its best was a magnificent vehicle for commentary on social, political and cultural changes. I wasn't overly concerned with plot – I wanted character development and great observations.

I loved doing these reviews, but they didn't quite manage to scratch the crime itch. Not long after I started reviewing at the *Herald*, I had an idea: to publish a kind of fanzine, but a little more professional, devoted to crime and mystery fiction. Well, it coincided with being asked for, or proposing, a 'Ten Questions' feature on Peter Corris for *Playboy*. If I'd suggested the story, I'm sure I was just looking for an excuse to meet the author – which I did when I wandered to his flat in Darlinghurst one day. It was around 11 am.

'Is it too early for a beer?' he asked. Of course, it wasn't.

I'd been harping on to my wife, Julie – whilst I should have been focused on an *Edge* magazine deadline – that I was really driven to start a crime fiction magazine. One day, she semi-snapped, 'So, stop talking about it and do it.'

I mentioned the idea to Peter. He was enthusiastic and promised that if I got the magazine up and running, he'd give me a previously unpublished Cliff Hardy short story for the first issue.

And so *Mean Streets* – subtitled *A Quarterly Journal Of Crime, Mystery And Detection* – came to be, with the first issue published in October 1990. Quarterly? That became a little bit of a joke. Sometimes there were three issues a year, other times two – I don't think there were ever four in a calendar year.

The first issue contained Corris writing about Hardy, along with the promised previously unpublished short story. There were interviews as well with James Lee Burke, James Ellroy and Marele Day – plus a feature in which film historian and critic Bill Collins talked about his favourite crime and mystery movies.

The magazine was launched at the Harold Park Hotel in Glebe, with readings by Peter, Marele and Steve Wright, as well as visiting American writers Andrew Vachss and Evan Hunter (better known as Ed McBain, author of the 87th Precinct book series).

The title, *Mean Streets*, was a homage both to Scorsese's film and Chandler's famous lines, 'But down these mean streets a man must go who is not himself mean, who is neither tarnished nor afraid.' It was an upmarket fanzine, lacking the sophistication of overseas publications like *The Armchair Detective*. It had a colour cover and 64 pages – all in black and white and on cheap paper stock. It featured interviews, articles and reviews, and its content very much reflected my own predilection for hardboiled American crime-fiction and an obsession with the post-1980 Peter Corris and Marele Day-led revival of Australian crime fiction. However, I was also keen to document the history of crime fiction in this country.

It was very time-consuming. In a pre-personal-computer world, all the copy had to be retyped and design done by sticking down the words and illustrations, as they would appear in the magazine, on boards that would then be sent to the printer. We created bromides for the illustrations, and when it came back from the printers all copies were individually wrapped and mailed to subscribers around the globe.

Had I opened a can of work for myself? Oh yes. Suddenly I was inundated with manuscripts – short stories and often very long novels – from every unpublished crime-fiction writer in Australia and many from overseas. News travelled fast amongst the crime-writing fraternity, who were very supportive of the new publications.

Shortly after the first issue, Julie and I had moved to Blackheath in the Blue Mountains. It was a good escape from our city lifestyle, which soon included our second daughter, Sara.

Piles and piles of unsolicited material flooded through the door at the new place. These would-be Chandlers and P. D. Jameses expected me to read every word, and offer comment, and ideally publish them in *Mean Streets*.

And the general correspondence was voluminous too. It all had to be answered in typed letters, with endless trips to the post office. There were queries about obscure Australian crime writers or books, requests about where particular novels might be found, letters from authors I'd approached about interviews, as well as mounds of impassioned pleas about which were the best book publishers to contact.

The magazine sold for $5 and later $6. Initially it was distributed through newsagents, but it soon became obvious that the number of copies that needed to be printed versus actual sales just wasn't stacking up financially. Despite my best efforts, there was no funding available to assist the magazine, and despite publishers wanting their books covered in its pages, very few were prepared to advertise – even at a knock down $100 for a full-page ad. There were – thank you – exceptions, but not many. We did manage to raise some funds courtesy of a rock'n'roll marketing aesthetic, producing a run of rather cool *Mean Streets* T-shirts.

There were eventually 17 issues of *Mean Streets*. That includes two which (how did we not notice!) had the same number – the final one appeared in December 1996. There was supposed to have been at least one more published. It was pretty much completed, and I carried the layouts around the world with me late that year, whilst on an extended overseas trip. I tried to find time to proofread them, but failed. I believe those pages are in the *Mean Streets* collection at the State Library of NSW, along with a huge array of correspondence and ephemera.

We ran into one spot of bother. A subscription ad for one issue read: 'Subscribe To Mean Streets – Or There'll Be Homicide.' The photo used to illustrate this was of Leonard Teale and other cast members of the legendary television program. I thought it was a nice little nod to the iconic show.

Crawford's – the TV production house that created and held the rights to *Homicide* – felt differently, and there was a rather stern letter from lawyers representing them, saying that they wished us to stop implying that they endorsed the magazine. I wrote a semi-cheeky letter to the lawyers, telling them how much I loved *Homicide* and that we sold only a few hundred copies of *Mean Streets*. One of the legal team replied, saying that he dug the magazine, but could we please not run that ad, or use imagery from any Crawford's television shows again? (In other words, don't think of using a photo from *Division 4* instead . . .)

Given that, at the time, what money I was very occasionally making on tour-promoting was being lost on *Mean Streets*, I decided not to do battle with Crawford's. Cool ad, though.

Times in the Blue Mountains were financially tough. That two hours from Sydney started to seem like a world away. I felt a little isolated from friends and the music industry, gigs were a hassle to get to and from, and there were no record shops anywhere nearby. But I kept doing anything I could to make a buck. There was the *Sun-Herald* stuff, and I was appointed the first editor of the Triple J magazine, created a widely syndicated music industry news column, wrote for *Pollstar* – the American concert industry magazine – and spent time in Melbourne working on the ABC TV show *Access All Areas*.

(This was a series based on interviews with musicians. I'd been hired as a researcher, so for six months I went backwards and forwards from Blackheath to Melbourne. I stayed at a hotel in St Kilda, then spent six weeks in America setting up interviews with the likes of John Lee Hooker, Randy Newman, members of the Grateful Dead, Tony Bennett and my old friend Sting, among many others.)

I'm proud of *Mean Streets* – we covered a lot of writers and books. I read a lot, learnt a lot, and it was a change from writing about and interviewing rock'n'roll stars. I used to say to friends that if you wrote a letter to, say, David Bowie or Mick Jagger requesting an interview, it was 175 per cent certain you'd never hear back. But if you wrote to their equivalents in crime-fiction world – think James Lee Burke and Lawrence Block – there was a very strong likelihood you'd get a response and a 'yes' to the request.

During this era, I became semi-obsessed with the history of Australian pulp paperback publishing and the authors – particularly Carter Brown, but also Marc Brody and K. T. McCall – who published voluminously and usually through Sydney-based Horwitz Publications. I was delighted to become acquainted with Denise Yates, the widow of Alan G. Yates, who'd authored the Carter Brown books. I tried to assist her in getting the rights to her husband's books back from the publishers.

Along the way, whenever a rock'n'roll band I knew was doing an interstate tour, I'd ask them to grab any Carter Brown they saw in a second-hand bookshop or Vinnies in country towns they were passing through. (As long as it was under about $4.) As a result, I have the majority of the 300 or so novels that Yates wrote – and a lot of duplicates.

Speaking of rock'n'roll bands, those few years are a bit of a gap in my musical life. I really wasn't as in love with – or across – new music as I might have been. It was kids, semi-rural life, crime fiction and older records. So the grunge era sort of passed me by. Years later, I found myself asking friends what Pavement, Buffalo Tom and Pixies records (to name but a few) I should be listening to.

In the wake of *Mean Streets* – and my reviewing for *The Sydney Morning Herald* – I became known to some as 'Mr Crime'. I began to contribute other crime-related pieces to the *Herald*. For a cover story for the *Good Weekend* supplement, I took five Australian crime fiction writers to look at the terrain where their fictional heroes plied their trade.

For another cover story, I hung out with real-life private detectives. These PIs were fascinating figures, and, as I discovered, very different from their fictional counterparts. There wasn't too much walking of the mean streets. And very few blondes in distress.

I sat in a stake-out van – an incredibly tedious way to spend a day where for the most part nothing happened – and it was cramped and, being summer, super-hot. I also visited a PI on the leafy North Shore with a replica Maltese Falcon statue on his desk, who told me that most of his work was finding missing kids who'd run away from wealthy families.

Then there was the guy who looked and acted like one of the Krays, the notorious, violent English gangsters from the 1960s. He lived in a faux mansion in Sydney's inner-west with a glamorous wife, a gym, a large, snarly guard dog at the gate, and all of his success ostentatiously on display. I wouldn't have wanted to cross him and I hope he doesn't read this. His caper was collecting debts, which made him more of a standover guy. He said he was a PI, though, as he had to find the people who owed money before getting heavy with them.

The day I went to interview him, he told me his address. He added that there was no number on the house and the gate was locked. 'My dogs will let me know you're outside,' he growled down the phone line.

There were sometimes surprising aspects to being 'Mr Crime'. I'd interviewed Nick Cave many times over the years and usually found him pleasant but intimidating, often at the same time. And we'd never been especially close.

One Christmas in the mid-1990s, I was at home with the family in Launceston. Sitting out the front in the sun, I heard the phone ring in the kitchen. Mum answered it, then she walked out and said, 'Stuart, there's a Nicholas Cave on the phone for you.'

Cave had tracked down my parents' phone number and wanted to talk about murder ballads and get some ideas of classics and obscurities in the genre for the album he was recording. I don't recall any Christmas greetings – it was just straight down to the business at hand.

I was also asked to interview visiting writers at festivals and other events. Among them were Walter Mosley, Lawrence Block, Michael Connelly, Ken Bruen and P. D. James, the latter being a total delight. I still carry with me her ruminations about the split seconds that can change lives. My interest in crime fiction has always been driven more by that than by whodunnit (even though I loved, and continue to love, Agatha Christie) – being in the wrong place at the wrong time, the snap decision, the vagaries of existence. The moment when the frying pan in the kitchen moves from the stove to someone's head, as P. D. James described it to me so memorably.

When the acclaimed American novelist and short-story writer Richard Ford came to Australia, I was invited to have lunch with him. This was a big deal. Ford had been best buddies with Raymond Carver. He was a giant for us.

When a few of my buddies heard about the upcoming lunch, rare book dealer Nicholas Pounder asked me if I'd get Ford to sign a 'few' books for him. The few books turned out to be two suitcases worth of largely hardback editions that he hoped he could turn a nice profit on once they were signed. I lugged them to the lunch and Ford signed them all without complaint.

Did I mention how I saved Ford's life that day? Lunch was at Rockpool in Circular Quay. We had a good chat and fine food on a really grey and wet Sydney afternoon. A few drinks were consumed, then we went to leave. Ford had only just arrived in the country, so he was probably jetlagged – and a few drinks would have enhanced that. Plus, it was his first time in Australia.

Ford went to cross the road, turning left to look for traffic as he would in America. Wrong way, dude. A car was bearing down on him at speed and on a wet road. I managed to grab him and pull him back onto the pavement. American literature owes me one for that.

Because of my work in the area I was frequently asked for endorsements, and I wrote blurbs for what seemed like dozens of Australian crime fiction novels. Peter Corris dedicated his book *Browning P. I.* to me. That was pretty special.

In the mid-'90s, I approached Corris about writing a book about him and he agreed. We signed a deal with Allen & Unwin and, over a couple of years, he gave generously of his time and allowed me access to volumes of correspondence, friends and so forth. I wrote around 90,000 words, then turned a draft in to Patrick Gallagher at A&U. Unfortunately, Patrick told me he no longer thought it right for a book about Corris, although he said I could keep the $2000 advance. Yes, those were heady times for would-be authors.

I suspect he was just being polite. Maybe he sensed there wasn't a big enough demand for the book, and to be honest my writing was a little rudimentary and lacking in flair. I don't think I was ready to write a significant literary biography. But Patrick was a gentleman. He didn't say any of that. The manuscript exists somewhere and one day I'd like to think I could complete it. I really admired Corris and think his achievements should be recognised.

However, I did get to co-edit three anthologies of crime fiction, two of them for Allen & Unwin. *Hardboiled* was just that – a collection of American hardboiled detective fiction. *Case Reopened* was a pet project – and clearly, I think, way ahead of its time. I had this idea that I'd approach Australian crime-fiction writers to come up with a fictional resolution to famous Australian murders and mysteries. The disappearance of Harold Holt, and the Wanda Beach and Easey Street murders and many others were 'solved'. What happened to the Beaumont children was resolved as well.

It was a fabulous collection of inventive writing and – as at least one producer agreed – ripe for a television series. A team was assembled, and meetings held. The political commentator, speechwriter, author and screenwriter Bob Ellis was called in for a day-long session at my home in Blackheath. Ellis was late, but when he swung into action my jaw dropped.

Bob paced around the living-room table – the same one that Guy Clark had sat at years before, doing lines of cocaine and singing songs (that table has seen some stuff: I'm writing on it today). He was fleshing out characters and their foibles seemingly off the top of his head, this stream of consciousness accompanied by frequent swigs from a flask of Scotch.

At the end of the day Ellis appeared in no condition to drive, but with his car parked outside insisted on heading back to Sydney. I thought he should rest at my place or even get the train, but that wasn't a conversation he seemed inclined to have.

Forty-five minutes later, he knocked on the door. He'd forgotten his briefcase.

'You always leave something behind at places you want to return to,' he said, before once again disappearing into the night.

Eventually, the *Case Reopened* TV series floundered. There appeared to be no-one interested in investing in such a project. Potential producer/director Don Featherstone and I kicked the idea around and refined and reshaped it for a couple of years, before it became obvious to us both that it wasn't going to fly. Imagine if it had been the era of Netflix and not the mid-'90s and networks were clamouring for content. Maybe it's not too late.

The third anthology was *Crosstown Traffic*, published by an independent publisher Five Islands Press. In it, writers were asked to start with a crime-fiction yarn and then veer off into another genre – romance, science fiction, horror and so forth. As a cross-genre exercise, again maybe ahead of its time.

One day – still in the mid-'90s – over a lunch at the Malaya restaurant in George Street in Sydney, a bunch of us decided we should be giving out awards for the best Australian crime fiction – similar to the

Edgar and Gold Dagger awards in the US and UK. What to call it? Various names were bandied about before I suggested the Ned Kelly Awards. I joked that they'd be shortened to the Neddies – so we were embracing Australia's most famous bushranger and another of our most infamous real criminals in Neddy Smith.

James Ellroy, who had taken to describing himself as the 'Demon Dog' of American crime fiction, presented the first Neddies in 1996 at a ceremony upstairs at Berkelouw Books in Paddington, writhing around the floor and barking like a Demon Dog. Some people got it. Many didn't. Most writers don't crawl around acting like a dog. The Ned Kelly Awards are still going and I was delighted to be awarded a Lifetime Achievement award in 2005.

During these years, people sometimes used to ask when I was going to write a crime-fiction novel myself. I used to laugh and say, 'Never. Superficially, they may seem easy, but doing them well is damn hard work. It requires real skill – and I'm not that good.'

Incidentally, this book was written with my computer perched atop (still) the most expensive book I've ever purchased – the third edition of *Twentieth-Century Crime And Mystery Writers*. It's 1291 (large) pages and was published in 1991. It set me back $245, but the only book I've probably used more in my life is Ian McFarlane's *The Encyclopedia Of Australian Rock And Pop*. I'd be lost without either. Music and crime. Crime and music.

# 33

# IT WOULD BE A CRIME

In the late 1980s, when I was working at *The Edge*, I heard that P. J. O'Rourke, the American satirist and political writer, was being brought out to Australia by his book publishers. As our biggest competitor was *Rolling Stone* magazine, I sensed the opportunity for a bit of mischief.

O'Rourke was best known for his journalism for *Rolling Stone*, so I thought it would be amusing if *The Edge* promoted a reading by him in Sydney. I offered him $1000 cash for a one-off reading and lecture, and he agreed.

Not surprisingly, the show, at Klub Kakadu in Darlinghurst, was extremely well attended, with a queue down Oxford Street of P. J. fans. O'Rourke delivered a good performance, I made a bunch of money and *The Edge* got – I shouldn't go there, but I'm going to – the edge on *Rolling Stone* by presenting a reading by one of its star writers. All in good fun – well, not totally. The competition between the two magazines was, at least from our end, pretty serious.

This performance opened my mind to an array of fascinating and (I believed) potentially lucrative possibilities. Music promoters were a dime a dozen, and the competition for tours was ferocious, but no-one was really applying that approach to writers.

The more I thought about it, the more I realised there was a lot to like about being a writer promoter. I loved the fact that writers usually travelled by themselves. Plus, from what I knew, they were a lot easier to deal with than musicians, because they usually didn't have managers and high-powered booking agents, and they didn't require road crews, expensive lighting and big PAs. I suspected they'd be easier to negotiate with, as most weren't very accustomed to being paid to read from their work. And I doubted that they'd have extravagant backstage rider requirements.

The way I figured it, the right authors were as big a drawcard as rock'n'roll bands and singer-songwriters. And, this being pre-internet, people were reading more; while listening to and watching authors on Zoom was several decades away.

So when opportunities presented themselves, I jumped right in. I organised some performances by Kinky Friedman. He was an established country singer and songwriter ('They Ain't Makin' Jews Like Jesus Anymore', anyone?), but was making a far bigger name for himself as a crime fiction author. Kinky was a cigar-chugging, self-obsessed performer, but extremely funny – at least the first time you heard the jokes. Both the cigars and the jokes stayed the same from tour to tour, and I promoted Kinky a few times.

Later, when I established *Mean Streets*, I organised a number of readings in conjunction with the publication. Usually, the authors were already in Australia for promotional trips or appearances at writers festivals, so essentially I subcontracted the likes of American writers Ed McBain and Andrew Vachss for *Mean Streets*-sponsored events. As I've mentioned, one of these was for the launch of the magazine.

But the really inventive one was when Elmore Leonard appeared at Kinselas nightclub in Darlinghurst. Leonard was in Australia to publicise his novel *Pronto*, which had a protagonist, Raylan Givens, who was a country and western (both kinds of music) loving marshal. Givens had always regretted that his wife hadn't had two male children, as he wanted to name them Hank and George, after country-music legends Hank Williams and George Jones.

The show was billed as 'A Night Of Country And Crime'. To that end I'd organised some Sydney musicians (who called themselves The Hoodlum Priests) to play all the country songs referred to in *Pronto*, and for music writer Clinton Walker to be DJ, playing country records with a crime-fiction theme. Leonard had no idea of this and arrived for the reading, sat at a table, and after 15 minutes or so, started smiling when he realised what was going on.

I was trying to bring a good old-fashioned entrepreneurial approach to presenting performances by writers. It was a successful night that ended in a satisfying moment. I approached the representative from Leonard's publishing company to ask whether I should give the payment for the performance to her or directly to Leonard.

'Oh, don't worry about it,' she said. 'Writers aren't used to getting paid for things like this.'

As far as I was concerned, Leonard should definitely be remunerated, so I paid him direct. I also fixed up everyone else, and then – in a rather extravagant move – caught a taxi back home to the Blue Mountains. That was $250, but I figured that a hotel would have been around $100 and I'd drink more, and then need to eat in the morning and get the train back. I'd had a successful night and, this way, I'd be home when the kids woke in the morning.

Over the years, I decided that writers I toured would have to fit two categories: (a) I really liked them, and (b) They had an audience big enough to warrant a national tour where people would pay to see them. To that end I approached a variety of writers over the years, sometimes without success. I was aiming sort of high, but why not?

On that front, Hunter S. Thompson's representative told me frequently (hey, they got back to me on stationery emblazoned with the 'HST' logo and the legendary Owl Farm as the address) that he was booked up but to contact them again 'next year'. Given the antics that Thompson had gotten up to on his one previous visit to Australia in the 1970s, maybe I was lucky that he was always booked up. I suspect that my time with Guy Clark might just have been a training run for an HST tour – even if Thompson's intake of illicit substances was only a 10th of what was claimed.

William S. Burroughs' minder told me the author was simply too frail to make such a long trip. This was even after I'd offered first-class air travel and all sorts of other inducements. We'd certainly got to the discussion about whether Burroughs' 'medicinal needs' could be taken care of before the idea was knocked on the head.

Two other Beat Generation writers – poets Anne Waldman and Gregory Corso – were mooted as well. The trouble was that, despite Waldman being very organised, Corso didn't have a current passport and seemed unmotivated to get one – even though he liked the idea of coming to Australia. Corso was the bigger drawcard, so it was explained to me that without him there was no tour.

I had a funny conversation with him when I phoned his apartment in New York. We got to the point where I asked if he'd feel more comfortable making the trip to Australia if Allen Ginsberg was with him. He liked the idea and said that if 'Ginsey' was in, he'd come. So I called the guy who looked after Ginsey. Unfortunately, as I expected, Ginsberg was, like so many writers, committed for at least a year in advance, and I never seemed to get him at the right time to find a place in his schedule for that trip to Australia – with or without Corso.

I also wanted to try to persuade Charles Bukowski to make a trip. However, after exploring a variety of possibilities I couldn't even get a message to him.

Hey, I even looked further afield than writers. I had correspondence with photographer Bunny Yeager about mounting an exhibition of her photos of model Bettie Page in Sydney – the idea being that Bettie and Bunny would both travel to Australia. That idea had legs for about seven seconds, before it became obvious, from what Bunny told me, that Page wasn't in the right state of mind for a tour and the idea of just doing Yeager's photos didn't stack up financially.

And around 1992, Andrew Vachss was in my ear about a theatre production based around one of his crime stories. I looked at pitching it to an Adelaide arts festival – but when I did, the budget was astronomical and it would have been very unlikely even to come close to breaking even. And what did I know about theatre productions? Nothing. A lack of knowledge hadn't stopped me doing things in the past, but I didn't have those resources. Unfortunately, Vachss, a terrific writer, didn't understand and our communication became increasingly tense and unpleasant.

That was a shame. By then, though, I'd already become pretty ensconced in touring another type of artist. You can probably guess what type.

# 34

# PASSIONATE KISSES

Having dipped a toe into touring with a couple of authors, I guess it was only natural that I'd have a crack at the same thing with the music business. Soon I was immersed – obsessively so, at times – in the precarious world of bringing international music artists to Australia.

In 1989, I formed a management company called BBC with two mates. Bicci Henderson was an experienced tour manager, who looked after the affairs of country band The Happening Thang. Rob Barnham owned a PA system and worked for me on Paul Kelly's live shows. That included booking vehicles, hotels, plane tickets and all the logistics behind keeping a touring band on the road.

We rented a two-storey house in Surry Hills, not far from the Sydney Trade Union Club. It just felt right. It was like saying your office was down the block from CBGB in New York. It was close enough for me to stroll between rock and management-business central and *The Edge* office.

It was early days for the magazine and we were finding our way with its content and style. There wasn't a lot of intervention from the publishers in the day-to-day running of *The Edge*, so no-one really cared if I wandered off for a few hours to attend to BBC business.

Bicci, Barnham and Coupe: BBC. That name was fine . . . until we brought Lucinda Williams to Australia on her first tour. Unfortunately, someone from the other BBC – you know, that English broadcasting company – then sent us a cease-and-desist letter. They reckoned they'd been getting phone calls, enquiring about where to buy tickets.

The threat was a little scary, but it was flattering too. Apparently, people all over the world wanted to do business with Bicci, Barnham and Coupe. Partly, we thought it was ludicrous that anyone could seriously confuse the two business ventures.

We came up with a solution, and started putting full stops in between the letters as a point of difference. So now it was B.B.C. – impossible to confuse with the other mob, surely?

The Lucinda Williams tour came about because I'd simply fallen in love with what I thought was her first album – but later realised was her third. It was on the Rough Trade label, who were distributed in Australia by Festival Records. So I contacted Festival, said I was interested in bringing Lucinda to Australia for a tour, and asked who I should contact.

At the time, I had no real idea what was involved in mounting a concert tour. Immigration? Visas? Taxation liabilities? Venue bookings? Tour contracts and deposit requirements? Well, Bicci and Rob knew a bit about that stuff, so between us we figured we could muddle through the process.

I was put in touch with Lucinda's manager, an affable New Yorker named Rob Koss, and a deal was struck – one that included Lucinda being accompanied by her guitarist Gurf Morlix.

Venues were booked. Posters put up. Did a lot of people come? Not really – although now you could fill a football stadium with people who claimed they were at Lucinda and Gurf's shows at the Bridge Hotel in Rozelle, the Annandale Hotel, Max's Petersham Inn, or the interstate equivalents.

During the tour, my mood oscillated – often quickly – between exhilaration that this was actually happening, and complete and total fear. What would happen if the whole thing stiffed financially? What obvious and important things might we have forgotten? Much of the time I was just rolling with it, because I had a lot of balls high in the air and they all needed to stay there if I was to have an income.

Lucinda was incredible, but unfortunately it was way too early for her to attract a big audience here. Her shows were of a consistently high standard, and although she played to comparatively small audiences, she was intense and powerful onstage.

This was niche music and, while the audience numbers reflected that, those who turned up loved it. We had some tour support money from Festival Records and everyone was paid – except us. Welcome to the world of concert promoting.

But I'd been bitten by the bug – hard. I loved the thrill of nearly every aspect of it (except the losing money bit). It had been exciting to see Lucinda and Gurf walk out from immigration at Sydney airport. They were here! First obstacle overcome. It was totally cool as well to hang out at soundchecks before the shows, and amazing to stand at the side of the stage watching them perform and gauge the audience reaction.

As a music fan, I was enthralled to be around them both and got a total kick when Lucinda would ask me, in that great slow Southern drawl of hers, what I'd thought of the show, or whether I reckoned she should perform a particular song that night.

That aside, though, there was the financial side of things to consider. B.B.C.'s fingers had been burnt and, in fact, the days of the organisation were numbered. Bicci and I were good friends and he was keen to continue doing bits and pieces in this area. (To his eternal credit, he covered many of our financial losses in the early days.) However, Rob had had enough.

He had a truck and a PA that turned over good money, as well as aspirations to do more management work. He eventually managed artists such as Paul Kelly and Christine Anu.

I wasn't too discouraged, though, and actually, my time as a tour promoter was only beginning. Keith Glass had a lot to do with me continuing down this path. He was independently promoting tours by American singers and songwriters he loved – people like Townes Van Zandt and Butch Hancock and Jimmie Dale Gilmore.

I'd known Keith for several decades, ever since he'd been a partner with David N. Pepperell in the groundbreaking Melbourne import record shop, Archie 'n' Jugheads in the 1970s. I think David was Archie and Keith claimed Jughead. They were both cool dudes and I bought a lot of records from them. Two essential stops on a visit to that city were Archie 'n' Jugheads in the CBD, and then over to North Melbourne to Hound Dog's Bop Shop. I'll tell you about that later.

As far as Archie 'n' Jugheads was concerned, it was hipsville. Neither of the owners suffered fools easily and they seemed to have an innate sense that they knew more than you. Keith was short but stylish, without being pretentious, and had an endearing smile. He had an acidic tone and a slightly patronising manner, though, when he thought you were buying the wrong album (something he considered manufactured or lacking in soul or substance – rather than, say, Billy Joe Shaver, The Amazing Rhythm Aces or James Carr), or, heaven forbid, expressing an opinion that was at odds with his. But I liked him and paid attention to what he recommended; both then and when he opened the country-music-oriented Deep South shop some years later.

Keith was also an accomplished songwriter, pretty good guitarist and not a bad singer. He'd been playing in bands in Melbourne since the 1960s. As well, he'd managed The Birthday Party, started the super-cool Missing Link indie record label and had an encyclopaedic knowledge of the history of country music. When Keith talked about country music, you listened. Then you bought whatever record or CD he insisted you absolutely needed. It was always a little like a scene from *High Fidelity*.

We drifted in and out of each other's lives, slowly becoming friends because of our shared musical passions. When Keith relocated to Sydney in the second half of the 1980s and worked at Virgin Records, we saw more of each other, simply through geographic proximity, running into each other at gigs, and knowing a lot of the same people.

By now, Keith had started bringing international artists to Australia – often in conjunction with Kevin Byrt and his cohorts from Real Groovy Records in Auckland. The idea was a good one – one party organised shows in New Zealand and the other Australia, and they split the international airfares.

Keith had managed to bring the legendary Texan singer-songwriter Townes Van Zandt to Australia and survived to talk about it. A hard drinker, Townes consumed the contents – all of them – of many mini-bars in hotel rooms around the country. It reached the point where Keith had to call ahead and ask the establishments to empty the fridges before they arrived. Townes frequently had to be corralled to get onstage and was always in danger of disappearing, so the tour tested all of Keith's patience.

In a less stressful venture, he also toured two of the great contemporary songwriters from Lubbock, Texas – Butch Hancock and Jimmie Dale Gilmore – who I'd seen play at the Three Weeds in Balmain. Paul Kelly was a fan and sang with them at one show, which was recorded and issued as a live in Australia album. Watching that performance and knowing the promoter only increased my desire to do some work in the area. All I saw was the end result – not all the work that went into getting to that point. But I loved what I saw and wanted to be part of it.

After Keith moved back to Melbourne, he called me. This was in early 1990. He told me he was organising an Australian tour with Guy Clark and wondered if I'd be interested in putting together the Sydney leg. This amounted to three performances at Klub Kakadu on Oxford Street.

Was I interested? Not only was it an opportunity to be involved with an international tour, but it was Guy Clark. I was a total fan of the Texas-born, Nashville-based singer. I loved his most famous song 'L.A. Freeway' and everything else I'd heard by him. Actually working with Guy and being part of the promoting team? Count me in.

And unlike the Lucinda Williams tour, Keith had done all the work in negotiating contracts, booking air tickets, venues and so forth. He was the overall promoter, so the financial risk was his. I'm actually not sure what our financial arrangement was – or even if such a thing existed. I just wanted to be involved.

The tour began in a straightforward fashion. On top of all the work Keith had done, there were things for me to attend to. I organised the PA, the support acts and the publicity campaign, which involved telling everyone I could that Guy was coming to Sydney and trying to convince them they should attend. Very sophisticated. Then, the day before the first show, I met Guy and took him to his hotel in Bondi – a less than salubrious joint, but he seemed OK with it. And it was convenient, as I lived not far away in Tamarama. Soon after this tour, I moved even closer, buying an apartment just up the road from where Guy was staying.

I was completely taken by Guy. He was tall and extremely handsome and had a presence that made me think of the first time I met Johnny Cash. Both carried themselves with a confidence that seemed to come naturally. When they walked into a room, there was an aura around them that commanded respect.

Keith and I had lunch with Guy and went back to the hotel, where former Redgum singer John Schumann – another big fan of Guy – dropped by and ended up singing him songs in the hotel room. Then I suggested to Guy that he and I head back to my apartment and we'd kick on. I sensed from the company I knew he kept in Nashville that cocaine was part of his world, so I let it be known that, not only did I too have an interest in the white powders, I had some back at my place. I soon realised that Guy *really* liked cocaine. Beer and vodka were procured. Guy liked vodka. He liked vodka *and* cocaine the best.

Guy, my wife Julie and me were in our living-room in Tamarama. Somehow, his guitar materialised (details are a bit hazy), but Guy sat at the table and talked and sang – and talked and sang. Come daybreak and we were still kicking on. Guy slept for a few hours in our spare room, still with his cowboy boots on, before heading back to his hotel.

Sometime that afternoon I crashed too, only to be woken eventually by the phone ringing. I looked out the window at bright daylight and panicked. That's the polite way to put it. I was beside myself. I figured I must have slept through the night and into the next day.

'Fuck! Fuck!'

I'd slept through Guy's first show in Sydney. Missed it completely. He didn't know what time he was on, where the venue was – I was meant to take him. I ranted at Julie for a while, before she calmly pointed out that it was five in the afternoon and I'd only been asleep for two hours.

The other Sydney dates proceeded in a similar fashion to the first night. Guy would play the show, then we'd go back to my house with some fresh supplies of cocaine, copious beers and a big bottle of vodka. Sometimes friends would join us as Guy sat at the table, and the mantra never changed: 'You chop me another one, my friend, and I'll sing another song.' And so it went, a drug and alcohol-fuelled house concert every night for an audience of three or four.

For a music fan – especially a Guy Clark one – this was as close to heaven as it gets: one of my musical heroes sitting in my living-room night after night singing songs to me, my wife and whichever friends had tagged along. And – I thought – I stood to make some money from this caper. How bad was this?

As it turned out, it took me at least a week to recover from the physical abuse and I dropped about $800 on my side of the tour – not to mention the cocaine costs. This was a not insignificant amount of money for me at the time. But Guy signed all my record covers, a pattern that would repeat itself pretty frequently throughout my promoting career – if you call it that. I'd do all this work and end up with signed albums or tour posters and a big debt.

But there were other things to take from this tour. I'd become good friends with Guy and I knew that he'd had a fine time in Sydney, and particularly at party central in Tamarama. And people who'd seen the shows completely loved them. Suddenly I was 'the guy who organised those incredible Guy Clark shows'. If only a few more people had come along for the experience.

Naturally, I was devastated to have made a loss. Keith was taking care of the outstanding bills, though, and the reality that the shows hadn't made money was easily overridden by an indescribable sense of having achieved something special. I was still in the headspace that if I loved an artist, everyone else would too. Essentially, I had the promoting bug.

And it had bitten hard.

# 35

# EVERYBODY'S TALKING

'There were no people around,' says Harry Dean Stanton to no-one in particular. 'Just us and the dinosaurs.'

It's May 1990, and Harry Dean is standing in his room at Sydney's Victoria Towers, his residence on and off for the two weeks of his Australian tour. He's drinking a lukewarm cup of coffee and flicking through Sam Shepard's *Motel Chronicles*, the book that inspired *Paris, Texas*, the film that has made Harry Dean an international cult figure.

Dinosaurs appeal to Harry Dean. The night before, he was at a barbecue thrown for him and his band, The Repo Men. It was towards the end of his first-ever full-scale tour as a musician and he was admiring the collection of plastic dinosaurs lined up along the arm of his chair by the daughter of one of the hosts.

'Kids are really into dinosaurs, aren't they?' he drawls slowly to no-one in particular. 'It's good. They're better than guns. I guess they're going back to their roots,' he says, returning to his plate of barbecued prawns, which he likes because 'they don't taste fishy'.

What was I doing being involved with an Australian tour by the legendary cult actor Harry Dean Stanton? Well, why not? I guess because I could. There wasn't a lot of thinking involved beyond that.

*

As you might have guessed there was also no real science to what I was doing as a tour promoter. Budgets, if you could call them that, were literally done on the back on an envelope. International air fares, performance fees for the artist, publicity, accommodation, etc: I'd add it up and divide by the ticket price and how many people I thought would turn up. Spreadsheets? Me? You must be joking.

The suggestion, no matter how vague, that a tour by someone I admired might be possible had me frantically making phone calls, and starting the hustle to make it happen. My decision to tour American actor and occasional, but passionate singer Harry Dean Stanton came about in exactly this way. One night during Lucinda Williams' tour, I was sitting at my home – now in Bondi – when her guitarist, Gurf Morlix, mentioned that he was also playing in a part-time band with Harry Dean. Being a huge fan of his movie performances – particularly in *Paris, Texas*, *Repo Man* and *Cool Hand Luke* – I mentioned to Gurf that I'd love to tour Harry Dean if that was ever a possibility. I expected that to be the last I'd hear of the idea. Wrong. Three months later, I had a call from Gurf to say that Harry Dean was, indeed, keen to tour Australia with his band. Here was his number, give him a call.

When I summoned up the gumption to dial the number, Harry Dean was friendly, if a little vague. However, we did establish that he was interested in an Australian tour. Naturally I was over the moon – this was such a coup. It would be the coolest tour to come to Australia since, well, ever.

It was also certain to make an absolute fortune. It was a no-brainer. Every way I did the numbers on the envelope, I came to the same conclusion.

Tour projections were made, venues called, budgets done. I'd done all of the negotiations and set-up for this tour. We were relaxed because this seemed like an obvious financial winner. The tour was going to make us (me and Bicci Henderson) at least $100,000 – no, easily $250,000. Thank you, Harry Dean Stanton. Thank you, Gurf Morlix. Thank you, linesmen. Thank you, ball boys.

It must be said that, at this point, the only musical performance by Harry Dean I'd heard was one song on the *Paris, Texas* soundtrack.

But it didn't really matter that I had no idea what he'd sing on the tour – or even if he actually could sing. Harry Dean was the business.

Over the years, I'd have many conversations with promoters in which they said they'd be reluctant to tour an artist if they hadn't seen them perform. Would I have toured Harry Dean if I'd experienced a show first? Probably. It felt good and I wanted to do it.

That's if I could actually get him out here. Negotiations dragged on. Harry Dean wanted to come, then he wasn't sure if he wanted to come. His combo didn't have a drummer, so I organised for a mate, Roger Ansell from the country band The Danglin' Brothers, to play with him. Then my phone rang at about four o'clock one morning. Harry Dean didn't do international time-zone conversions. He told me he'd found his own drummer. Still, he wasn't totally committed to coming. Venues were put on hold and 'Call me next week' became a joke around my house.

It got to the point where I had to call Harry Dean and say, 'Listen, is this tour going to happen or not?' I received an affirmation that I'll never forget: 'Stuart, you can assume that you and I are riding together in one big, black limousine.'

But it wasn't going to be that simple. Harry Dean then decided that he wanted everyone in the band – he and the four musicians – to fly business class to Australia. This very definitely wasn't part of the thinking from our end. We suggested a compromise: Harry Dean would fly business class and the other guys in economy.

This didn't wash with Harry, who was no longer a movie star (and presumably a pretty financially comfortable one) but a member of a band – and everyone in the band flew together. The gang mentality writ large. In a moment of craziness, we agreed. At this point we didn't think we'd have any financial problems, though – we were just going to make $20,000 less than we'd bargained on. No real drama.

Then Harry Dean started vacillating about the exact departure date, which made us just a tad nervous. After a few days, this nervousness turned into panic. Harry Dean was also confused and a bit flustered about having to go and get his visa stamped. It all seemed too compli-cated for him.

In the end, Bicci flew to LA to sort things out and make sure Harry Dean and the band actually got on the plane. A bit of insurance from our end. Another expense. Are you starting to see a pattern here? Anyway, after much stress, nerves, gnashing of teeth and waking in the middle of the night panicking, they finally arrived.

I met Harry Dean at Sydney Airport. He was a quiet, unassuming figure, shorter than I expected and so unobtrusive that initially I didn't recognise him.

He was enigmatic too. As he was filling in a form that required his date of birth, he wrote down that day's date.

'You weren't born today,' I joked.

'Who knows?' he laughed as he changed it to 1926.

The media were clamouring for him to arrive, get settled and start doing interviews. Clive Robertson was highly intelligent, probing and loved to ask left-field questions. Harry Dean described a TV interview with him as one of the greatest conversations he'd ever had.

'We're trying to work out what part Harry Dean played in *Alien*,' Clive said during his introduction. 'We've decided he must have been the alien, the blob that emerged from Sigourney Weaver's chest. Can you imagine emerging from Sigourney Weaver's chest?'

Harry Dean thought that was amusing. After all, apart from *Paris, Texas*, in his 50 previous films he'd usually been the character you remember seeing but couldn't quite recall who or what he was. The audiences who turned out to see Harry Dean in Australia weren't film buffs, though. They were hip pop-culture buffs – and Harry Dean was about as hip as pop culture got in those days.

Early one morning we did breakfast television with Kerri-Anne Kennerley. She didn't appear overly engaged with Harry Dean, beyond spending the brief period before cameras rolled telling him about musicians and actors *she* knew who may also have been in his circle of hipsters.

As the interview got underway, she seemed to feel that Harry Dean wasn't doing the appropriate amount of fawning over her. At one point, she asked him what his attraction to people was.

'I guess I have a certain animal magnetism,' answered Harry Dean, deadpan.

'Well, you obviously left it behind this morning,' she retorted.

Animal magnetism it certainly was, after dark and after shows. Women well under half his age fell all over him both backstage and at clubs.

'Why have you never been married?' radio personality Mike Gibson asked him during an interview in a hotel bar. 'Oh, just lucky, I guess,' replied a smiling Harry Dean.

In business terms, the tour started extremely well. The first show was at the Rose, Shamrock and Thistle hotel in Rozelle, a comparatively small Sydney pub, licensed to hold around 300. Fans had started assembling at 5 pm and, by the time Harry Dean and the band were due to perform, the place was packed shoulder-to-shoulder with nearly 600 people.

The 'Three Weeds', as it was fondly known, didn't have a backstage entrance, not being the sort of venue used to hosting such a big name. So for Harry Dean to get backstage, he had to push his way through the packed crowd. I was carrying his guitar case and I'll never forget their reaction. The whole venue turned, ignoring the hapless support act, and gave him a standing ovation, chanting 'Harry Dean! Harry Dean!'

An hour later I finally got my first opportunity to see my touring artist in action. The band, which Harry Dean had let us call The Repo Men, was great – it included rockabilly/country semi-legend Billy Swan in its ranks. The star himself, though, was a pretty average singer and harmonica player. He was the sort of performer you'd pay scant attention to if he wasn't legendary cult actor Harry Dean Stanton. But the crowd loved him. And he sang *that* song from *Paris, Texas*, which was all most of them wanted to hear. We counted our loot and prepared for the next night.

The Paddington RSL Club was a massive success, with more than 1100 people crammed shoulder to shoulder inside. We decided to push tickets up to $20 each – at the time a pretty hefty figure for a pub/club show in Sydney. I recall saying a 'fuck you – no' to representatives from Michael Hutchence, when they rang requesting 20 complimentary tickets. I figured they could afford to pay. Hutchence turned up anyway, milling around backstage with all the other cool cats. Fashion designer Jenny Kee was intent on inviting Harry Dean to her place in the Blue Mountains. Everyone wanted to hang with Harry Dean. And hang, many of them did, Harry Dean spending most nights in bars with hangers-on, nursing one, maybe two, Scotches for hours.

Before the Paddington show, Bicci and I sat in a quieter bar at the club and worked out that we'd already grossed over $35,000. We started muttering about the serious tax problems we were likely to face. What could we do with the money we were going to make? How little could we get away with declaring?

We'd been just a fraction premature. Ten days later, we were struggling to pay the tour bills.

What went wrong? For starters, contrary to what I'd expected, Harry Dean was far less well received in Melbourne than he'd been in Sydney. In fact, after those first two shows of the tour, attendances plummeted everywhere. And we were greedy.

Early on, we'd booked a series of return shows in Sydney, figuring that because we'd done so well at the first gigs we'd do the same at the end of the tour. Nice idea. But we'd overestimated – significantly – the number of people who wanted to see a cult American actor sing – and not very well.

A fairly damning review in *The Sydney Morning Herald* from Bruce Elder – a critic who could make or break a tour in the days when people really did pay attention to newspaper reviews – didn't help our cause one little bit. Particularly in the early 1990s, Elder wielded a lot of power, the sort of influence journalists today can only dream of having. With a well-chosen 800 words, he killed off our return dates. Elder called it as he saw it: Harry Dean was, at best, an ordinary musician.

So while the cost of the tour was going up, the amount of money coming in kept shrinking . . . and shrinking more. We quickly realised that breaking even was maybe the best we could hope for – and it wasn't long before we were staring at a loss. We just didn't know yet how big the deficit would be. When we said goodbye to Harry Dean and The Repo Men at Sydney Airport, we were facing a sizeable debt.

The final figure was around $25,000 – a massive amount of money for us. I have a signed tour poster that hangs on my wall and I've always ruefully joked that it cost me 25 grand.

But I did get to hang out with Harry Dean Stanton.

Very much a night person, he rarely went to sleep before sunrise. He'd retire to dance clubs and late-night bars virtually every night. 'If I get five hours tonight,' he said, 'that'll do me for the next three days.'

And for a man who had apparently spent much of his life in bars, and described them as being more religious places than churches were, Harry Dean didn't appear to drink a lot.

'Give me one of those beers that makes me cry,' he smiled one night in the hotel bar. It was his roundabout way of asking for a Victoria Bitter. Otherwise, there was the occasional shot of tequila or Scotch. On only one night did he appear to overindulge. That was after the second-last show when, as we drove back to the hotel in Kings Cross, he was leaning out of the van window, *yeah-haw*-ing at the late-night hordes in the Cross. Then, he unpacked his guitar at the hotel, headed off to the Site nightclub, acquired a group of newfound best friends, went to a party and ended up staying awake till daybreak.

It was great to spend time with Harry Dean and hear his thoughts about life. He was deeply involved with the philosophies of the American Zen Buddhist Alan Watts, along with Krishnamurti, a number of Chinese thinkers, and the writings of Wilhelm Reich.

'It just makes a lot more sense,' he told me at the barbecue laid on for him and The Repo Men, 'and it's a lot more of a life-positive religion than the Western world religions, and the Middle Eastern religions.'

Harry Dean, who travelled with a large dictionary in his suitcase, was also enamoured at the time with the politics and ideas of the Russian leader Mikhail Gorbachev, and was reading his book *Perestroika*.

'He's challenging the whole planet. The guy is the first world leader. He states very clearly that he wants to stop the nuclear arms race, to stop war and save the planet. The guy's either a liar . . . but his actions speak louder than words.'

A few minutes after expounding these thoughts, Harry Dean was sitting on an armchair with five-year-old Coby – the owner of the aforementioned dinosaurs – tuning her pint-sized guitar and strumming a few chords for her. Then she climbed up as he piggie-backed her around the living-room.

For the majority of his tour, Harry Dean went unrecognised walking the streets, or at bars. My theory was that because every second person in the Cross had that down-on-their-luck, weathered Harry Dean look, he didn't stand out.

Essentially it was hard work to get a real fix on him. He was absent-minded and maybe just a little bit disconnected from reality, existing on some other cerebral planet. It was hard to reconcile that – or the image on the screen in so many memorable movie appearances – with the man worried about recalling the chords to a particular song, what time the soundcheck was, or whether his guitar was in the van.

Probably my favourite memory of the whole tour came at the barbecue. As Harry Dean departed, he turned to Coby and said, 'I love you, Coby.'

'I love you too, Harry Dean,' replied a young voice.

I kept in contact with Harry Dean, and in 1996, when I was in Los Angeles, working on the *Access All Areas* series, I called him up about doing an interview for the show. Prior to the crew and co-host Paul Grabowsky arriving, I caught a cab to Santa Monica to see Harry Dean and a guitarist playing in a cigar lounge. Remember when that was a thing? He was pleased to see me, mentioned me during his performance – which included many of the songs he'd done on the Australian tour – and drove me back to my hotel.

Harry Dean and I kept a connection for a few years. He'd call every month or so and at one stage he offered to make good on some of the tour losses. That kinda didn't seem right, though. Promoting is all about taking chances. Would I have considered paying him extra if the tour had made a killing? Maybe. To shore up his loyalty to return to Australia with me again as promoter.

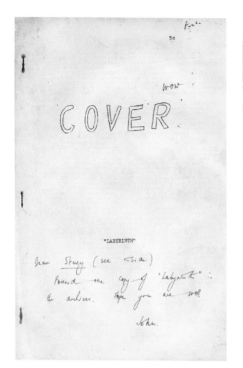

The one and only issue of *Labyrinth*. My first-ever writing about music, in a magazine I created at school.

Thin Lizzy's Phil Lynott atop the barrierless Boulevard Hotel in Sydney. I was there too – and terrified.

Heady days at Benny's, early 1980s. Recognise the guy in the Stalin t-shirt? Who thought that was a good idea?

Blondie's Debbie Harry with potatoes in Hindley Street, Adelaide, in 1977 . . . and some dag photo-bombing. (Photo: Victoria Wilkinson)

AC/DC's Bon Scott, with a drink, natch. And who's photo-bombing again?

Roger Grierson and I were housemates, as well as partners in a record company and other misadventures.

Hey, Mum and Dad, I'm a real journalist. Here's the proof – my press pass, *The Sun-Herald*, 1981.

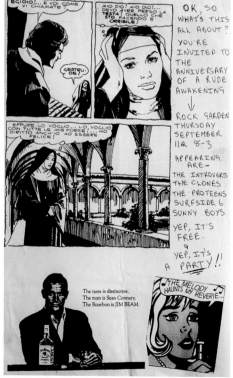

It's my 25th and I'm throwing a party. Incidentally, it was also one of the Sunnyboys' first-ever gigs.

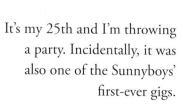

Fellow journalist Clinton Walker and me, riveted by Gary Numan, at the infamous Sebel Townhouse. (Photo: Philip Mortlock)

Read closely: Bruce Springsteen promises to catch up with me when he reaches Australia.

August 5, 1983, #216

Registered by Australia Post — Publication No. NBP 1333 (USA: $1.25/ NZ: $1.25) *$1.00

# RAM

**THE CHURCH**
**EDDIE GRANT**
**NONA HENDRYX**
**WEATHERGIRLS**

**MARK HOLDEN**    **CECIL TAYLOR**
**HAYSI FANTAYZEE**    **FLASHDANCE**
*KILL CITY* — *Surviving* **Wollongong**

# THE BIG KISS OFF

PHOTO: OPTIC NERVE

Win POLICE Jackets plus TEARS FOR FEARS Albums

Hot on the trail of the 'rematch' interview with The Church's Steve Kilbey – arm-wrestle and all.

*Top left:* Working on an early issue of *Mean Streets*, assisted by daughter Jay.

*Top right:* Children Frankie-Rae and Eddie.

Me with Eddie. (Photo: Jon Lewis)

The gang's all here to launch Paul Kelly's *Gossip* album, 1986: me, Toby Creswell, Ed St John, Paul, and Clinton Walker.

I've seen KISS without their make-up and The Residents without their eyeballs. The eyes are intact as they pose with Snakefinger at the Southern Cross Hotel in Sydney, 1986.

After a sell-out Paul Kelly show in Melbourne, his drummer, Michael Barclay, looks to Mr Party Central for guidance as to what happens next. A bemused booking agent, Gerard Schlaghecke, looks on.

Talking Heads' David Byrne, making sense. I'm recording our chat on my trusty cassette player, Sebel Town House, 1979.

With Mick Jagger in Paris on the balcony of the George Cinq hotel – seems quite tall, doesn't he?

Soapie extra, extra, read all about it – that time I had a role in *Sons And Daughters*.

# Dolly

JANUARY 1986 No 183 $2.00

MICHAEL J. FOX POSTER

MEET A-HA, HOODOO GURUS, PARTY GIRLS

STUART COUPE IN SONS AND DAUGHTERS!

BEAUTY — THOSE NEW YEAR'S RESOLUTIONS

CONTRACEPTION — WHAT DO YOU KNOW?

## HAPPY NEW YEAR!

Me in jeans doing my best 'Born In Australia'. *Dolly* profiles the contributor readers love to hate.

Trying to be too cool for school. *Dolly* days with fellow contributor Barry Divola.

# I was a soapie extra

**It had to happen: Stuart Coupe *finally* got to meet his favourite. Bruce? Nope. Madonna? Hu-huh. Ralph the Wonderdog? No way. Simon LeBon? Not even close, boyo, No, it was Abigail, and all the other stars of *Sons and Daughters*. Yep, our Stuart Coupe posed as an extra for his fleeting five seconds of fame and fortune.**

"It's a dog's life," Alison remarked to me as I prepared to walk down the hospital corridor for the tenth time in succession.

It was getting on for 6pm and I'd been walking backwards and forwards along the hospital corridor for the past four hours.

Don't get me wrong, there was variation. During one half hour I'd pushed an empty wheelchair around a corner eight times. Then a few hours later I'd been able to carry a few boxes of surgical implements.

And there were other redeeming features. I'd heard the hospital staff say the same things over and over again. And seen them make sure that the reading on Gordon's heartbeat machine was correctly erratic. Then I'd winced as Caroline had repeatedly messed up her conversation with Alison.

By this time you're probably wondering exactly what I'm talking about. It should be clear if I explain that a few weeks back I spent a day as an extra on my favourite TV soap opera, yes siree, the wonderfully addictive *Sons and Daughters*.

When it comes to *Sons and Daughters* you can shove your *Dallas* or *Country Practice* — *S&D* is the real thing! I have a friend who claims to have seen virtually every episode (more than 700) since this classic Australian soapie started and, after initially being a cynic, I must admit to having been addicted for the past two years.

So when the idea of a story on A Day In The Life Of An Extra was first mentioned, I was real keen — as long as the extra was on *S&D* !!!!

But before I get into the nitty-gritty of whether Alison did or did not bribe Caroline, and how serious Barbara's condition is, and confront the very relevant question of whether or not Alison has stepped into Gordon's shoes, let's go right back to the beginning.

Anyone who wants to be on TV as an extra has to be a member of Actor's Equity, the acting profession's union. It cost a little over $30 for me to join for this appearance and I was warned to have my receipt or membership card with me at all times on the set just in case there was a spot check on the cast.

Most extras are represented by an agency, of which there are several. Extras for most TV shows come from the books of these agencies and the typical situation is that the available work is reasonably fairly shared amongst the major agencies.

When I was notified that there was possibly work for me I was told to front up at the Grundy building at 10am on a Tuesday morning so that the powers that be could see whether I was suitable for the work they had in mind.

Arriving at Grundy's was not as I had expected. There was no red carpet. No cameras wanting to interview this future sensation of Australian TV.

"Fill in this form, give it back to me and take a seat till you're called," said the receptionist.

Another shock was to follow. I suddenly realised how little I knew about myself, maaaaaannnnn. I didn't know how much I weighed, or what my waist measurements are. Even had to think about the exact colour of my hair. I knew I couldn't drive, that I didn't want to do stunt work, and under "Unusual Skills" I wrote "journalism"!!!

Then I was shoved against a wall and photographed by the receptionist.

"That's one thing that actors have to know a lot about: all their physical characteristics," Grundy's manager, Sue, told me.

"We need to be able to go to the files and know exactly what we're getting. There's no use getting a 183cm tall woman to stand next to a 140cm man in a wedding scene, and things like that."

As Sue was telling me this, she was pulling out file after file after file, jam-packed full of information on extras. Literally thousands of would-be bar drinkers, hospital attendants or crowd scenes.

The idea that being an extra was just a possible bit of sideline work for people was soon dispelled.

"Actors on the way up take being an extra very seriously," Sue said. "They see it as their possible big break, and do it for the experience in the hope that they're going to be noticed by someone and offered more work.

"You'd be surprised at the number of aspiring actors and actresses who go on shows like *Perfect Match* just hoping to be noticed."

Sue and the people in her office watch *every* episode of *Sons and Daughters* on video to check the performances of everyone — even the guy sitting right on the far side of the screen who's seen for five seconds drinking a glass of beer in a 30 second bar scene.

They also conduct regular auditions of people who sound or look interesting and keep all these on video so that they can be referred to from time to time.

Initially I was being considered for a bar scene and I was amazed to find that if six bar drinkers are needed for an episode of *Sons and Daughters*, Sue doesn't just close her eyes and pull six actors out of the extras file at random. No siree, getting the *right* six bar drinkers is important.

Eventually it's decided that I'll be a hospital orderly because the bar scene is being shot at an outside location, and they figure I'll experience more of the typical day of an extra by appearing in a studio location.

While at Grundy's I'm also informed that it's part of actor's etiquette not to blab to all and sundry about what happens in future episodes of a show so, unfortunately for all you *S&D* fans, I'm not at liberty to tell you whether Caroline makes it through . . . come to think of it, I'm probably in the bad books for letting on about the car accident. But then again, I might be making all this up!!!!

It wasn't necessary for me to turn up for the rehearsals that happen a few days before shooting, but it's essential for anyone who has a speaking part. You see, there are even levels of extras. I was at the bottom and then there are 50 Worders, who are extras who say between one and 50 words in a scene. They get paid more money, and then there are featured extras, like rock stars and well-known actors in the show for a brief appearance.

OK, so my big day as a TV Star was a Monday when the cast of *Sons and Daughters* were recording parts of episodes 725-728.

Now believe me, this is no easy, glamorous life. The first call for Caroline Morrell (Abigail) and Samantha Morrell (Sally Tayler) was at 7am in the morning. That was make up and costumes, with the shooting of the scene in Caroline's town house starting at 8am.

The rest of the cast involved in Monday's shooting were due at Studio A, at ATN 7 in Epping at various times during the morning.

Although I wasn't due to appear until after lunch I fronted by mid-morning just to see what was going on . . . and to spend as much time as possible around my favourite soapie stars.

Tentatively walking into the Green Room (relaxation room for the stars), I glanced around and there they were — Abigail, Charlie Bartlett (Sarah Kemp), Alison Carr (Belinda Giblin), David Palmer (Tom Richards), Gordon Hamilton (Brian Blain) plus a bunch of nurses — my fellow extras!!!

There are snapshots from past episodes all around the walls, a TV so everyone can see what's going on on the set, a few tables, chairs and tea and coffee-making facilities.

There was a form on the door asking for names for the *Sons and Daughters* Christmas Party — drat, Abigail's already taking someone!!! It was almost enough to make me walk out of the

PHOTOS ▸ ANDREW SOUTHAM

92

93

No-one's going to recognise me so cunningly disguised. Here's that *Sons And Daughters* piece in *Dolly*, with me in my favourite *Get Smart* windcheater.

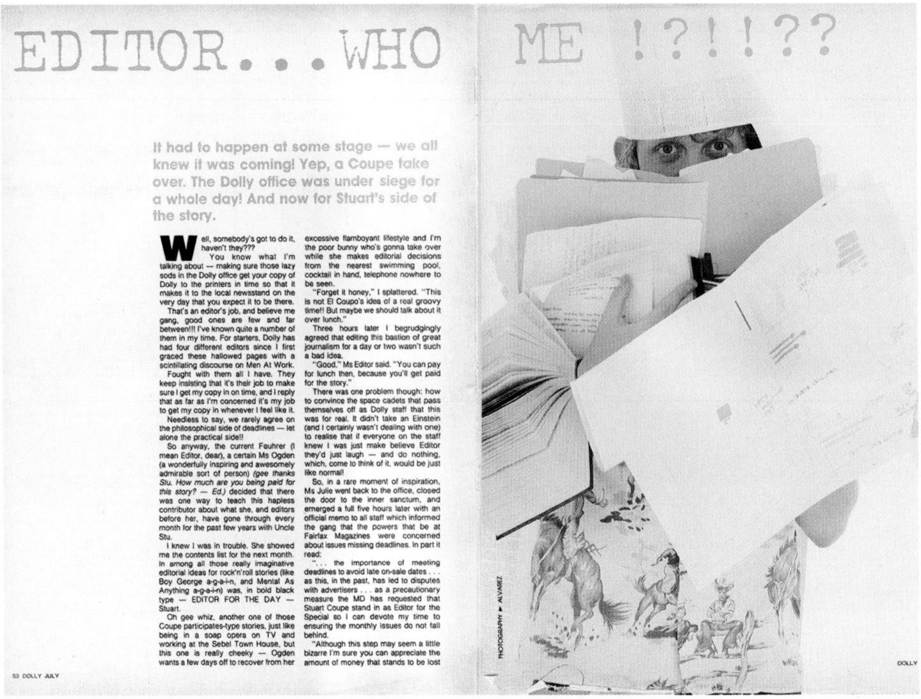

# EDITOR...WHO ME !?!!??

It had to happen at some stage — we all knew it was coming! Yep, a Coupe take over. The Dolly office was under siege for a whole day! And now for Stuart's side of the story.

Well, somebody's got to do it, haven't they???

You know what I'm talking about — making sure those lazy sods in the Dolly office get your copy of Dolly to the printers in time so that it makes it to the local newsstand on the very day that you expect it to be there.

That's an editor's job, and believe me gang, good ones are few and far between!!! I've known quite a number of them in my time. For starters, Dolly has had four different editors since I first graced these hallowed pages with a scintillating discourse on Men At Work.

Fought with them all I have. They keep insisting that it's their job to make sure I get my copy in on time, and I reply that as far as I'm concerned it's my job to get my copy in whenever I feel like it.

Needless to say, we rarely agree on the philosophical side of deadlines — let alone the practical side!!

So anyway, the current Feuhrer (I mean Editor, dear), a certain Ms Ogden (a wonderfully inspiring and awesomely admirable sort of person) *(gee thanks Stu. How much are you being paid for this story? — Ed.)* decided that there was one way to teach this hapless contributor about what she, and editors before her, have gone through every month for the past few years with Uncle Stu.

I knew I was in trouble. She showed me the contents list for the next month. In among all those really imaginative editorial ideas for rock'n'roll stories (like Boy George a-g-a-i-n, and Mental As Anything a-g-a-i-n) was, in bold black type — EDITOR FOR THE DAY — Stuart.

Oh gee whiz, another one of those Coupe participates-type stories, just like being in a soap opera on TV and working at the Sebel Town House, but this one is really cheeky — Ogden wants a few days off to recover from her excessive flamboyant lifestyle and I'm the poor bunny who's gonna take over while she makes editorial decisions from the nearest swimming pool, cocktail in hand, telephone nowhere to be seen.

"Forget it honey," I splattered. "This is not El Coupo's idea of a real groovy time!! But maybe we should talk about it over lunch."

Three hours later I begrudgingly agreed that editing this bastion of great journalism for a day or two wasn't such a bad idea.

"Good," Ms Editor said. "You can pay for lunch then, because you'll get paid for the story."

There was one problem though: how to convince the space cadets that pass themselves off as Dolly staff that this was for real. It didn't take an Einstein (and I certainly wasn't dealing with one) to realise that if everyone on the staff knew I was just make believe Editor they'd just laugh — and do nothing, which, come to think of it, would be just like normal!

So, in a rare moment of inspiration, Ms Julie went back to the office, closed the door to the inner sanctum, and emerged a full five hours later with an official memo to all staff which informed the gang that the powers that be at Fairfax Magazines were concerned about issues missing deadlines. In part it read:

". . . the importance of meeting deadlines to avoid late on-sale dates . . . as this, in the past, has led to disputes with advertisers . . . as a precautionary measure the MD has requested that Stuart Coupe stand in as Editor for the Special so I can devote my time to ensuring the monthly issues do not fall behind.

"Although this step may seem a little bizarre I'm sure you can appreciate the amount of money that stands to be lost

52 DOLLY JULY

PHOTOGRAPHY ▸ ALVAREZ

DOLLY

Cowboy for hire. Guest-editing *Dolly* magazine and still undercover.

# KNOCKIN' ON DYLAN'S DOOR

**"Climbing Mt Everest is easier than interviewing BOB DYLAN" — just the sort of talk that's guaranteed to spur the intrepid reporter in search of an exclusive. Unlike Mohammed, STUART COUPE goes to the mountain. Why? Because it was there...**

'IF Hank Williams was sitting here now, what would you ask him?" I said to Bob Dylan, who has listed Williams as one of the people he'd most like to have interviewed.

"I'd probably ask him where he gets his drugs," Dylan replied, laughing for the only time in our half-hour interview.

"What else would I ask him? I think that would be enough. I always liked his clothes, and I probably would have wanted to know where he got these.

Dylan was sitting in the downstairs bar at Auckland's less expensive Regent Hotel after his recent Australian concert, a magnificent outdoor performance in front of nearly 40,000 people thankfully free of the sound problems that were to plague subsequent Entertainment Centre concerts in Sydney.

Dylan seemed relaxed and in a playful mood, probably sensing as somewhat nervous journalist sitting opposite him, he threw me one of his casual (and ignored for another verbal sparring match.

Interviewing Bob Dylan — even in 1986 — is something different to your ordinary run-of-the-mill pop-star encounter.

Questioning the likes of Bruce Springsteen Sting, Johnny Rotten's yarn, Boy George or this week's have-halfpa-gone-tomorrow pop sensation rarely requires the awe-laid let's face it, downright trepidation that accompanies an audience with the most influential song and saga man of the last quarter-century. Then again, there's not too many people who get to test that face Bob Dylan doesn't often give interviews. Why should he?

Lincoln Hall, one of the three Australians who climbed Mt Everest, wanted to interview Dylan whilst he was in Australia for this third concert tour. Through Dylan's Australian publicist, Patti Mostyn, Hall sent a copy of the book he'd written about his Everest adventure to Dylan's manager, Elliot Roberts, hoping that its contents might encourage Mr Zimmerman to talk to him. The answer was a definitive no.

"Tell him that climbing Mt Everest is easier than getting an interview with Bob Dylan," Roberts replied.

Hall invited out on an audience with Dylan. Lauren Beard got one after the second Sydney concert, the two remained chatting for hours. Greg Matthews, Aus-

*Page 14, RAM, March 12, 1986*

I interviewed Bob Dylan, twice. He wanted to know where Hank Williams got his drugs – and would I pass on a compliment to Brett Whiteley.

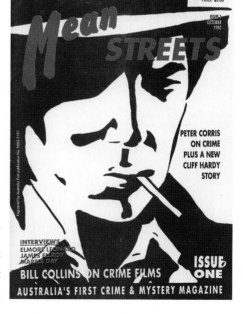

The first edition of the 'quarterly' *Mean Streets*. We did 17 editions in six years – including two that carried the same edition number.

Marlboros, mobiles and motor-mouths. Breakfast of champions with Anthony Bourdain, Brasserie Les Halles, New York, 2001. (Photo: Victoria Wilkinson)

In 1990, my business partner and I toured Harry Dean Stanton – surely that would make us our fortune. Nope. We lost $25,000. At least I ended up with a great signed poster.

When I interviewed this guy from CSN&Y for my *Dirt Music* radio show, he approached me at the 2SER studio and said (unnecessarily), 'Hi, I'm Graham Nash.' (Photo: Susan Lynch)

Cigarette break – and concept meeting with myself – at the doorway of Laughing Outlaw Records. (Photo: Chris Pavlich/ Newspix)

With actor Samara Weaving and my daughter Sara, outside Laughing Outlaw and heading to the ARIAs, 2006.

At my *Promoters* book launch, making sure that 'Chuggi' and Michael Gudinski don't come to blows.

In conversation with Tex Perkins, whose book I ghosted/co-wrote. And don't forget, my G.R.E.E.N. label released the Beasts of Bourbon's *The Axeman's Jazz*. (Photo: Susan Lynch)

*Left:* Me and Barnesy at his place, interviewing him about the legendary roadies for my book, 2018.

*Bottom left:* 'Haven't seen you for 22 years, but I'm writing a book about you. Hi, Paul Kelly.'

*Bottom right:* One of these people is the greatest songwriter ever. On the balcony at my home with Steve Kilbey. (Photo: Susan Lynch)

Getting racing tips from recent Melbourne Cup winner Michael Gudinski. We were making an appearance together at Mumbrella, Paddington Town Hall, in 2016.
(Photo: Susan Lynch)

Back on my balcony with Hoodoo Gurus' Dave Faulkner after a radio interview. Relations with my former clients have always been good.
In 1992, they presented me with a gold CD plaque in recognition of my contribution to their career.
(Photo: Susan Lynch)

DJ Anthony Albanese knew a photo op when he spotted me at Bluesfest 2022.
(Photo: Toby Zerna/Newspix)

Backstage at the Factory Theatre in Sydney with Tim Rogers, as well as Glenn A. Baker, with whom I wrote my first two books.

With legendary rock writer and longstanding friend David Fricke, and Hugh, New York City, 2019.

Me in NYC, outside the Niagara bar. I love this mural of The Clash's Joe Strummer. He was grateful I kept their manager, Bernie Rhodes, occupied during their 1982 Australian tour.
(Photos this page: Susan Lynch)

# 36

# THE GAMBLER

At this stage, I was more fascinated by the notion of being a promoter than by the reality. I'd always had a lifestyle of flying by the seat of my pants and hadn't learnt to worry too much about where the next dollar came from. Probably still haven't to be perfectly honest.

With a notoriously short attention span – particularly when drugs were involved – and a low boredom threshold, I was up for anything new and exciting, particularly when it involved music. And, of course, I totally believed that any losses were a mere hiccup on my inevitable road to being Australia's most astute concert promoter.

Still, 25 grand was a lot of money. How do you get out of a financial bind like that? Well, you do what other promoters do and promote another tour. If you'd lost on the third race at Randwick, the chances are you'd try to make good in the fourth race of the day. It's exactly like gambling. If you're behind the eight-ball on the day's punting, there's no other solution but to plonk down more money on the next race – and pray.

Bicci and I tossed around some ideas for tours. In what I thought was a stroke of genius – and it sort of was – I recalled a series of shows that had been doing the rounds in the States. They were low-key events, featuring Rosanne Cash (yes, the daughter of Johnny), Mary Chapin

Carpenter and Nanci Griffith, three extremely talented country-oriented singer/songwriters.

I thought this was a good concept and decided to try to bring them to Australia. However, I'd never been overly excited by Nanci Griffith (which I know is a terrible thing to say, especially as she's now passed away, but I just didn't totally engage), so I thought we'd put Lucinda Williams in the mix instead.

We dubbed them 'The Highwaywomen', in a pretty damn obvious allusion to the country-bloke supergroup of Willie Nelson, Johnny Cash, Waylon Jennings and Kris Kristofferson, aka The Highwaymen, who were big news at the time.

I don't think I've ever worked harder setting up a tour. For starters, no-one in Australia had heard of Mary Chapin Carpenter – and that included her record company, Sony. I had to try to convince them to release her first two albums (which I grew to totally love). Until that point, they'd had no intention of doing so, because sales in America had been far from spectacular.

I already had the relationship with Lucinda and her manager, so it wasn't too hard to convince her to return. But Rosanne Cash – by far the biggest name of the three – proved extremely difficult to nail down.

A major difficulty was dealing with three different sets of artist managers. Naturally, they all wanted the best deal for their clients. There were issues of billing (was there a headliner?), fees (who was to be paid what) and transport (if one artist demanded business class international travel, did we offer that to them all?). And if so, were we paying or would that come out of the artists' fees? There were so many things to juggle.

The costs were out of Bicci's and my financial range, so we brought in two partners. One was the established promoter Adrian Bohm, the other a manager/booking agent John Sinclair. John was the only person I knew who had ever won the big prizes on the TV show *Sale Of The Century*: $250,000 in cash, two upper-range cars, etc. 'I don't know a lot about anything – but I know a bit about a lot of things,' he quipped to me once.

In the end, we managed to sort it all out. I snared Mary Chapin Carpenter for a fee that, within months, would be laughable. I told her manager that $US500 a show was the most I could afford – which it was – and he accepted. Some months later, Carpenter broke big time in the States and wouldn't leave home for less than a couple of hundred thousand dollars a show.

Opening night was at the Enmore Theatre, and despite extremely poor ticket sales it was an astonishing performance. Mary Chapin Carpenter appeared first, to a smattering of applause, which was to be expected as she was unknown to all bar real obsessives. Rosanne came onstage next and was well received: daughter of Johnny Cash, established songwriter and all that.

Watching them in the few days since they'd arrived in the country before opening night, it had been obvious that Rosanne thought she was the star of the show. She was the one who had insisted on business class air travel, *plus* a personal assistant (also in business class), to look after hair, make-up and so forth. So when Lucinda walked onstage and a standing ovation erupted, the 'What the fuck have I gotten myself into here?' look on Rosanne's face was priceless. She quickly realised that the show was most certainly 'Lucinda Williams plus friends'.

The tour was remarkable, not only because of the women's individual talents, but because of the extraordinary dynamic that grew between them as the tour progressed. Prior to their arrival in Australia, Lucinda knew Mary Chapin but didn't know Rosanne – who in turn knew Mary Chapin but didn't know Lucinda. After 10 days on the road together, though, visiting Melbourne, Adelaide, Canberra and Brisbane, they really seemed to bond.

At the first show, each artist watched politely as the others performed, but by the time of the three return performances in Sydney they were interacting superbly and with great affection, singing each other's songs, cuddling each other onstage. It was a beautiful thing to behold – despite, you guessed it, less than spectacular attendances at the gigs themselves.

Life on the road in Australia – and maybe I can take some small credit for this – had also begun a major career leap for two of the singers. Prior to the tour, Mary Chapin had never heard Lucinda's song 'Passionate Kisses', but she fell in love with it and had a massive hit with her version of the song when she returned to the United States, winning a Grammy for the performance. Mary Chapin had become a star, Lucinda's name was now everywhere and her publishing royalties from the cover version were enormous. Lucinda joked to me a few years later that she owed me half the house she'd bought in Nashville with the songwriting royalties from that track.

But while the tour was great for Lucinda and Mary Chapin, it wasn't so great for my bank balance. Actually, it came close to breaking even, but costs were still greater than income – about $10,000 greater. Although reviews had been terrific, as had word of mouth, again I realised that my fandom was getting in the way of solid business decisions. Seriously in the way.

I tended to have a number of friends who knew this area of music pretty well. Before the tour, most of them had said we were going to clean up, and that the combination of the three was inspired, and a real coup. However, my friends don't always (if ever) reflect mass tastes, and I was still dealing with artists who had, at best, a cult following here. Plus, all my friends expected free tickets, and you have to have a real lot of (actually paying for tickets) friends to fill the Enmore Theatre and the like.

The tone had been set at the Enmore, when we only sold 900 tickets out of a possible 1800. One upside was that Kasey Chambers was taken to the show by her father, Bill, and she's said many times that this concert changed her life and consolidated what she wanted to do with it.

Bicci now moved on to less speculative ventures, and Keith Glass and I started doing most of the tours together. He and I had an almost perfect working relationship, because he was pragmatic and down to earth, as well as blunt about the possible economic viability of tours I suggested.

After we'd agreed on a tour, I did the majority of what I loved most: the hustle and bustle of the actual deal, as well as the publicity. Meanwhile, Keith had an infinitely better understanding than I did of the mechanics of touring, so he took care of venues, air tickets and hotels, and dealing with other logistics. It probably goes without saying that he was better at keeping financial records than me. Plus, he had an American Express card that we used to bankroll our tours – so at the end of the day, the economic stress was on his shoulders. I always approached it as if we were partners, though – in both losses and wins (if we managed to achieve such a thing).

Our partnership also worked well because Keith loved being on the road, while I rarely attended anything other than the Sydney shows. Julie and I had two young daughters, and preferred to be at home in Blackheath. As a working musician, Keith frequently performed as the support act – both saving us money and gaining exposure for his performing and songwriting career.

I didn't really expect to find myself promoting really large-scale international tours; and when I later observed such undertakings, I was glad I hadn't. And that was without considering the stress involved in the financial risk of such ventures. Even the tours Keith and I did were starting to come in at over the $100,000 budget mark. That's a lot of money at the best of times – and a massive amount when the two promoters have no real money between them and a credit card that has to be paid off.

We had enough on our hands touring the likes of Chris Whitley.

# 37

# BIG SKY COUNTRY

Some tours stick in your memory banks more than others – often not for the best of reasons. Such as the saga of the first time American blues/country artist Chris Whitley came to Australia in 1993.

The call came through early in the morning from Auckland. 'The fuckwit's been busted.'

The fuckwit in question was Whitley, who Keith and I were touring in a joint venture with New Zealand promoter Kevin Byrt and his partners at Real Groovy Records. It had been their idea and they'd done most of the negotiations. Keith and I were presenting a bunch of Australian shows and splitting the international travel expenses with the Kiwis.

Everyone in the international touring game knew that New Zealand customs officers were amongst the most ferocious on the planet. Before the tour, Whitley had asked about the availability of marijuana and had been assured that there'd be a bag of grass waiting for him in a car at Auckland Airport once he'd cleared customs – with plenty more where that came from. Evidently, Whitley hadn't trusted us folk on the other side of the globe and had hidden a joint in one of his boots. This was beyond stupid and then some. Naturally, the sniffer dogs went ballistic as soon as they got near him and Whitley was hauled off for a search.

Almost anyone can work out that it's stupid to try to bring drugs into a foreign country – and doubly stupid to have them in a boot.

If the joint had been in his jacket, for instance, he could at least have argued that he'd been at a party the night before his flight and someone had surreptitiously slipped the joint into his pocket. But in your boot? Dude, you put it there yourself. Game over.

The end result was that Whitley was held at the airport until he could be put on the next flight back to Los Angeles. At this point it seemed pretty certain that the tour wasn't going to happen, and I wish I'd taken notice of the glaring early warning sign. It was only a taste of things to come.

Whitley was clearly not going to be allowed into New Zealand any time soon, but Keith and I decided we'd at least have a shot at getting permission for him to enter Australia. We told Whitley to stay put in a Los Angeles hotel, then started an endless round of calls and faxes to the Australian consulate in LA.

A friend in Los Angeles was enlisted to take Whitley for an interview at the consulate. Then another. Then *another*. Copious paperwork was filed and, lo and behold, our felon-in-waiting was given the green light to grace our shores. I still wonder exactly how this came to be.

That was one problem out of the way. But that was just the start of the problems. Whitley appeared vague and disorientated and clearly wasn't a stickler for even the most basic of details. Before he could be booked on a new flight, I made two-hourly calls to the reception desk to check that he was still in the hotel. Three hours before Whitley was due to leave for Australia, I called again.

'Could you tell me if Mr Whitley has left the hotel?'

'Yes, sir, he has checked out.'

'That's good news. Did he look like he was going to the airport?'

'No, sir, he did not.'

'He didn't? Why didn't he?'

'He was only carrying a plastic shopping bag, sir. And his condition and appearance did not suggest that he was about to take an international plane flight.'

This was not the news I was hoping for. We knew Whitley's vintage guitars were somewhere in transit between New Zealand and

Australia – at this point officially lost – but we'd expected him to be carrying *some* baggage.

Keith and I had no idea what was going on. We were panicking. Had Whitley forgotten he was supposed to make a 13-hour plane trip? Or had he abandoned the tour and headed home? Or was he really undertaking an intercontinental expedition with only a plastic bag for luggage?

Some hours later, all was revealed.

'Hi, Stuart, I'm in Hawaii.'

I was massively relieved, and only briefly confused. Joining the dots, I realised that Whitley was calling reverse charges from the airport there, these being the days when international flights from LA to Sydney always stopped there to refuel.

'That's good news, Chris. When do you reboard?'

'There's a problem.'

'What problem exactly?'

'The plane left without me.'

It transpired that Whitley had once again taken a joint on the plane with him – at this point he was officially a *very* slow learner – and during the refuelling stop in Hawaii had walked out of the airport to smoke it, thereby necessitating going back through immigration and customs to reboard the flight.

In a wave of drug-fuelled vagueness, though, Whitley had seemingly forgotten he was meant to return to the terminal and get on the plane. And once he'd remembered, unfortunately the aforementioned aircraft wasn't operating on Whitley time, but Qantas flight schedule time.

Okay, what now?

We called Whitley's manager in New York, telling him that we had a big problem. This constant rebooking of flights, we said, was costing a fortune and we weren't going to pay; these stuff-ups were well beyond our responsibilities. The deal for the tour was hurriedly and torridly renegotiated, before Whitley boarded yet another flight – this time direct to Sydney, and without any accompanying marijuana or drug of any kind. (At least as far as we were aware.)

Keith and I met Whitley at the airport. We were, as you'd imagine, somewhat relieved to see this diminutive and dishevelled figure, thin to the point of emaciation, wandering out of the customs area. We shook hands and I asked him where his luggage was. He looked down at the plastic shopping bag he was carrying and said, 'I need to go buy a toothbrush.' We got him one from the airport chemist. Another crippling tour expense to deal with.

We installed Whitley at the Cosmopolitan Motel in Double Bay. There, he appeared to take care of himself by actually eating a little and focusing on interviews with the local media and then the actual shows. His first gig wasn't for a couple of days, and his first day coincided with Melbourne Cup festivities, so we installed ourselves in a prime position at an outdoor restaurant to watch upmarket, born-to-lunch Double Bay in action.

Keith and I spent hours with him in his room, in the reception area and walking around the leafy streets of the suburb, as he recovered from the jetlag and his circuitous journey to this part of the world. He talked constantly about his child and recent break-up with his partner, and listened to the Smashing Pumpkins album *Siamese Dream* as if it was the only album ever made.

The CD must have been in that plastic bag (which didn't appear to have contained much else beyond a shirt and maybe some underwear). There was no evidence to suggest he'd brought any other albums with him. I guess he figured *Siamese Dream* was all he needed.

Happily, his guitars were finally located (in one piece) and everything was under control, at least for the time being. Curiously, for someone who seemed to have an obsessive need for marijuana, he never asked me or Keith to get him any. And at this stage, as far as I could tell, we were the only people he knew in Australia.

On the night of his first show at The Basement, I went to collect him at the Cosmopolitan and he'd obviously done a bit of damage to the contents of the minibar. But the show itself was extraordinary – and well attended. He was the real deal.

From this point, the tour began to proceed fairly uneventfully – although Whitley seemed to be attracting an increasingly large group of new best friends to his hotel room, all of them partying through the night.

One morning, I got a call from the Cosmopolitan: they wanted to throw Whitley out. A honeymooning couple had checked into the room next to his and hadn't appreciated the Smashing Pumpkins being played at full volume at 4 am. We smooth-talked the hotel, assuring them it wouldn't happen again, and tried to convince Whitley that he needed to tone things down – which he appeared to do.

The shows were drawing good audiences, and we looked set to make a good profit. By the time of the final gig, however, Whitley was in very bad shape. The partying had clearly taken its toll. The show was at the Three Weeds, and Whitley turned up for soundcheck four hours late, barely coherent. He was slurring badly as he stumbled around the venue.

Keith and I were worried. We needed something to straighten him out – and fast. It seemed obvious that the only option we had – outside of cancelling the show – was to get something stronger than coffee into Whitley, to cut through the booze and at least keep him upright for the gig.

I started calling cocaine dealers I knew to see if I could get supplies sent over. My phone book was pretty good in this department, but . . . nothing doing. Whitley was erratically careening around the backstage area, continuing to drink anything he could lay his hands on from the hospitality supplied by the venue. There was an almost-capacity crowd in attendance and Keith and I were becoming more concerned by the second.

The support acts finished and it was showtime for Whitley. This was so far from being good, it wasn't funny. He staggered onstage, dropping guitar picks and struggling to hold his guitar. Three songs into the set, it was clear he could barely perform. He fell over. He was helped up by a roadie and performed a few more songs – badly – then fell over again. At this point, he was assisted offstage by the same roadie and a friend.

People in the audience were yelling out, heads were shaking, some were laughing. Others looked like they were about to head for the door and demand a refund.

I rushed backstage to see what I could do. As I reached out to Whitley to help him onto a chair, he tried to punch me – totally unaware of who I was. He was restrained by a road-crew member and given a few minutes to try to get himself together, before somehow staggering back onstage.

But things weren't about to get better. Whitley slurred, dropped his guitar, and seemed to forget mid-song what he was playing. Amazingly, none of the audience – obviously fascinated by these antics – left. And in the end, no-one asked for their money back. The train wreck they'd witnessed must have been enough to justify their ticket price. Or maybe they just felt sorry for us hapless promoters.

The next day, Whitley was booked on a plane back to the States. I went to the hotel to check him out. At the front desk, the receptionist looked up, with her eyebrows raised and with a bit of 'This doesn't happen in Double Bay' disdain. She asked who was paying my client's room-service bill for the previous four days. I said it was Whitley's responsibility, but I'd put it on my credit card and sort it out with him later.

'Sir,' the receptionist said, 'do you realise the total is just over $1400?'

I took a deep breath and looked at the piece of paper she pushed in my direction. It appeared Whitley had been keeping the hotel staff relentlessly on the go during the midnight-to-dawn shift. Three mornings in a row, as well as ordering bacon and eggs, he'd requested six bottles of house wine, which left little doubt as to why he was in the condition he'd been in the night before.

As Keith and I negotiated a reduced fee with Whitley's manager in New York to cover the problems with travel, the artist himself, after paying all the expenses he'd incurred, left Australia pretty much as he'd arrived: with a plastic shopping bag and a few hundred dollars in his pocket. Well, at least he had his guitars – and a newish toothbrush. Who said show business isn't glamorous?

Sometime later, I saw Whitley in New York. Sony Music had asked me to interview him while I was there – on their dime – along with other artists of theirs who had new albums on the way. He was friendly and looked in better shape, confessing that he didn't remember much about his first trip to Australia. Years later – after I'd written about my experiences with Whitley – he was often asked about that tour and always denied everything. I'd made it all up, he said.

Though Keith and I made money on the Whitley tour – a rarity for us – it wasn't a lot, and certainly not compared to the anxiety of the experience. Whitley came back to Australia several times, and from all reports was much less problematic on subsequent visits.

Whitley died in 2005. He was just 45. A prodigious talent gone way too soon. Fundamentally, I think he was a really good person, going through a bad patch during that time in Australia. And I'll always remember his amazing first show at The Basement.

# 38

# LONG AS I CAN SEE THE LIGHT

Always on the lookout for new tour promotion ideas, I was surprised in early 1994 to receive a package from Geffen Records containing an advance copy of an album by Ted Hawkins. It was accompanied by a press release saying that he was coming to Australia in a few months for a 'promotional tour'.

My jaw dropped. I'd been a fan of Hawkins since I'd heard the early albums of this amazing middle-aged black singer. He'd been discovered busking at Venice Beach in Los Angeles in the early to mid-1980s, after performing there for many years before that. Hawkins sat on a milk crate with his acoustic guitar and sang his own material, along with versions of classic soul and country songs. I was not alone in being stunned that he'd been signed by a major record label – and was coming to Australia.

I immediately called Geffen in Sydney to find out exactly what form this promotional tour was going to take.

'Oh well, he'll come out and do a few interviews with people like you, and then maybe sing a few songs one day in the boardroom here,' I was told, by someone who was very off-hand about working on this album by an unknown singer who sang sitting on a milk crate. This was very definitely out of sync in an era heavily dominated by grunge – particularly another band on Geffen called Nirvana.

So I went to Geffen with a proposal. They were bringing Hawkins out to Australia, anyway, and would be paying for airfares and accommodation. What if Keith and I put on a run of club dates and paid Hawkins for his performances?

Geffen were delighted. Stuart and Keith were delighted. As promoters we'd just scammed (or should I say 'negotiated') to have all the major costs for a tour by an international act paid by someone else. There was a lot to like about this arrangement.

The deal was negotiated with Hawkins' management and the promotion started, as both Geffen and I tried to get media excited about the upcoming visit. The problem was that he was essentially unknown in Australia, so radio stations weren't interested. We did posters and persuaded a few sympathetic friends to write stories for the street music press, but Keith and I began to get nervous that, even with such a great deal, we might actually drop money. We were pretty good at that.

Hawkins arrived that September and did one morning television appearance – pretty much all that could be organised. He was a big man, quiet, humble and clearly surprised that there was interest in him touring Australia. The most distinguishable thing about him was a fingernail on his right hand that looked like it hadn't been cut in 50 years, and which he relied upon to pluck the strings on his battered guitar.

The first night at The Basement drew a respectable crowd, but a large percentage were record company and media types who, naturally, had been given free tickets. Bastards. But the show itself was breathtaking. Hawkins had a presence, a commanding softness that could build to a room-grabbing intensity. He really was something special, something I already knew as a fan.

We'd booked three nights at the venue, but in a move that would later haunt us, we decided to cut our potential losses and reduce it to a two-night stand. Then something totally bizarre happened. It was what every promoter dreams of: an unknown artist strikes a chord, word of mouth spreads, and things go crazy. Really crazy.

On the second night I was frightened to go down to The Basement, expecting it to be nearly empty. For the whole journey in to the city, the taxi driver and I chatted and, after I told him about Ted Hawkins, he was in my ear about touring Tony Joe White, which I thought was a good idea.

I was contemplating the driver's advice – and reflecting ruefully on how much more lucrative a TJW tour might be than Hawkins' – as the cab turned in to Reiby Place at Circular Quay. I was stunned. There were people *everywhere*. What the fuck was going on? Did I have the day wrong and someone majorly popular was booked to perform at The Basement? Maybe Elvis had been found alive and was doing a surprise show?

People were milling around excitedly as I fought my way through to the entrance. I arrived just as a guy plonked down $100 on the counter. He asked if that was enough to get in. Tickets were $25.

Inside it was mayhem, with over 500 people crammed into every corner and hovering around the entrance, hoping to get into a room licensed to hold maybe half that number. I believe that we still hold – to this day – the house record for the venue, now known as Mary's Underground. It was so crowded that I watched Hawkins' show on the video screen in the back bar as it was beamed through the in-house camera set-up – a single camera focused on the stage.

The tour was an instant success, for reasons the two promoters just couldn't work out. Suddenly, as promoters we were flavour of the month. Two days earlier, Keith and I had been having a quiet meal in Kings Cross, thinking the tour *might* work, and then it had all just gone crazy. Ted Hawkins mania had hit. I remember one of the owners of The Basement getting Keith and me in the back room of the venue after the second show and saying, 'Boys, tell us your dreams and we'll back them.'

The tour worked everywhere. The shows in Adelaide and Brisbane went well, and three nights in Melbourne, one more in Sydney and one in Perth all sold out. We recorded the final night of the three-night stand at the Continental Café in Melbourne for a possible live in Australia album.

Hawkins left the country having sold nearly 14,000 albums and was far more successful in Australia than anywhere else. He seemed thrilled about this – in a subdued and gentle kind of way. I hadn't felt as though

I'd gotten to know him that well. He kept to himself and did the shows. No partying. Certainly no drugs.

In the aftermath of the tour, Keith and I became obsessed with getting him back here as soon as possible, this time for something bigger, which we were certain would work. We booked a national tour for February the following year in theatres like the Enmore. We were close to confirming Jimmie Dale Gilmore as special guest, with Archie Roach as the opening performer. Pretty much everything was signed and sealed. The venues were booked, deposits paid, Hawkins' fee agreed, the advertising designed. There was just one thing we hadn't planned on – something for which there could be no contingency plan.

On 2 January, my phone rang. It was Hawkins' manager, Nancy Meyer. She was calling to tell me that Hawkins had died on New Year's Day after a stroke. He was 58.

I rang Keith in a state of shock.

'I guess the tour's off,' he said with remarkable understatement.

# 39

# LOS ANGELES, I'M YOURS

Over the years I've often reflected on a career hanging around artists – interviewing and writing about them. I always come to the conclusion that, for sheer off-the-dial intensity and surrealness, nothing will ever top the 48 hours I spent in Los Angeles a few days before Christmas, 1995.

As well as the tour promoting, as ever I'd been earning a crust via various other means. One of those means was the occasional overseas excursion funded by a record company – the latest, a trip to America courtesy of Sony.

The principal reason for the trek was to go to Philadelphia to see an early show on Bruce Springsteen's tour to promote his Woody Guthrie-esque album, *The Ghost Of Tom Joad*. I'd flown in to Philly and been met by a chauffeur driver for Sony, who took me to my hotel so I could deposit my bags.

From there, I was taken to the venue where another Sony-affiliated act, silverchair, were performing. There was no interview planned, but the label was keen for me to file a live review for my outlets in Australia.

I went back a while with silverchair – not that there was far to go back. In 1994, as editor of the fledgling Triple J publication *J Mag*, I'd gone to Martin Place in the centre of Sydney for a lunchtime perfor-mance by a band named Innocent Criminals, who were tipped to go on to big things. At the time they were managed by their mums, who I sat through the show with and interviewed for the piece.

The mums were enthusiastic, a little bit bemused but proud about what was happening with their kids. They were very much a team and joked about how they'd go on one tour and the dads would go on the next. It was all rather cute and endearing. The band were pretty good too. In all honesty they didn't blow my mind – but it was outdoors at lunchtime in Martin Place, which is a tough gig for anyone. I could sense they had something going for them which was potentially impressive. I just wasn't sure they'd get there.

By the time I arrived in Philadelphia, the young Australians I'd seen in Martin Place were in the midst of mini-Beatlemania, and their *Frogstomp* album was going nuts on the American charts. Tonight was one of the shows hastily put in place after the postponement of their spot on a Red Hot Chili Peppers tour. It was an all-ages gig (and unlicensed) at the comparatively small Trocadero, a venue that held 1800 fans.

Even backstage, there was only water or Coca-Cola on offer. Ah well, what can a thirsty Australian journalist do, except deal with it, dude. I pestered the band's friendly but firm manager, John Watson, for a band interview but he declined. I tried at least a dozen different tacks and he fielded each one with 'Not tonight.'

But I digress. Silverchair put on a pretty incredible performance – one that didn't seem anything out of the ordinary for the seemingly unaffected band members, who had larked and goofed around backstage like the teenagers they were. At the end of the night, the silverchair bus zoomed past me, with hundreds of kids screaming and chasing it, amid general mayhem. I wandered the streets of Philly looking for a cab.

The following day was 'Bruce Day'. I wandered about beneath sleet and rain with 'Streets Of Philadelphia' in my head, before heading to an early evening/pre-show gathering of Springsteen nutters, who I'd encountered via an internet news group. There was a mass of them, maybe 100 obsessives who'd converged from all over America, and in some cases far-flung places around the globe.

There were trivia quizzes and lots of bonding and the usual conversations you'd expect at these gatherings: 'Is this your first show on the tour?' 'Do you have tickets for New York?' 'How popular is Bruce in Australia?' I got some applause and an honorary award for being the person who'd travelled the furthest to be there, easily beating out a lightweight who'd flown in from Germany.

The Springsteen show was good. Probably great, but I guess I wasn't in the mood for acoustic Bruce, and it did seem to go on for a long time. Also, I was seated in the front row of the first tier of the theatre, which did nothing for my fear of heights. I was glad when it was over.

No interviews this night. I'd get to chat with Springsteen a few nights later in New York at a gathering after the show in that city. It was a low-key affair with the usual drinks and nibblies. Maybe there were some heavy-hitters there, but I didn't recognise any of them. Bruce and his wife, Patti Scialfa, held court in a cordoned-off area, but with no real security to keep the riff-raff like me away. It wasn't the sort of gathering where Bruce was likely to be mobbed. New York was too cool for that.

As I was leaving the party, I remembered a young woman who had written to me a year or two earlier at one of the magazines I wrote for. Her name was Cheryl, and she lived in regional Victoria. She was wheelchair-bound after an appendix operation gone wrong, and she lived for Springsteen. Adored him. Cheryl and I never spoke, just emailed, but I was the closest person she knew to God, because I'd actually met God.

Anyway, I dashed back into the party and past security. I interrupted Springsteen, who, having moved away from his secure area, was mid-conversation with a group of people as he did the rounds. I'd said hello to him earlier in the evening, but I'm pretty sure he had no recollection of our discussion about 'Friday On My Mind' in Paris a decade and a half earlier – and nor did I expect him to.

In our second exchange of the evening, I told him a garbled story about this young woman in Australia and asked him to sign a scrap of paper I'd located in a pocket. He wrote, 'To Cheryl – Happy Christmas – Bruce Springsteen.' Mission accomplished, I thought, as I said goodbye and vanished into the night.

I managed to get it to Cheryl's parents to give to her on Christmas Day. She wrote to me soon afterwards saying that *nothing* else mattered that Christmas. It was, and remains, a wonderful feeling to have done that, given what it meant to her.

A few days later, I interviewed one of my favourite American crime writers, Lawrence Block, at the White Horse Tavern in Greenwich Village. This was the author of some of my favourite crime fiction novels ever, particularly the ones featuring weather-beaten private detective Matthew Scudder.

The other central figure in these novels is New York. I'd learnt so much about the different areas of the city from Block's writing, so to hang out with him in one of NYC's most legendary bars – where Dylan Thomas drank his last whiskys in November 1953 – was a big deal.

I then flew to Toronto to see and talk to Oasis. I interviewed Noel Gallagher around soundcheck, as he and the band hung out a few hours before showtime. We were ushered into a small room away from the cacophony of pre-show PA and equipment testing. Noel was thoroughly entertaining and opinionated, and scurrilous in his comments about his brother Liam and just about anyone else I mentioned. I wasn't really into Oasis, but it all made for good fodder for newspaper stories I'd later write.

It was snowing as I got back to the hotel. I went to the restaurant on the top floor to get some dinner and stare out the window at the lights of Toronto. It was freezing outside and I was lulled by some good food, with every mouthful seeming to say, 'Stay here, stay here.' I had a glass of red, a second, a third. Of course, I had a ticket for the Oasis show and was no doubt expected by the record company to attend. Snow was bucketing down. Fuck this, I thought. I didn't go.

With a red-wine-induced blinder of a headache, I caught a crazily early taxi to the airport. It was 7 am, miserable, almost pitch-black. I asked the cab driver when the sun would come up. 'It won't, sir – it'll be like this all day.'

The plane was delayed by storms. After everyone had boarded. Note to self – *never* get stuck on a plane on the tarmac for four to five hours, with a hangover, and without access to alcohol. It was hell. And then some.

Everyone had a theory about when we'd take off. As the hours went by, strangers started talking to each other. The guy behind me muttered loudly about how they'd have no choice but to disembark us soon. Everyone was sharing their stories of where they were meant to be, and why this was a disaster.

Finally, the wings were de-iced, which, if you've never seen it, was a weird-arse thing to observe. Trucks drove out to the plane and shot orange liquid onto the wings.

'Now they have 25 minutes to get into the air, otherwise they ice up again,' a booming-voiced, middle-aged passenger behind me said – like he knew about this shit. After 30 minutes, I was checking for more ice.

I was getting even more nervous than I usually was in planes and the hangover was not helping one bit. I had no idea if this guy knew what he was talking about or not, but it was playing havoc with my psyche. 'If the plane takes off now, are we all going to die?' I wondered. I seriously did think about this as an outcome.

I decided I needed to use the onboard phone. In big planes in those days, believe it or not, in every seat there was a phone in the panel below the tray table in front of you. I spent a fortune calling Sony in Los Angeles, no doubt sounding like an arrogant and pretentious Aussie, as I yelled, 'Look, I'm not going to get there for lunch with Neil Diamond! Can you move it till the next day?'

*Eventually*, we took off. The wings stayed on. The plane landed in LA. I went straight to the Sofitel Hotel, across the road from the massive shopping emporium, the Beverly Center. This would be home base as my breakneck 48 hours in LA were about to commence.

They began with me heading to the famous Chateau Marmont. It was a home away from home to movie and music-world hipsters, and the scene in the 1970s of legendary, over-the-top, indulgent and decadent parties, involving the likes of Led Zeppelin. I was going there for something a bit less decadent – breakfast with Iggy Pop.

I'd interviewed Iggy a few times and, as I walked into his room, I knew it was OK to start the interaction with: 'Iggy, you look like shit.'

Which I did, because he did. He laughed. The night before, he'd been at a party for Lemmy from Motorhead's 50th birthday. That explained everything.

Iggy always gives good interview. He's smart, as funny as all get out, and he doesn't shut up. It's always an easy and enjoyable conversation. Did he eat? Did I eat? I honestly can't remember, because with Iggy it's nonstop verbiage and gags. You can ask him how the weather is and sit back for 45 minutes, as that's the only jumping-off point he needs to discourse on whatever subjects are on his mind. It's a conversational roller-coaster – with similar intensity to his gigs – so mere details are quickly forgotten. I know I had a ball and loved every second in his company.

From there I caught a cab to Neil Diamond's studio and office. They were situated in a faceless building around the corner from the Beverly Center. There were no signs on the door to identify its owner, or huge image from *Hot August Night* in the window. All the blinds seemed to be permanently pulled. It was the sort of building you could walk past for 20 years without realising that it housed Diamond's multi-million-dollar empire and the state-of-the-art studio where he'd recorded countless albums.

Diamond himself apparently lived within walking distance so he could wander into his studio day or night to tinker away on songs. The studio was never hired out to other groups or musicians which was the way Diamond liked it. He never knew when the inspiration to write another 'Solitary Man', 'Kentucky Woman', 'I'm A Believer' or 'Red Red Wine' was going to occur.

Inside the building it was a veritable hive of activity as publicists, assistants and technical maintenance staff went about their business of keeping the Diamond machine oiled whilst his two dogs meandered from office to office. The walls were covered floor-to-ceiling with memorabilia.

I admired Diamond as a Brill Building songwriter and had spent many hours listening to *Hot August Night*. But I wasn't reverential. This wasn't Leonard Cohen, Joni Mitchell or Bob Dylan – all of whom I'd met in person, interviewed and been in total awe of.

Diamond had a new album out. That didn't overly excite me. What excited me even less was that, before I was introduced to Diamond, I was told I needed to sit in the studio and listen to the album. Not once. Not twice. But three times. I had a fix on this album after a few minutes of the *first* play through, so this was tantamount to extreme torture.

I still can't remember a song on it. It seemed bland, uninspiring and frankly dull. And I was also still on an Iggy Pop post-chat high, so this was just a little bit of a comedown. Uncle Google tells me it must have been *Tennessee Moon*, which isn't a bad album and one I should have been into more. But I wasn't feeling it. And I felt it less with each listen. I just wanted to talk to its famous creator.

Fortunately, Diamond himself was thoroughly affable and fun to chat with. I liked him a lot. Sitting in a room in his office, we ate meatball and noodle soup. We talked a lot about his love for motor-cycles (he had two Harley-Davidsons in his office) and how, on his last Australian tour, he and some of his buddies from his band and crew had hired Harleys and taken a trip to Mount Victoria in the Blue Mountains and stopped at the Hydro Majestic hotel.

'It's a very strange place,' Diamond said. 'It reminded me of the hotel Stanley Kubrick used in *The Shining* – some ancient relic that had a lot of ghosts in it.'

We also talked about Frank Sinatra, songwriting, Diamond's love of poker and – of course – that bloody new album. After the earlier tedium of sitting alone in the studio listening to *Tennessee Moon*, it ended up being a most enjoyable hour.

OK – Iggy and Neil done. I then headed back to the hotel. There, I got a message that an invitation to hang out with Cypress Hill was on the cards. With their notorious consumption of pot, anything could have happened if that had gone ahead. Maybe it was for the best that it ended up falling through.

Instead, I had a chat on the phone with Jeff Buckley. I have to admit I dug his dad more. And I was soooo tired of *that* version of 'Hallelujah' (OK, it's pretty good). It was a fine, but perfunctory chat. Phone inter-views are like that. It's hard to establish a rapport. But I remember his soft voice and friendly, unpretentious tone, and his gentle, thoughtful answers to my questions.

Then I went for a walk, returning to find a series of messages saying that Geffen Records had managed to secure an interview with Brian Wilson. Could I be at his home in . . . 45 minutes? I didn't drive. And I had no idea where the Wilson residence was. Everything in LA seemed a long way away. How long would it take me to get there? How much would it cost?

I raced up to my room, grabbed my cassette recorder and notebook, raced back downstairs and sprinted out of the lobby. There, I frantically hailed a cab (never the easiest thing to get in Los Angeles), spluttering Brian's address to the driver between half-choked gulps of breath. Thirty-five minutes.

This was a '*Fuck me*' moment of some magnitude. Brian Wilson! I hoped we were going in the right direction. Were we going in the right direction? Half an hour to go. There was Iggy and Neil and Jeff – but this was Brian Wilson, creator of some of my favourite music in, like, forever. The *Pet Sounds* guy. Should we run these lights? Run these lights! Twenty minutes to go . . .

Eventually, we drove through the entrance of a gated community and I knocked at the door of a faux mansion – which I *really* hoped was the right address, as the taxi had already driven off. Yes, it was the right address. I was ushered by an assistant into the house. Glancing around the opulent surroundings, it was impossible to ignore the fact that each visible room had at least one, if not two or more, floor-to-ceiling, fully decorated Christmas trees. (Admittedly, the festive season wasn't far away.)

The assistant directed me into a massive room that was sparsely furnished (if you ignored the white grand piano dominating the space). There, yes, Brian Wilson was sitting in a big armchair, cuddling a large pillow. We were introduced. He told me to sit down.

He didn't, however, point to where I should sit. He also didn't look around and express surprise that there was no other chair in sight. And he certainly didn't call for an assistant to actually bring a chair in. So I sat on the floor, literally at the feet of the master.

I slumped down on a cushion in front of Brian, trying to get as comfortable as possible, and not look surprised or thrown by the fact that he hadn't offered me a seat. You know, trying to act like I was used to doing interviews sitting on the floor, whilst the subject sat in an extremely comfortable-looking armchair clutching an oversized pillow. Wasn't this how interviews always happened?

And how close to get to Wilson? He wasn't speaking loudly, so I wanted my cassette recorder to pick up his voice. I didn't want to crowd in on his space, though, so I edged as close as seemed comfortable for both of us.

Brian wasn't an easy interview subject. Clearly damaged. The answers were short. He seemingly believed in only using three words if two wouldn't do. And every six or seven minutes, he'd stop mid-sentence and stare at the ceiling for 30 seconds or so, before regaining his concentration and asking me to remind him what we were talking about.

Wilson talked about getting guest vocalists on an upcoming Beach Boys album of country music songs. 'We're going to try and get Dolly Parton, who I adore. I think Dolly is one of the greatest . . . of course, very big breasts . . . very alluring . . . she's a very alluring girl. And maybe we'll get Julio Iglesias.'

'What about George Jones?' I ventured.

'Who . . . maybe . . . is he a country singer?'

Informed that 'The Possum' was, in fact, probably the greatest living country singer on the planet, Wilson replied, 'Oh yeah, right, right . . . and what's that guy's name who was "Entertainer Of The Year" for two years . . . Garth Brooks? We're going to try and get him too. Can you imagine us with all those country people? *Can you imagine it?* It's almost impossible to understand. I think it'll be wonderful.'

At one point I asked him what songs the Beach Boys were going to include on this new album, and he said it would include a version of Creedence Clearwater Revival's 'Proud Mary'.

'I'll show you,' he told me, getting out of the chair and walking over to the giant white grand piano that dominated the room.

He motioned for me to sit next to him and told me to put my tape recorder on the piano. 'If this ever gets out, I'll know where it came from,' he said, sounding surprisingly serious but trying to make it seem like a joke.

He then sang and played the song. OK, OK, I was sitting next to Brian Wilson in his home in Los Angeles, whilst he performed 'Proud Mary'. It was very, very surreal.

Later, we were chatting more, me still at his feet, and he asked if I'd like a drink. At this stage I would have killed several people for a cold beer, so I said yes.

'Get this guy a diet cherry cola!' he bellowed to an assistant.

So now Brian Wilson and I were both sitting, talking and drinking diet cherry cola. The stuff was hideous.

Throughout the conversation, there were occasional glimpses that things were still not exactly wired up correctly in Wilson's head. At one point he asked me if I smoked cigarettes. Telling him I did and that I had a packet in my bag if he'd like one, he looked furtively around to the other rooms with the panicked look of a 12-year-old caught with their first *Playboy*.

'I'd really like one,' he whispered. 'But I'd better . . . I'd better not . . . I've given up.'

I asked if it was true that he burnt the tapes to the legendary, much-mythologised and, at the time, unreleased album, *Smile*. At this suggestion, Wilson became emotional and almost whispered, 'I wish I had,' before getting up and telling me he couldn't talk anymore now and walking out of the room.

After this, Wilson's assistant came and showed me to another room and talked with Wilson's wife, Melinda, who was sitting there. She was playing me tapes of her husband's demos of new songs (but not offering to let me record them on my cassette machine), when suddenly The Ronettes' 'Be My Baby' thundered through the house.

It was, Melinda explained, Wilson's favourite song, which he listened to almost constantly. He was playing it on a jukebox in what felt like the next room. I suggested to Melinda that she must get sick of hearing it, and she told me it was OK tonight, because so far he was only playing it on one jukebox. Often, she said, Brian would have it playing simultaneously from three or four different sources in the house, all just a little out of sync with each other.

When Brian joined us in the room, to make conversation I remarked that I'd never seen so many Christmas trees in one home before. He looked wistfully at his wife and said softly, 'We should put another one up in the bedroom tonight.'

After about two hours, a large percentage of it with the very friendly and talkative Melinda chatting and listening to music, I took my leave. As I headed back to the hotel, I reflected upon the fact that I'd just sat on a piano stool next to Brian Wilson. I was struggling to take it all in. Had that actually happened, or had I just gone to interview Cypress Hill and smoked some *really* strong pot?

As the LA action continued, the next day I had an interview with Larry Flynt, the wheelchair-bound publisher of *Hustler* magazine. Of course, I knew about *Hustler*, but until the *J Mag* publisher had suggested I try for an interview, I had absolutely no idea who was behind the magazine; no idea about Flynt being paralysed from the waist down after an assassination attempt in 1978; and no idea that there was a film on the way about his life (which was maybe why he agreed to do the interview). *The People vs. Larry Flynt* would appear just days later, with Woody Harrelson playing Flynt and Courtney Love his late wife, Althea.

Friends in Los Angeles had informed me that Flynt was notorious for being highly selective about what interviews he granted. So, when I cold-called his office I was completely taken aback when I was told that Flynt would see me. The reaction of my friends was universal. Their jaws dropped, followed by: 'You're going to meet Larry Flynt?!'

So the morning after my chat with Brian Wilson – and the day of my return to Australia – I headed down to the offices of Flynt Publications, a 10-storey building on Wilshire Boulevard in Beverly Hills. I took the lift to the top of the building, where, immediately, any preconceptions about what the offices of a magazine like *Hustler* might look like were thrown out the window. This was opulent in the extreme, a circular building full of antiques, oil paintings and, in particular, Tiffany lamps, which I'd read were an obsession of Flynt's. That was weird. Then things became just a little other-worldly.

I was sitting on a luxurious couch, taking in the activities of the office. Suddenly, an extremely attractive woman who I guessed to be in her early 20s appeared in the waiting area. She was wearing a white dress. A very (very) short one. She was surrounded by three guys who fitted my stereotypical image of LA photographers. They had a studied cool, were understatedly well dressed, well tanned and, well, smooth, confident and exuding a slight arrogance.

Flynt's staff started emerging from offices and from behind desks and began congratulating her. There were at least five minutes of 'well done's and 'great's and 'you must be so pleased's.

Bemused, I needed to find out what all the fuss was about. What had she done? Why the excitement? I lifted myself off the couch and walked to the reception desk to ask.

'Oh, honey, she's this month's "Beaver Hunt" winner,' Flynt's secretary told me, with a look that suggested she thought I'd just arrived from Mars. How could I not know why the woman in the white dress was there?

One of the photographers walked over and asked who I was. I explained that I was a journalist from Australia and about to interview Mr Flynt. Everyone seemed to call him Mr Flynt.

'That figures,' he said. 'You look a bit different from the white trash that usually hangs around here.' He delivered those lines with a grin, before sauntering back to the star of the afternoon.

The centre of all the attention had been selected from presumably hundreds – maybe thousands – of women who sent explicit polaroids of themselves to the magazine each month for the Beaver Hunt pages. It was a good lurk – four or five pages of photos each issue, ranging from the good to the bad, that cost not one cent.

The best 'beaver' won $US5000, a *Hustler* travel bag (gee!) and the opportunity to do a real spread for the magazine. Plus, they got to meet Mr Flynt, who would personally present them with the cheque and the travel bag.

Speaking of which, after I'd been waiting on the couch for 45 minutes, I finally got that opportunity myself (minus the spread, the cheque and the travel bag). His secretary directed me into an office that was expensively furnished and absolutely massive. The MCG was bigger, but only just.

Flynt himself looked very Californian. Very monied. And almost plastic. It was as if he was cleaned and buffed every day, before being wheeled into the office. He was sitting confidently and with a real air of power and influence in an 18-carat gold wheelchair, his desk built high enough that it wasn't visible to anyone else in the office. As for me, I'd been seated so far away from Flynt that a pair of binoculars and a loudhailer wouldn't have gone astray.

But while he oozed money and power, he appeared to be lacking in anything approaching an engaging personality. It was hard to imagine him laughing – and I certainly couldn't get one out of him.

Speaking in a muted tone – another legacy of the bullet wound that had gone through his throat and severed his spinal column – he addressed the issue of whether *Hustler* was pornographic or not: 'One man's art is another man's pornography . . . We have a law in this country which says if you publish something it must have socially redeeming value. I feel that sex within itself is socially redeeming.'

As I noticed that there was nothing sexual on display – with the exception of a sculpted replica of a man and a woman having sex placed on a sideboard behind Flynt's desk – he explained what lay ahead for the lucky Beaver Hunt winner. 'She'll be in the magazine. There's a bonus of $5000, which is in addition to her original fee for posing. My competitors, they pay almost 20 times that.'

Overall, Flynt seemed happy enough to answer my questions – even questions I didn't ask. Unbidden, he explained, 'The thing is that I don't push my own preferences in the magazine. With Mr Hefner, who publishes *Playboy*, it's obvious that he likes blondes with big boobs. I really like petite brunettes myself, but I always go out of my way to keep my own preferences out of the magazine.'

The interview was a performance piece where he seemed unlikely to deviate from an internal script, conducted for an audience of two – me and one of his assistants, who sat at the side of the room the entire time.

We talked about censorship, what could and couldn't be shown photographically in magazines, the readership of Hustler (he estimated 20–25 per cent were women) and the upcoming film about his life and relationship with fourth wife Althea.

Another thing I hadn't realised until *J Mag* asked me to interview Flynt was that, aside from *Hustler*, Flynt Publications produced magazines devoted to everything from knives (*Fighting Knives*) to boating (*Ski Boat*), from tattoos (*Skin & Ink*) to computers (*Ultimate Gamer* and *PC Laptop*, among others). And up in Sunset Boulevard, there was a Hustler shop which sold sex toys, DVDs, clothing, books, and other bits and pieces – plus it had a café. Quite an empire.

At the end of the interview, I walked the two or three miles across Flynt's office to the exit. And that was that. As I was about to head to the elevator, his secretary handed me about 25 copies of *Hustler*.

'Research for your story,' she smiled. What, no copies of *Fighting Knives* or *Ski Boat*?

I didn't know what to think about Flynt. He was clearly smart, but very guarded. He was a vigorous campaigner against censorship. Just because it was good for his business, or was there more at play? I wasn't sure.

I made it to the airport later that day, buzzing from the assault on the senses from the previous 48 hours: courtesy of Iggy Pop, Neil Diamond, Jeff Buckley, Brian Wilson and Larry Flynt (and nearly Cypress Hill). It had been exhausting, but thrilling.

And, on returning to Australia, it was inevitable that I'd be pulled over for a baggage check. There were some grins and 'Yeah, right's when I explained that the magazines in my suitcases were . . . research material.

# 40
# DON'T STOP 'TIL YOU GET ENOUGH

**K**eith and I continued to do tours through to the mid-1990s. We brought Guy Clark back to Australia, this time with his son Travis. We figured that the word of mouth from his first visit would be such that the audiences would be significantly greater the second time around.

We were wrong. The attendances were pretty much the same. The new fans replaced those who had grown older and didn't go to live shows anymore – or simply thought that seeing Clark once was enough.

In 1995, at the end of that tour I remember being backstage at The Basement after three magnificent nights. As some friends and I went to leave, Clark turned to them and said, 'Take good care of Stuart – he's fragile at the best of times.' The drawl on 'fragile' was magnificent. And heck, this was a tour where Guy and I didn't do drugs, as I'd quit the powders. OK, maybe we had one or two small lines, for old times' sake.

Keith and I were running out of ideas. We talked about heaps of possibilities before realising the chances of them making money were at best slim. And there was an increasing amount of competition. It seemed as if new promoters were emerging every second day – many of them with more financial resources than we had.

And maybe we were getting just a little tired and worn out by the stress. I was feeling increasingly fragile as maybe Guy had seen something in my demeanour. The constant worry about money was starting to take its toll – and my drinking wasn't helping.

But like old prize fighters, Keith and I kept climbing back into the ring. One more tour. Just one more. And then, OK, maybe just this one.

Tours by guitar legends Dick Dale and Link Wray in 1995 and 1996 were pretty much the end for me and Keith. Both came close to breaking even – notice I use the word 'close' – but the budgets were creeping up.

Also, we fell for a bunch of the same old ruses used by artists. Both Dick and Link were accompanied by their bands and partners. In the case of Dick, who was undergoing a career renaissance thanks to the inclusion of his song 'Misirlou' on the soundtrack to Quentin Tarantino's *Pulp Fiction*, we were sold on his romantic partner being his manager. Once they landed in Australia, we realised she did as much managing as I did space travel.

Dale was demanding and egotistical. He insisted that we pay for him to freight his vintage Fender amplifiers to Australia, and it seemed as if every time we woke up there was a new request that was going to cost us money.

When Dick arrived in Australia, one of his merchandise items was a badge. The Grateful Dead always described their fans as Deadheads. Dale handed out a badge that said 'I'm a Dickhead'. I wasn't sure if he was referring to himself or what he thought of his fans.

His shows were great, and oh so loud, and the attendances were larger than we were used to. But so were the overheads. So, in the end we broke even, or close to it. We were usually *close* to breaking even.

Link was accompanied by his wife, Olive, who proceeded to drive everyone completely crazy – including, it seemed, Link – with her demands and moods. It's a terrible thing to say, but when we received news that her mother had died and she had to return to Europe, there was a collective sigh of relief from everyone involved. That seemed to include Link, who suddenly appeared to be enjoying the tour more, once Olive was on a plane home.

Link was a lovely man, accompanied by a much younger band of German musicians, who looked and sounded like they'd grown up on a steady diet of The Ramones and other punk bands. If Dick Dale was loud, Link was *much fucking louder*. Ear-splittingly louder.

Dressed head to toe in black leather, he looked wonderful and performed superbly. It was only when we were backstage and he peeled off the leather, and I looked at his skin, that I realised he was 67 years of age. Not exactly old, but showing all the signs of a man who'd lived, played and worked hard.

As far as tour promoting was concerned, that was the end. After Link departed, it wasn't as though Keith and I sat down and decided no more music tours. We just drifted into our own worlds. We'd had a great run and some incredible experiences that I wouldn't trade for anything. But I was beginning to realise that my aspirations of becoming one of Australia's most successful concert promoters were a mere dream.

Keith then did a few low-key tours that didn't really require a partner. I dealt with a variety of upheavals in my life and tried to keep my soul and psyche together. And the stress of promoting tours and risking so much money didn't have a part to play in that.

# 41

# I WANNA DIE IN LOS ANGELES

I'd just about extricated myself from the tour-promoting world, but I still wasn't completely done. I had one more author tour in mind, with the one guy who fitted my two requirements (as you might recall, I needed to love their books, and they needed to be able to draw an audience across Australia). That writer was the self-styled Demon Dog of American Crime Fiction, James Ellroy.

I considered Ellroy to be the only writer to have done anything new with the genre since the heyday of Ross Macdonald and Raymond Chandler in the 1940s and 50s. Plus, I was aware that Ellroy was a total publicity junkie. And via friends overseas, I'd become aware that he did performances that were much more than just him reading from his books. These were events.

As soon as I read that he'd done an American tour with aging piano accordion player Dick Contino, on whose story he'd based the novella *Dick Contino's Blues*, I wanted to bring him to Australia; Contino too, as I loved the idea of him playing an accordion set before Ellroy read. Keith Glass and I worked together on what became a tour of massive and mythic proportions.

I made initial contact with Ellroy through his publisher, Random House. The author was apparently keen to come, but unfortunately Contino couldn't make it. I thought that his mate Edward Bunker, a criminal, crime writer and 'Mr Blue' in *Reservoir Dogs*, would be another perfect choice to tour with Ellroy – but he was tied up with film commitments in France. So Ellroy would make the trip alone.

I was in America around that time and offered to visit Ellroy at his home in Kansas. 'Stuart,' he responded via fax, 'there is never a reason to visit Kansas – unless you are flying over it to get to somewhere else.'

Random House agreed to pay for Ellroy's airfare to Australia (good news) and his accommodation (even better), on the assumption that he'd be available for a series of bookshop signing sessions. Keith and I would pay Ellroy for his appearances.

This was another of those tours – hello, Harry Dean Stanton – where it appeared impossible not to rake in the loot. This was the one that was going to dig me and Glass out of a financial hole. This was our all-or-nothing bet on the last race at Flemington, after a tip that our horse was a dead cert. How many of those do you hear about? And how many of them come true?

But we were convinced. We booked a run of dates in 1996 in large-ish venues with an average seated capacity of 600, starting in Brisbane and finishing up during Writers Week in Adelaide. Soon, though, things became complicated. Ellroy wanted to price tickets so that a copy of his current book, *American Tabloid*, was included. Not such a bad idea except, I argued, anyone who wanted to see him do a performance had already bought a copy.

'Well, then they've got a copy to give to a friend,' he countered. 'And I sign every copy at the show.'

Of course, Ellroy had his eye on the bottom line. Each book added another $3 or $4 to what he would eventually receive from this caper, given what I imagined his royalty rate was. He wouldn't get it straight up – but he would get it.

When it came to the promise of signing every book at the appearances, I did the maths and worked out that if he said hello to each person at a show, which I expected would sometimes be up to 600 people, at a book a minute he'd be signing for 10 hours.

'I do at least 30 a minute,' Ellroy replied. Which he did – the signature usually being a slash and the initials 'JE'. Some lucky people got 'Kill – JE'.

Then Ellroy announced that he wanted to perform one or two songs/raps with a band. We decided to take a Western Australian outfit called The Jackson Code, who were Ellroy fans, on the road with us. Costs were going up. Next came the request that we screen a BBC documentary about Ellroy, *White Jazz*, during the show. I had to negotiate with the BBC over rights, get the film sent to Australia (these were the days when film was actually, literally, film in cannisters), and organise projectors and screens for each performance in venues that didn't have such stuff at their fingertips. Costs kept going up. And some venues, such as The Metro in Sydney, needed to be changed to seated mode, instead of the usual standing one. More costs. And reduced capacity.

Ellroy arrived in Sydney and was all swagger and bluster. He was tall and robust, with glasses and a receding hairline. As I dropped him at his hotel, I asked him what he was going to do when he went to his room. 'Watch some hardcore pornography,' he said, 'and work out for a few hours.' It was only when I accidentally overheard him talking gently to his wife back in Kansas that I realised most of the persona was show.

Away from the glare of performances and interviews, Ellroy was comparatively quiet and serious and totally besotted with his wife, who he constantly phoned. He didn't drink, smoke or take drugs, had a phenomenal intellect and was consummately professional.

I organised for him to be a guest presenter at the inaugural Ned Kelly Awards, which were held upstairs at Berkelouw Books in Paddington. The recipient of the first Lifetime Achievement Award, to be presented by Ellroy, was going to Jon Cleary. In a slightly whispered tone, the Australian literary legend said he couldn't stand Ellroy's bravado and carry on. As I mentioned earlier, the American visitor didn't endear himself to many of the conservative attendees by getting on all fours and walking around the crowd barking. The Demon Dog – get it?

As for Ellroy's own shows, they turned into epic productions. We'd screen the documentary, then, in nightclub-crooner style, Ellroy would come out and sing songs about murder, slashing people with knives, and all manner of seemingly semi-spontaneous lyrics. After that, he'd talk to the audience before reading from *American Tabloid*. Next was an intermission, then a short set from The Jackson Code, a lengthy question-and-answer session with Ellroy, and another song from the band – all before the book signing. The actual show often ran for more than four hours.

And when Ellroy was on, he was *on*. He was unstoppable. One evening we'd done a book signing at Ariel Books in Paddington. The shop had ordered in hundreds of books and Ellroy did a signing session before we had to leave. He signed a *lot* of copies, but there were still many boxes unsigned. For the next few days, he kept bugging me about going to the shop to sign the remaining books. I asked why he was so intent on doing this and he explained that, once they were signed, it was impossible for the shop to return them, because they were considered damaged stock. So, every book he signed clicked over his royalties, regardless of whether anyone bought it or not.

Media interest in Ellroy was fanatical. I fielded request after request for interviews. It didn't hurt that the New South Wales Premier Bob Carr was a self-confessed Ellroy tragic. Ellroy and I were even invited to dinner at the Premier's residence in Maroubra, to which Ellroy responded, 'Never heard of the guy – you tell me if I should go or not.' I advised him that if the premier of the state invited you to dinner, it wasn't a bad thing to accept.

At the dinner were author Frank Moorhouse, bookseller Nicholas Pounder, Carr's wife Helena and a couple of Carr staffers. Whilst Helena busied herself in the kitchen preparing the meal, I wandered in to say hello and thank her for having us in her home, as the fawning over Ellroy by the otherwise male dinner companions was getting to me.

Before dinner, Carr insisted that everyone sit and watch portions of the television series *Blue Murder*. At the time, it was banned in New South Wales. The show dramatised the corruption within the New South Wales police force and, in particular, the relationship between criminal Neddy Smith and Detective Roger Rogerson. Ellroy would have had no idea who these people were and seemed bored. It may have been a big deal for the Premier to have a copy, but basically Ellroy couldn't have cared less.

Dinner over, Carr brought out his collection of Ellroy first editions from a glass-fronted bookcase and had them all signed. Before we arrived, I'd told Ellroy that he should kick me under the table when he was ready to leave. Soon after he'd signed the books, Ellroy almost broke my ankle with a swift, well-timed thump. The author and the Premier posed for photos on the stairway of the house and we were soon in a taxi heading to Kings Cross for our next engagement, a meeting with a photographer and journalist from *Rolling Stone*.

A couple of nights later, the Premier and his wife were prominently seated at the first performance in Sydney at the Metro when Ellroy started making gags about Carr being 'the bagman for the NSW government'. It was in good (albeit slightly malicious) humour. Carr loved it.

The tour started relatively smoothly, despite the show's length. The crowd was small in Brisbane and the venue not totally suitable, but that gig at the Metro was almost a sell-out.

Meanwhile, Ellroy was also hanging out with Russell Crowe, who was preparing for his role in the film version of Ellroy's book *L.A. Confidential*. It was typical of Ellroy's approach that when he wasn't doing stuff for me, he was immersing himself in another project. He was excited about the film and keen to spend time with Crowe, talking about the characters, their vernacular and so forth.

It was in Melbourne that we came unstuck: through no fault of our own, mind you. We had a sold-out show the first night at the National Theatre in St Kilda – the audience including Guy Pearce, who was also preparing for his role in *L.A. Confidential* – but the second night (the bring-it-home, bring-us-the-money night, in theory) coincided with a federal election. I blame Paul Keating.

A few weeks earlier, when the Prime Minister decided to go to the polls, we'd already confirmed all the Ellroy dates and flights. On the Saturday night, the theatre was virtually empty, as were the streets of St Kilda. Everyone was at election night parties or at home watching the results on television.

It's amazing how things can come out of the blue to mess with you. The previous year, when we'd announced dates by Dick Dale, Keith called me. He cut straight to the point: 'We're fucked.' I asked why and he said that Chris Isaak – super-popular at the time – had announced a tour, and not only was he playing just down the road from where we had Dick Dale performing in Melbourne (on the same night), it looked like that situation would be mirrored around the country. My only response was, 'What if we delay Dick coming on, so people can come from Isaak to our show?' That was never going to work.

Attendance-wise, Adelaide was also slow, because Ellroy was doing free appearances at Writers' Week. Canberra was a disaster. Then, a final show in Sydney didn't work well. Again, somehow we'd lost money on what had seemed a no-brainer. And we'd lost money when someone else was paying the international airfares and the hotel bills for the talent.

Where had we gone wrong? Aside from the election, which we obviously had no control over, when Keith and I reflected on it afterwards we decided we'd let Ellroy do far too many free bookshop appearances. They'd eroded the attraction of the paid shows, because, for many people, meeting him and getting their books signed was all they wanted. Also, perhaps the concept of a music/film/reading performance by a writer was a little beyond what many people could comprehend. Or maybe Ellroy just wasn't as big a drawcard as we'd thought.

It was depressing. During the tour, I'd been physically and mentally exhausted. I was drinking far too heavily, and not eating or sleeping properly. In Adelaide, it had caught up with me. I had to send Ellroy to Sydney alone to be met by Keith, while I went home to Blackheath for a few days to recuperate.

Every tour had its stresses – that's the nature of the caper – but by this stage it was really starting to have an impact. I craved a bit of financial stability and every time it had seemed within reach with a tour, it had slipped away. And these tours took up a lot of time and energy – which could have been spent on more consistently paying and less precarious (but not as potentially lucrative) work in journalism.

I'd never handled stress all that well. I'd usually think I could counter it by drinking, which always seemed to result in me not eating as well as I could, and falling into a spiral. Not that I realised it at the time.

I was disillusioned now about the whole thing. To watch another tour that I'd thought would be a sure-fire money maker fall in a financial heap knocked me for six. Friends were telling me how great it was that I was bringing these people to Australia, but it was beginning to dawn on me that the audiences in this country were just too small to make these tours viable.

The financial stress certainly didn't make my domestic life easier. Sitting in a hotel room in the middle of a tour that was losing money, with Julie on the phone telling me she'd just had to borrow $20 from a neighbour, was downright horrible. I'd had some astonishing experiences, ones that most people didn't get to have, but I was concerned that, the way things were going, I might be adding 'homeless' and 'bankrupt' to that list.

A few months later, Keith reflected on the tours we'd done. He was more upbeat about it than I felt at the time. In retrospect, though, I can agree with him.

'The thing that sticks in my mind is the memory of the crowd stretching around the block for Ted Hawkins. That's a far stronger image for me than a big empty room for Ellroy. It's the fact that you know you've lost money because you can't fit all those people into a show that hurts the most. If you've done your best and no-one turns up, it's bad, but it's worse if people want to give you their money and you can't get them in.

'Ellroy was a big disaster. That was something that on paper couldn't lose money – and yet we managed to lose five grand. That's when you know it's time to get out of the business, when it's starting to slip away from you.'

Although we kept coming up with ideas for money-making tours, after Ellroy the idea of international promoting had lost its allure. There were a couple of very low-key shows we promoted, but by artists who were already in the country or prepared to pay their own expenses. However, I was only peripherally involved with those shows, by the likes of American singer-songwriters Chris Smither, Tom Russell and Dave Alvin.

Occasionally, Keith and I would have a conversation about whether life would have been different if Ted Hawkins had lived and we'd made a huge swag of money on his second tour. Keith was adamant it would only have delayed the inevitable.

'We would still have managed to blow it. We would have brought out somebody incredibly stupid. We were thinking of enough stupid people as it was.'

There was just one more tour for me – about a year later. I had a friend, Andrew Bowles, who had a bit of money from a successful lighting business he ran with his wife, Wendy. He was keen to experience the vicarious thrills of concert promoting, so I organised a series of shows for Scottish folk singer Dick Gaughan. He was someone I'd admired since Stefan Markovitch had sold me his *No More Forever* album in Launceston in the early 1970s.

Yet again, it was a tour that *might* have made money. But there always seemed to be something to get in the way of that. Unfortunately, Gaughan's health wasn't great, and he had to cancel many of the shows. He arrived with throat problems that only got worse, as he smoked constantly, drank industrial quantities of coffee, appeared to eat very little, and never opened the windows of his hotel rooms to allow in that thing called fresh air.

Again, there was a sold-out show at The Basement late in the tour when Gaughan's health was really, really shot. To his credit, he gave it a go but after three warbling songs it was obvious he couldn't continue. He offered a croaky apology to the crowd and trudged off the stage.

We had to refund the whole venue. That tour lost a few thousand dollars, but Andrew was kind enough to write it off against his tax.

And that was that. Some years later, I wrote a book called *The Promoters*, which drew on my experiences organising and mounting tours. It netted me much more money than any of the actual tours did.

# 42

# I'M AN OUTLAW

During Harry Dean Stanton's Australian tour, he was asked to sign a photo for a two-month-old boy, whose father had named him, you guessed it, Harry Dean. He seemed genuinely touched before scribbling 'Don't join anything' on a poster for Harry Dean Carter. 'That'll probably screw up his whole life,' he chuckled. In 1998, Jules R. B. Normington called me up. I was about to break the Harry Dean Stanton Law. I was about to join something.

Jules was one of the founders of Phantom Records – one of Australia's finest and most influential independent labels of the era – and the shop in the CBD of the same name, in which I'd spent more than my fair share of money in the 1980s.

I hadn't seen Jules for a few years, probably since I'd organised for Dick Dale to 'do an in-store' at Phantom for an ABC TV news segment on the guitarist. Through that little endeavour, Jules had met his wife, Polly, who was a producer at the ABC.

Anyway, Jules called and muttered something about starting up a new independent record company, with me joining the couple of others in the team for this venture. Phantom had ended badly for him – with both the label and shop closing – and he'd been persuaded to try another label by his musician friend John Rooney, from the band Coronet Blue. This, combined with his ongoing business selling collectable records, seemed like a good idea.

Jules said he recalled that I liked reading contracts – which oddly enough was true – and wondered if he could have a chat about what to include in one. Phantom may or may not have done contracts. If they had, he didn't seem to have copies. He also correctly figured that aspects of them may have changed over recent years.

I don't think we'd ever done contracts during G.R.E.E.N days, but I'd needed to read a lot of them for my management duties, because the likes of Mushroom Records naturally insisted on them. Times were changing, though, and artists were nowadays, quite reasonably, requesting that the arrangements be written down.

A week later, Jules came over and we had a rambling discussion. I say it was rambling; actually, it was a conversation that might have saved my life.

At the time, I was struggling – with just about everything. Julie and I had separated, and I'd moved to Balmain after a stint in the centre of Sydney. A good friend had observed the toll the expensive rent was taking on my finances, and that I wasn't coping well being in an anonymous apartment by myself.

A friend of hers was looking to rent an apartment in a friendly, almost communally orientated block in Balmain. So there I was with neighbours, shops and cafés nearby, living by myself in a rather lovely little flat – except that it was also right next to a pub and 10 feet from a bottle shop. It was definitely better than being isolated in the city, but I had plenty of other issues to deal with at the time.

Call it melodramatic, if you want to – but at the rate I was going, if I hadn't already lost the battle with alcohol, I was pretty damn close to it. (It would still be years before I wised up totally about the impact of alcohol on my body and psyche. But then there are a lot of things I'm a slow learner about.)

I was also suffering from agoraphobia. The bottle shop and the deli across the road were about as far as I could go without crippling and frightening anxiety, but I'd need a few drinks to attempt it.

To make things worse, I was struggling to write. I was beginning to think I'd lost the ability. I wasn't sure what I wanted to do with my life – or if I wanted a life at all.

That's why the conversation with Jules was crucial. It provided a focus, a new activity, potentially some much-needed discipline, and the chance to earn an income from doing something I loved – working with artists and music. If this opportunity hadn't come along – well, I try not to dwell too much on where I might have ended up.

Andrew Bowles came to a couple of subsequent meetings with Jules in Balmain and, despite the Dick Gaughan experience, still seemed keen for a bit of the excitement that the rock'n'roll world presented. And the label presented a possible investment option.

Andrew did spreadsheet after spreadsheet, all of which confirmed that starting an independent label wasn't the smartest way to invest money. But Jules and I weren't particularly good at listening to researched and sensible advice. We weren't wired that way.

They say it can't be done? They're almost certainly right. OK, let's do it then. I had no money that I could invest, but I said I was in if there was a way to make it work.

Without my involvement, a bunch of investors were found. John Rooney's brother Terry worked at the accounting firm Deloitte. He had a bit of spare cash. So did a former musician who was doing well in real estate. Another friend of John's, Darryl Mather, had moved from the Lime Spiders to his own power pop project, The Orange Humble Band, as well as – and most importantly – becoming a very successful manager of rugby league players. Between them, they came up with $70,000. Soon after, Terry pulled in fellow music-loving finance guy Paul Glover, who in turn extracted some financial commitment from an American friend on secondment to Australia to work at Deloitte.

The label was up and running. I was to be paid $500 a week to run it, from a desk in an office in the city, in the Pitt Street building where Phantom had previously been. The record shop had been replaced by Revolution, a second-hand CD and computer-games shop. I'd spend quite a bit of money there too.

Jules still had his well-established Phantom Collectables business on the third floor of the building. It was absolutely crammed with thousands of records and magazines and music ephemera (I bought an REM jumper there). Somehow, we managed to clear a tiny area for our new label, near the never-cleaned bathroom.

So, we had a phone and a few desks. Now we needed a name. People sometimes compliment me on 'Laughing Outlaw' – with its nods to country music, but with a punk attitude. Well, it cost us a fortune for a marketing company to brainstorm for weeks and come up with that. OK, I'm kidding. And I had nothing to do with it.

Jules gets flustered easily, and everyone involved was giving him grief about a name for the company. He'd been desperately trying to conjure up something as potentially iconic as Phantom Records, but nothing was coming. Shit. Shit. Shit. Then one day, he was looking after his young son and reading him a story. There was a character in it who was an outlaw – and he was laughing. He was a laughing outlaw.

Houston, we have a label name. And 70 grand.

The name endured, but the money went very, *very* quickly. A Coronet Blue album came out. It didn't sell.

Meanwhile, Jules and I fell in love with an emerging band, Lucy Beegle, comprised of three women from Brisbane. The songwriter and singer was Alyson Locke, who wrote songs pitched somewhere between Jonathan Richman and The Runaways. She and her bandmates played with a naive approach that was better than The Shaggs, although probably not quite as good as what I imagine the first Ramones rehearsal sounded like. They were rudimentary and basic, but with lots of attitude and good intentions.

We loved them. We loved Alyson. We flew to Brisbane to meet them and see them play. Then we signed them and paid for them to make a record in Sydney, to be produced by Ted Howard, better known for his country music recordings.

Most people didn't like the finished album nearly as much as we did. It had a glorious simplicity that reminded me of early Jonathan Richman – particularly on songs like 'Coke Machine', about the reality that the closest dispenser of the soft drink was a three-kilometre walk from Alyson's home. That was rock'n'roll dealing with the important issues of life.

There are several pages on Discogs devoted to pretty much all the releases on the label. Lucy Beegle isn't amongst them. Note to self here: maybe we need to give it a few more years, then press 500 copies on coloured vinyl, get a few music critics – or invent some – to say it's a long-lost Australian classic, and we'll clean up.

Psychologically, the early days of Laughing Outlaw in 1999 were great for me. My relationship situation had changed. I had a new partner, Vicki, and the week the label started, I moved out of the place in Balmain and relocated with her to her house in Victoria Street, Lewisham. It was pretty much right across the road from the train station. 'Pretend you're in New York,' she said, when I commented on the constant noise and rail grit coming through the windows.

Anyway, as I've mentioned I was an office drone now. With the new stability in my life, I managed to get a bit of a handle on the agoraphobia, to the point where – initially with trepidation – I could catch the train from my home to the city, and walk the few blocks to the office.

Actually, soon I found I was enjoying it. It was a huge relief to have made major progress with the condition. I'd get up early and almost excitedly get onboard that train into the city each morning. It was a novelty, because apart from a brief period with *The Edge*, I'd never really had what you'd call an office job. I bought a semi-respectable shoulder bag to carry all my stuff to and from work. Each day felt like an adventure. My friends were bemused at my excitement. ('Why has the 8.28 to the City Circle been cancelled? Could I still make it to the office by 9 am on the 8.43?!')

I was having a great time as a commuter, but I was still drinking way too much. Lunch with another guy – who was using a desk in the office to run his own independent label – usually started at midday, with drinks and a little food at a nearby Japanese restaurant, before beer and often vodka was purchased from a nearby pub.

So there was mixed news on the psychological and health front. Unfortunately, there was no mixed news on the business front. It was all bad. Before too long, Laughing Outlaw was on the verge of collapse.

In the first 12 months, a lot had gone wrong. We'd invested in a succession of bands and albums that we adored, but which hadn't sold a cracker. And in reality we didn't have a lot of money to play with, given the cost of making albums, wages and other overheads.

So if things didn't turn around, there was going to be no label, no office, no need for a commute. By the end of 2000, things were dire, and the investors were getting restless. They figured Jules and I had no idea what we were doing. We were enjoying having no idea, although they may have had a point.

But there was light – in the form of Paul Glover, an obsessive, nerdish music fan, lover of Radio Birdman, punk rock and the idea of being part of an independent record label. Paul worked at Deloitte in a pretty significant role. He had disposable income and decided that he liked disposing it on things that made him happy.

Two things made him happy – investing in Laughing Outlaw and in bars. So, with two friends he also bought the licence to the O Bar in Devonshire Street in Surry Hills – and acquired a really expensive DJ set-up, so he could DJ in his pub on weekend afternoons. That venture didn't end so well, though, with unexpected costs quickly knocking the stuffing out of the partners and their relationship.

Laughing Outlaw, on the other hand, was just one endlessly long cash drain. A thousand here, three thousand here, another thousand here – OK, ten thousand here. Fortunately, Paul seemed to have an endless fount of financial resources and appeared to enjoy spending it releasing CDs on Laughing Outlaw. And if you want to get rid of money, an independent record label is a damn fine way to do it. There's none better, beyond leaving the cash on a corner of a street in the CBD. It might disappear slightly faster that way. Maybe.

In 2001, I brought the South By Southwest music conference in Austin, Texas to Paul's attention. I thought it might open up a whole new world of musical possibilities for us – obscure, exciting international acts we could release in Australia and (no doubt) make a fortune doing so.

'We should go,' he said.

And so we did.

# 43
# EAT TO THE BEAT

On the way to South By Southwest, I managed to tee up an interview with Anthony Bourdain. Oddly enough, he was going to be in
Australia when the conference was on, but we arranged to meet in New
York. I'd read his book *Kitchen Confidential* and loved it. He wrote with
such engagement and spark – and made me, and pretty much everyone
else who read it, actually give a shit about what happens in kitchens in
NYC restaurants.

I wanted to interview Bourdain as he seemed like a particularly
interesting individual who'd be fun to write about. Hell, I was even
prepared to get back into promoting writers and try to organise
some readings for him in Australia. That was not to be, but I did
arrange to meet him one morning at Les Halles, the brasserie where
he worked.

It was early when I arrived. The thin, lanky, strong-boned Bourdain
was already there, directing staff and doing the other sorts of things that
were necessary as preparation for lunch and dinner craziness. He took
a break for an extended conversation.

We sat at a table in the front of the brasserie, the tape recorder went
on and we started chatting. Bourdain had the air of someone who had
plenty of time – others had been drilled to take care of everything in the
kitchen. He was there if there was a disaster.

Bourdain oozed New York City cool. He was brash, opinionated, intelligent and talkative. We both smoked Marlboros and were carrying clunky mobile phones that were still an expensive rarity in NYC. The collapse of the Twin Towers six months later would change that, as every American suddenly wanted to be in constant, immediate contact with their loved ones.

During our chat, Bourdain and I didn't talk much about food or restaurants or cooking. It was much more about punk rock, CBGBs, Lester Bangs, and the glories of New York City rock'n'roll in the 1970s.

At the end of the conversation, which he seemed to have enjoyed, he said, 'Come and meet my crew.' He took me on a trip through the kitchen to see his team all busily preparing for the later onslaught. Things were being chopped and cut up, ingredients mixed. It was all seemingly being done with precision and everyone understanding their tasks. The craziness described in such detail in *Kitchen Confidential* would happen later in the day.

It's a shame I didn't manage to get Bourdain to tour. I think some reading performances in Australia would have ruled. Maybe the Beasts Of Bourbon or The Cruel Sea opening proceedings. I reckon he would have dug that.

After Bourdain, I headed down to South By Southwest, which was a hoot for any music fan. Hundreds and hundreds of bands performing in every nook and cranny, one of the world's greatest record shops in Waterloo Records, people everywhere.

I love Austin. It had great food and ambience, terrific weather, and it was easy to get around. Paul and I would go to the annual conference most years, usually with our partners. We had endless meetings with other labels and artists who wanted us to release their material in Australia. They were strangely silent when we suggested a reciprocal arrangement.

In the first couple of years, we did deals to release the great songwriter Alejandro Escovedo and country/bluegrass hybrid Split Lip Rayfield from Bloodshot Records, and signed country punk band Slick 57, who were a trio from Dallas. That was after drinking too many beers one afternoon, whilst watching them play at SXSW. And then of course they had to come to Australia and tour. On our dime.

In 2001 we signed The Dictators – who Paul loved – and they had to come out too. We had a bash for them at the O Bar, when that was still a thing, and they played a boat cruise on Sydney Harbour. Nice people, and very happy to be in Australia and doing a tour.

We also signed quirky pop singer-songwriter Spike Priggen from New York, and what seemed like the entire roster of the psychedelic power-pop label Rainbow Quartz. We were everyone's friend. After getting a distribution deal in the UK and Europe, we employed a publicist to deal with our releases in those parts of the world.

In 2002, we organised for American country rock band Last Train Home to tour the country. They played everywhere from an outdoor Americana music festival in Erskineville in inner city Sydney through to the bar at the White Cockatoo hotel in Petersham, a five-minute walk from where I lived. I loved the band. The fact that lead singer Eric Brace convinced his buddy, acclaimed novelist and screen writer George Pelecanos – who I was a huge fan of – to write the sleeve notes for the album was a bonus.

Through all this, we also began to release a seemingly endless array of Australian independent artists. Nothing really came close to breaking even. We did make some good money after I signed Melbourne alt country artist Dan Brodie ('the missing link between Johnny Cash and Nick Cave' was the catchcry). When Tony Harlow, who ran EMI at the time, heard him and decided that, yes, he needed a male Kasey Chambers and that Dan was, in fact, the one, we on-sold the contract to the big guys.

Of course, we used that money to sign more and more artists. We didn't stop. We didn't know how to. 'No' was not a big part of our vocabulary.

Naturally, we signed some wild cards. One band let everything go to their heads once we did a deal for them with a major label. One of the members was also a partner in another independent label. He took me aside one day and admitted he couldn't really commit to the band for the next month. I asked why, and with all seriousness he said, 'Well, I need to be on call to just drop everything and fly to sign Radiohead.'

OK, Radiohead had put it out there that they were considering signing with an independent label, so I guess there was a possibility. I told him I wasn't going to do anything for Laughing Outlaw for the next month – just be on standby in case I got the call to sign Bob Dylan. He didn't get it.

Then there was the drummer from another band, who called me from his hotel room in Melbourne to complain that his pillow was too hard. And what was I going to do about it?

I've never laughed whenever I've watched *Spinal Tap*. I actually thought it was a documentary the first time I saw it in a cinema in New York. I know these people. They walk amongst us. They call and complain about how firm a pillow is. They think this is what you do.

Incidentally, prior to the Laughing Outlaw days, there was an occasion – at about 2 am on Christmas morning – when the drummer from a band I was managing phoned from a telephone box and insisted that I get out of bed – like *now* – catch a taxi to meet him and bring my hole-in-the-wall card, as he and I were going to withdraw several hundred dollars of my money, go and find a cocaine dealer, and kick on. He was flummoxed when I told him this wasn't a great idea and explained that this was not how the rest of the night was going to play out, that I was going back to sleep, and that he should at least try to do the same.

Although I wasn't much help as a pillow-fixer, I did fulfil a few different roles at Laughing Outlaw. Over the years, I guess I was sort of a publicist for the label, and for some artists I did a good job of talking them up. I wasn't really into it, though – the lack of enthusiasm for most of our releases was frustrating – and I began to despair of the Australian media. Every new release I'd sit and address 100 to 120 envelopes, stuff them with a CD and bio info – plus scribble a personalised note on most of them – and march to the post office. But it often felt like they were all lost in the mail system given the amount of coverage they didn't receive.

It seemed that all I was doing really was providing stock for Australia's second-hand CD shops, as that's where most of them appeared to end up after being on sold by the media folk I sent them to. OK, I used to do it too – but I never sold releases by Australian independent artists.

You have to have some principles.

# 44
# BIG WHEELS KEEP ON TURNIN'

Although I was busy with Laughing Outlaw, I'd returned to a bit of writing. One day in 2001, I got a call from Matthew Kelly from Hachette, suggesting a book on concert promoters. He'd been watching the *Long Way To The Top* television series about the history of Australian rock and pop, and had noticed that managers and other industry figures were prominent – but not so much the promoters.

I was still doing crime fiction reviews for *The Sydney Morning Herald*, but it had been a number of years since I'd done any serious writing, and the last time I'd muddled through a book had been in 1998. At a low ebb I'd done enough – just – to cobble together my half of the text for Triple J's *Internet Music Guide*, which I'd co-written with Richard Kingsmill from the station. Yes, there was a time when you could write a slim book, pretty much covering all the music resources and sites on this thing called the internet. The book had been published by ABC Books, with Matthew the publisher.

In all honesty, I thought the idea of a book on concert promoters was a pretty dull idea and told Matthew as much.

'Isn't that about as interesting as writing a book on bank managers?' I quipped.

Then I thought more about it, said yes, banked the advance, and got to work. As I reflected upon the idea and the individuals involved,

I began to realise that it was a much more compelling project than I'd initially thought. And Matthew resisted the 'I told you so' line as I immersed myself in the researching and interviewing.

Through the process I realised even more what a gamble promoting was, and what deep pockets – and discipline – were required to survive in that business. I remember having lunch with one of Australia's most successful promoters, Michael Coppel. He explained that when he started, he only wanted to tour artists he loved. It cost him so much money, it would have been cheaper to fly overseas first class, and hire a limousine to drive him around to see them play four or five times. That resonated!

I wrote about my own experiences at the end of the process, but Matthew suggested the book should start with that.

'Talk about how you tried to be Australia's most successful promoter and failed,' he said, 'and then tell the stories of the people who got it right.' It was a masterstroke.

While working on the book, I did sometimes wonder if I'd bitten off way more than I could chew. Who knew that simultaneously writing 80,000 words and running a record label could be a bit time consuming? I certainly found out and there were many times I thought juggling all this was beyond me. But I persisted and was proud of *The Promoters* – and the label didn't collapse. Everything was done in a blur of too much drinking and too little sleep.

Once the book was finished, a launch was organised. This was back when publishers coughed up for such events. We picked the Hopetoun Hotel in Surry Hills, and I asked Michael Chugg to make a speech to launch the book: successful promoter, former Launceston boy etc.

'I don't fucking like a lot of what you said in it, but I'll launch it for you,' he barked down the phone. Chugg always barked.

Recently, Chugg had parted company with Michael Gudinski in a fairly acrimonious fashion. Their long-standing partnership had been dissolved and now they were intense business rivals, instead of a power-house team. The relationship between the two was tense – and very competitive.

Naturally, I'd written about the rift in *The Promoters*. And I think some of what I'd said about his business relationships with various partners since the split – which hadn't ended well – had touched several nerves. But I knew Chugg wouldn't have agreed to do the launch if he was seriously angry. If he was, you'd hear him bellowing from several kilometres away and you wouldn't want to be anywhere in the vicinity.

Other invitations went out to media and friends to attend the event. Then one day my phone rang. It was Gudinski. I hadn't actually invited him yet – and certainly not to speak. I figured if I had Chugg involved, he'd give it a wide berth. Wrong.

'So, Chugg's launching your book – I'm coming too. I'll be giving a speech. See you there. Bye.' That was pretty much the conversation. No asking if it was OK with me, or anything of that nature.

When I arrived at the Hopetoun, Chugg and Gudinski were already at it, talking angrily in a corner. I'd been nervous enough about the book launch as it was – this didn't help. This was a very, very public spat. Everyone was watching – or pretending not to, as they snuck looks at the two of them and tried to hear everything that was being said. I later realised they were fighting over a proposed Elton John tour.

Once the argument had been put on hold, Chugg took to the stage. He said a bunch of nice things about me and the book, despite being heckled by songwriter John Kennedy, who muttered something disparaging about him. So far, so good.

Then Gudinski got up. His opening gambit was something like this: 'You know there's going to be a film made about this book. Who's going to play me? Probably Sting. And Chugg – he'll be played by Marlon Brando.'

This was clearly a reference to the fact that, at the time, Brando was extremely overweight and, as far as most people were concerned, a fading star. Chugg tried to ignore Gudinski, but I sensed that if there was one more gibe, things could get ugly.

Speeches over, I sat at a table and signed books. Meanwhile, Chugg and Gudinski continued their stoush. At one point, a photographer from *The Sun-Herald* grabbed me to get a photo in the middle of the two promoters. Gudinski made it very clear he wasn't having his photo taken with Chugg.

'Fuck you, Gudinski,' Chugg snarled, 'it's Stuart's night. Have your fucking photo taken.' Eventually, he was convinced to be in the photo – the two standing on opposite sides of me and briefly smiling before resuming their fight.

The final encounter I witnessed in Chugg v. Gudinski was a few minutes later. Gudinski – in full flight – was pushing his finger right at Chugg and yelling, 'Don't make it easy for me, Chuggi. Don't make it fucking easy – don't fucking die on me.'

Gudinski then turned and marched out of the pub. He propelled himself out the door and almost into oncoming traffic. One of his trusted staffers, head of his music publishing division Ian James, grabbed him and pulled him back onto the footpath. Chugg had already moved on to another conversation.

It was a bit more dramatic than I'd intended my launch to be. But there was an upside: Gudinski ended up buying close to 200 copies of the book. I asked my friend Gerard Schlaghecke from Gudinski's touring company, Frontier Touring, what he did with them and he said, 'He won't tell you, but he loves this book. He thinks he comes out better than all the other promoters, so he signs it and gives it to people.'

There you have it. My book was, in effect, a business card for Gudinski. I smile sometimes, thinking about the bookshelves of high-profile industry figures around the globe that might have a copy of *The Promoters* – signed by Gudinski.

Chugg and Gudinski would eventually patch things up, and they were once again working together when Gudinski passed away in 2021. They both had to admit they were like bickering siblings. Deep down, they loved each other. They just weren't that good at expressing it.

# 45

# SAW YOU AT THE RECORD SHOP

It will come as no surprise that I love record shops. Cannot pass one without going in. It's been that way all my life – ever since the first one I ventured into in Launceston as a teenager. It was in Charles Street, a furniture and white goods shop that had a selection of records in a corner at the back. That's where I went.

Much as I loved record shops, though, I'd never really thought of running my own. And then I did. My very own *High Fidelity* Mid-Life-Crisis Record Shop – or that's how I described it. And it was a lot of fun. When it was fun. And when it wasn't, it was horrible.

So how did I come to be running my own enterprise? It was simple, really. By the early 2000s, Jules was reassessing Phantom Collectables. Income was sporadic, largely because it took him a long time to get catalogues completed and mailed out. Also, the pressure on businesses like ours was enormous, because the lower end of Pitt Street had begun to be gentrified. Up until then, it had been a bit rough.

It hadn't been a really scary area, but there was one sunny afternoon when I was walking back from the nearest bottle shop – a sixpack in one hand and my mobile phone in the other. I didn't notice the guy behind me till I was up one flight of steps of our building and felt arms around me.

He grabbed me, threw me against the wall, wrenched the mobile phone out of my hand and ran back down the stairs and out into the street. Mobile phones were easy to sell in pubs in those days and fetched a bit of cash. It took me a few months to regain confidence walking up those stairs.

So, anyway, as I say, the rent was going up at an astonishing rate – or that's how it seemed to us of little fortune – so Jules decided to relocate Phantom Collectables to his home. He took an axe (literally) to all the shelving in the office and carted it downstairs, as we vacated the warehouse.

That left a small issue – where to run Laughing Outlaw Records from. I looked at various properties around the inner west and within walking distance of my home in Lewisham. There were a few options, but they weren't cheap, as the label wasn't exactly making real money.

I was starting to despair. I didn't want to run the label from my home. For starters, it was far too small and my now wife Vicki was far from inclined to compromise the space she had downstairs. As far as I was concerned, she needed about an eighth of what she took up – but she didn't view it that way.

I was bemoaning the situation one afternoon to a neighbour, Mary. She was always on the lookout for a deal, and said, 'Well, we don't really use the living room, so why don't you rent that?' The room in question was big enough to fit myself and the two Laughing Outlaw staffers in the back third, and then have, yes, a record shop at the front.

Mary's idea was that she, her husband, and their two young kids would live, eat and play in the kitchen and upstairs, and for $100 a week I'd have that front room. And it was an actual shopfront – and right near the entrance to the Lewisham railway station, with a lot of passing foot traffic, at least early in the mornings and late in the afternoon.

So Laughing Outlaw Records – the label and the shop – moved in. I managed to buy some old record and CD racks from the independent distributors and label Didgeridoo Records (who actually handled the distribution of Laughing Outlaw). I also ended up with the new releases CD rack – which weighed a tonne – from the iconic independent record label and shop Waterfront Records as an historical monument. (It's currently at RPM Records in Marrickville, if you want to check it out and maybe touch it and pay your respects to great record and CD shops of the past.)

I covered the walls with my memorabilia. There were lots of weird and wonderful objects, signed record covers, posters and the like. That was enough reason for a lot of people to drop in, and I started getting CDs and vinyl from Didgeridoo and Inertia, who operated as wholesalers. As well, I put some of Laughing Outlaw's CDs and those of friends in the racks. Soon it was a functioning little record shop that was easy to manage, as there was always at least one person in the office looking after label stuff and making sure nothing got pinched.

It didn't take long for me to realise that record shops are – amongst other things – a mecca for the lonely and the nerdish. I was next door to a laundromat/dry cleaner, so what would anyone do whilst waiting for their clothes to be washed, or after they'd dropped them off and had time to kill? And I was two doors from a corner shop that made hamburgers and toasted sandwiches – rather slowly. Waiting for your burger – what you going to do? Missed your train? That means 15 minutes in the record shop. There were also a lot of tyre kickers in various states of disarray.

As well, the area was home to a large collection of halfway houses for people down on their luck, recently out of prison and/or on various types of medication. They loved having somewhere to hang.

There was a lot of drug dealing around the station too (a phone box at a railway station entrance almost always means to expect drug dealing). The transactions were usually done in the laneway 10 feet from the shop door, or in the front seat of a car that would pull up outside, allow the customer to hop in, drive around the block, then the customer would get out.

The erratic arrival times of drug dealers and their habit of keeping the customer waiting meant that the majority of customers were edgy, furtive and in need of distraction. Smack dealer running late? Hang at the record shop. They were also on the lookout to grab anything that could be turned into cash.

It was definitely an interesting part of Sydney. A lovely Vietnamese family ran one of the corner shops. One day, their pet turtle went for a walk. An unaccompanied AWOL walk. It made it two blocks and was ambling – as turtles do – past the shop when I spotted it. I knew I hadn't taken drugs (in fact, I'd stopped taking them years earlier), but it's not every day a turtle walks past your record shop.

Naturally, given the nature of the business, you'd often come across those who wanted to sell records. I was good with most of that. Many people just dumped bags and boxes and milk crates of records at the front door. I arrived one morning to find a shopping trolley full of *really great* records at the door. Anyone could have pinched them. They were seriously good records: Devo picture discs, Culture Club albums, early Kraftwerk albums. Seriously good.

I had no idea where they'd come from, until a few days later a guy from down the road walked in and asked if I'd liked the records. He was clutching a FedEx package, which he asked if he could open in the shop. He did and I observed some sort of fluffy toy that looked as though it had been chewed by several ravenous dogs in the middle of a muddy paddock. It could have been a doll. Or a rabbit. It was hard to tell, actually, given the mangled condition. He told me he'd bought it on eBay for $300. Each to their own, I thought. (Mind you, there was – and still is – no record that I'd pay $300 for.)

I asked him what the deal with the records was. He said they were mine, no charge – he just needed to get them out of his place. 'Space,' he said. 'It was either the records or the toys. One collection had to go and I decided to get rid of the records.' More room for the mangled, moth-eaten, apparently collectable objects, I guess.

Every so often, things became a bit hairy. The son of the owner at another corner shop had been held up at knife-point and, a year or two later, a guy moved in down the road and set up a gambling-cum-gym business, with what seemed like a team of underlings. He was a tough piece of work. One day he drove past the shop, while I was standing outside, and yelled, 'Hey, Mr Laughing Outlaw, we're taking over the street!'

He and his cohorts persuaded the gentle family from Vietnam to move on. When they did, the new team opened their own corner store and café in the space. The guy and his mates who were apparently taking over the street tried to get me to go and gamble with them. Two of them came into the shop one day and asked if I played poker. I said I had no idea how and they said they'd teach me. Yeah, right.

No-one seemed to take this street domination seriously, and in all honesty there wasn't a lot in the street to take over, unless you'd set your sights on two stationery businesses, a dry cleaner and a record shop and label. I never felt seriously threatened, as it seemed as if they talked loud, but kept to themselves and whatever they were up to down the road.

One day, in October 2008, there was a ruckus outside. Within minutes, it was pandemonium – streets blocked. As the helicopters circled overhead, and snipers appeared on the roofs of nearby houses, I had no idea what was going on. Neither did anyone else I asked.

Over the next couple of hours, though, I managed to observe some of it and piece the rest together. Apparently, after an altercation of some description at the new gym, the takeover guy had boarded himself inside and refused to come out. Some people said he had guns and was threatening to shoot himself – or other people. Were there hostages? It was all whispers and suggestions. The police weren't saying much.

During the siege, the police asked if his girlfriend could use the bathroom in my home, as they weren't letting anyone past the barricades at the top of the street. Two cops stood outside the door (I couldn't work out if they were guarding her or making sure she didn't make a run for the site of the siege). Either way, whilst in there she shot up, not even bothering to flush the bloodied tissues she'd used.

Guns and ammunition were found, according to talk on the street, and he lay low for a few months as no-one saw him anywhere and the doors to the building were always closed. He didn't seem to have received the jail term others might have expected. Slowly, activity returned to their premises, but gone was the swagger and bravado if I saw him on the street.

In 2020, a couple of years after I'd moved from Lewisham to Petersham, I was collecting some records from a friend, and saw a helicopter hovering over that area. It seems that the guy had shot and killed one of the young blokes who worked for him, then turned the gun on himself. It was just your average, quiet inner-west neighbourhood.

Actually, though, I didn't have much trouble at the shop. The only time I really sensed things might get nasty was the day a guy came in clutching a copy of the Who's *Live At Leeds*. To my surprise, it had some of the original inserts with it. In case you're not aware of the history of the album, various items came with the first pressing: photocopies of record contracts, gig booking agreements, promotional photos, posters, handbills, correspondence and so forth. Twelve items, if my memory is correct.

If the record was in good condition, and had all the inserts, it might have been worth $150–200. But this copy was battered and scratched and filthy, and only contained some of the extras. Maybe I'd have offered $20 for it and tried to sell it for $30.

The problem was that this guy didn't believe they were photocopies. As far as he was concerned, they were original documents – he had the *only* copies. They were priceless. My questions about how he managed to have original Who documents in his possession were countered with, 'Well, I had a friend who . . .'

There was no way known I could convince him these were photocopies and not worth the thousands of dollars he thought they were worth. I think his bargain-basement, I'll-take-it-in-cash, price was about $1000. Things turned potentially nasty when he realised I wasn't buying. I thought for a minute he was going to throw a punch, but I escaped with a 'FUCK YOU!' as he stormed out of the shop. I never saw him again.

A lot of genuine music lovers came into the shop, but every now and then, someone would enter the premises and . . . let's just say, we weren't on the same vibration. This was just a bit before the boom and the crazy prices that people are now expected to pay for old vinyl. I had no real concern about the price of records, so I'd take a stab at what they were worth and that was it.

I didn't check Discogs (which wasn't yet the massive resource it is today) or eBay. I really didn't care that much – and vinyl records were yet to make the comeback they did a few years later. Most things in the Laughing Outlaw shop were $8–$20 for second hand and $30 for new. There were boxes everywhere. If you found a bargain, good luck to you.

One afternoon, this annoying guy came in. He went through everything and found a record – I can't remember what it was, but it was $6. He insisted I look the album up on some collectables website, where it was apparently valued at $75.

He had this supercilious look on his face that was basically saying, 'You're an idiot, and I'm a smart dude who knows his records.' For some reason, he gave me the complete shits. I wasn't irritated that the record was worth a lot – not to me, it wasn't – but that it was so important to him to point out to me that it could be sold for more than we were asking for. Good luck to him. I wish you could still walk into record shops and find a total bargain, but those days are gone. Discogs is just a click away.

A few days after this encounter, someone brought in a crate of records. Now, if you do the second-hand thing long enough, you can flick through a crate and, even after you see The Eagles' *Greatest Hits*, *Hot August Night*, *Frampton Comes Alive*, a Simon and Garfunkel album, and a few other mainstays of your typical collection of the era, you can still name pretty much every other record that will be in there. Fleetwood Mac's *Rumours,* maybe an Angels album, a Culture Club record, and so forth.

This particular day, I was flicking through all the obvious titles, and there, in the middle of them all, was a mono pressing of John Coltrane's classic *A Love Supreme* on the original Impulse label. Stereo copies of this album aren't all that common (am I sounding like a record-shop owner here?), but *mono* copies? Get out of here. I was aware of one copy being sold for around $300.

I had no way of contacting the crate donor and asking the question that still bugs me: how did this get in here? Where did it come from? Who owned it? It had clearly been played and relatively well looked after. Those little mysteries stay with you. Maybe one day someone will come up to me and say, 'Did you like that mono copy of *A Love Supreme* that I snuck into that crate of bog-ordinary records?' That will probably never happen, but one lives in hope.

Eventually, running the shop started to wear me down. Being partially in a service industry, naturally I was meant to welcome anyone who came in. The only issue was that I was also trying to run a record label, and from time to time do some writing. However, you couldn't predict who was going to come in and how much time they were going to take up.

And there were strange people. One Saturday morning, a guy came in who told me he'd travelled up from Wollongong to check the shop out. As he flicked through records, I made small talk, but I noticed he was becoming increasingly agitated. I asked if anything was upsetting him and he regarded me with a not totally friendly stare.

'You don't remember me, do you?'

I looked closely at him. Nothing was coming up to connect him with anything or anybody I'd ever met. I mumbled something about meeting a lot of people and having a bad memory for faces.

'I met you in the front bar of the Southern Cross Hotel in 1981,' he said. There was no humour, or 'Gotcha', in the way he said it. No follow-up about how he played drums in Tweeny Weeny and the Midgets, who'd played in a Battle Of The Bands that night. Nothing.

All I could do was mumble more about being sorry and try to keep him calm, whilst thinking to myself, 'Exactly how many people did I meet in that bar . . . over forty years ago?' Music nerds can be a bit like that. And it comes with the turf, I suppose, when you have some sort of profile.

As the shop side of things started to wear me down, I began to relate so much to the TV series *Black Books*, and the perpetually furious, jaded and cynical bookshop owner, played by Dylan Moran. We were remarkably similar, except I usually had a bottle of vodka under the desk, rather than red wine.

There were basic questions that increasingly annoyed me. No, we don't sell batteries. This is not a newsagent – we don't sell papers. No, you can't leave your name, take the album home, record a copy, then bring it back. I even coped – just – with requests about whether we had any Kylie albums in stock.

Then came the cruncher. One day, a head appeared at the door. It spoke. 'Do you have the new Matchbox 20 album?'

I lost it.

'Does this look like the sort of shop that would have the new Matchbox fucking 20 album? Go away!' I snarled with a venom that surprised even me. The poor bloke sulked away, probably wondering precisely what he'd done wrong.

I had officially become the *Black Books* of inner-west record shops.

# 46
# A CHANGE IS GONNA COME

The siege in Victoria Street wasn't the only significant event of 2008. There was also a seismic shift at Laughing Outlaw. My business partner, Paul Glover, had fallen in love, and his new girlfriend wasn't as enthusiastic about the label as he was. One day, early that year, he announced that he was pulling out of the label. Immediately. Just like that.

Paul's new love had convinced him of something he already knew very well – that over a decade he'd spent what I'd estimate to be close to a million dollars on an independent record label. And he had very little to show for it. She was convinced that he was almost like a junkie, and at one point she described me as being akin to the indie-label version of his dealer.

Paul stated that the label was to be wound up. Not sold. Not run by me. But crushed. Destroyed. As far as his partner was concerned, it could no longer exist, in case the junkie was tempted to go back to the dealer.

Of course, I was furious. And stunned. I was desperate to keep the label going. Find other investors. Do *something*. Laughing Outlaw had become my life – that, and drinking. In no way was I emotionally or intellectually engaged enough to go back to writing as the basis of my income: and the freelance journalism caper wasn't what it used to be, anyway.

If anything, pay rates were decreasing. As well, the media landscape was shrinking and, with retrenchments on the rise and plenty of people taking voluntary redundancy packages, there was a lot of competition in the freelance world. And there still wasn't a lot I felt like writing about – or publications I craved to contribute to.

Eventually, towards the end of the year, Paul allowed Vicki to buy the company for a dollar and to take over the name and all the assets. Why didn't I do that myself? We needed to move quickly and Vicki suggested using her existing business structure.

I've not exchanged one word with Paul since then. I hear from a mutual friend that he's happily married and has a child. We did a lot of cool shit together over those years, but his then-girlfriend, now-wife was probably right. More than anything, I'm glad he's apparently content and doing well.

Laughing Outlaw Mark II was – by necessity – leaner, but not particularly meaner. And really not much smarter. If at all. We continued to release too many recordings and under-market and under-publicise them. And of course, we had less money to do things with.

One problem was that, within about 12 months, the owners of our office/shop decided to sell their home. How inconsiderate was that? Then, the new owners, who were lovely people, figured that a living-room was, well, a living-room. So we needed another office.

Fortunately, that problem was easily fixed. Next door to the house was a decrepit two-storey building that had been squatted in and was slowly becoming even more uninhabitable than it already was. The last occupants had been a floating population of guys, some of whom I suspected worked either as male prostitutes or members of a Chippendales-like outfit – judging by the woman who frequently collected a few of them in her red convertible. And things regularly seemed to spiral out of control there. Fights would break out, furniture – chairs and such like – would come flying out of the upstairs windows, and police were regular visitors.

According to talk on the street from people who had lived in the area for a long time, a young woman, who I occasionally saw outside the place, was looking after the building for her elderly father and his brother. Apparently, the two men owned almost every second unoccupied house in the inner west.

She eventually managed to move them out. Then, caring citizen that I was, I explained to her that it was only a matter of time before another bunch of undesirables squatted in the property. I added that, as an habitual hoarder, I wouldn't mind having a little extra space for storage. And given that I lived just up the road, well . . . maybe I could be a surrogate caretaker, and, hell, in the spirit of generosity that oozed from my very being, why shouldn't I also give her $100 a month?

It was a Hot Chocolate moment. Everyone's a winner, baby.

Laughing Outlaw stumbled along. One of the heads of our distributors, Inertia, said he believed it was only a matter of time before we discovered an artist who became huge. How much time was that going to take, I wondered. There was no shortage of people knocking on the door and wanting the label to release their music, and there was the occasional sniff that something big was just around the corner – but the trip to that location increasingly seemed just beyond our reach.

However, we stayed in business and all was well and (more or less) good for a few years. That was until 2012, when the young landlady and her financial adviser again took an interest in the property. The advisor muttered something about it being a commercial premises and the rent needing to go up to market value.

Unfortunately for Laughing Outlaw, this was measured in many, *many* hundreds of dollars a week – not $100 a month. Trying my old strategy, I mentioned to her that the place was falling apart and that I was doing them a favour looking after her real estate. This time it was no dice. I suspect it was financially better for her if the building was vacant (people who know about this stuff mutter about negative gearing and all sorts of concepts that are beyond me). And so it became for the next five years, before being sold as a renovator's delight.

By necessity, the label moved up the road to my home. That was the end of the shopfront side of things and the beginning of the end for the label. Did I miss the shop? Not so much, particularly as the last location was a bit too run-down and spatially constricted for my liking. And I was beginning to realise that customer relations wasn't my strong point.

I was also feeling a bit beaten down by the label itself. A couple of artists we'd had high hopes for – and in one case invested significant (for Laughing Outlaw) amounts of money in – decided to part company with us. That knocked my faith in artist loyalty, as well as having me question whether the label would ever become seriously financially viable. Overall, I was tired and wanted a change: so I started to think about what life after Laughing Outlaw would be like.

By this time, my marriage to Vicki had ended. She continued with the label, which still operates as a mail-order business.

Would I ever start another record label? Funny you should mention it. I think about it often, but it's probably wise that I think, but don't *act*. There are great things about indie labels – working with artists and releasing all that music you love – but the downsides can be massive. They're also a massive amount of seemingly never-ending work, financially extremely precarious, and you're often destined to be the villains if things don't work out for an artist and their releases.

But I had some great, great times with Laughing Outlaw and its coterie of fellow travellers. I'm proud of much of what the label achieved. However, in what appears to be an ongoing pattern in my life, I don't actually own a copy of everything we released. If you have a spare copy of the CD by the Melbourne duo The Long Weekend, I'm in the market.

# 47

# RADIO RADIO

**S**trange now to think that, during my early years, there was no television in the house. I grew up with radio, as did most of my generation and those that preceded it. When televisions did appear in Australia – in the year of my birth – my grandparents were comparatively early adopters.

My earliest memories of engagement with TV were Sunday evenings, when we visited them and I was allowed to watch the Walt Disney show. I recall the devastation of being banned for some period of time after apparently referring to my grandfather Len as 'an old bugger'. I can only imagine I picked that one up from my father. But the period of separation between me and Sunday-evening TV stung, such that it looms larger in my mind than even the totally alluring, all-American singing gal, Annette Funicello. And I'm pretty sure I had Mouseketeer ears around this time.

But in the absence of television, I listened to the radio, particularly after I'd turned 11. I could have listened to the local stations, 7LA and 7EX, via a regular radio, but I had a crystal radio set. It was a curious device – a bunch of wires, circuits, diodes and coils attached to a thin plywood board – that managed to pick up radio signals. It was connected by metal clips to a telephone. You'd then listen through a single earpiece. Sounds weird, I'll admit – but all that really mattered to me was that it worked, and I was connected to radio waves on the mysterious – to a young Tasmanian – 'mainland'.

In those days, the family telephone was beside my parents' bed, so I sat on the floor in their room for hours immersed in whatever sounds and songs I could pick up. I loved the mystery of the crystal radio set, that it was mine alone and felt like a personal connection with the music beaming in from the outside world. There was a real sense of adventure listening to radio from so far afield.

In Launceston, 7LA was pretty conservative. I listened to 7EX, which was more adventurous and rock'n'roll oriented in its programming. The station was located about 20 feet from the Wills & Co record shop.

By 1968, I was hooked on songs and radio. I still own some of the singles – Tammy Wynette's 'Stand By Your Man' and the Detroit Wheels' raucous and thinly disguised punky ode to psychedelics, 'Linda Sue Dixon' ('LSD to me') – that were amongst the 10 I won in a competition on 7EX. The proximity of the crystal radio to the telephone worked here.

The competition involved ringing the station and, if you got through, you had to sing a few lines of a popular song lyric. I couldn't sing to save my – or anyone else's – life, but I did get put to air and managed to warble tentatively a small portion of The Who's 'I'm A Boy'.

My reward for participating was those 10 singles, most likely records they'd been sent that were never going to feature on the station playlist. It always surprised me that a song celebrating hallucinogenic drugs was amongst them, and I've hung onto the two that mattered to me most: country music and punky rock'n'roll were already in my psyche.

After I moved to Adelaide, I had my first encounters with radio, other than as a listener. As I've mentioned, I'd somehow managed to scam my way into getting the ABC to pay me $50 a week to store my records. Around the same time, I wrote a few scripts for specials on my friend David Woodhall's radio show. One was on Lenny Bruce, another on Randy Newman, and a special on the Beat Generation poets and jazz.

A year or so later, I had an opportunity to actually speak on the radio as a presenter, and to find out whether I enjoyed it and had any aptitude for it. For a brief period – probably less than six months in 1977 – myself and a friend and fellow music obsessive, the opinionated and amusing Dennis Atkins, co-hosted a two-hour show on the Adelaide University radio station, 5UV.

The show was called *Modern Love Songs*. Dennis and I gagged around and played usually new music that we were digging. We also played some classics from yesteryear, and gave what information we had about the songs and bands, combined with a few superlatives about how you really needed to hear whatever it was we were spinning.

It was fun, but I didn't feel like it was my calling. I preferred quietly reflecting about music to the fast-paced, spontaneous requirements of radio. Writing was my thing.

Around 1980, after I'd moved to Sydney, I was hanging around with a couple of friends who lived a street or two away in Stanmore, John Potts and his girlfriend, Virginia Madsen. They had a connection with the fledgling 2SER station, run by and from the University of Technology.

Somehow the idea was mooted about me and John and doing a radio show together. A few years had passed since my stint at 5UV, and I thought I'd see if I felt more of an affinity with being on the airwaves. John could operate a panel at the studios – on the 26th floor on Sydney's ugliest building on Broadway – while I had the records and knowledge. We decided to call it *From Punk To Funk*. A version of the show with a slightly different name is still going more than four decades later.

Every week, often after dashing into the nearby *Sun-Herald* office, or before or after an interview with a musician or whatever other activity my frenetic and erratic work schedule involved, I'd catch the super-scary lift to the top of the building. It always felt like its doors wouldn't open, or that it might plummet 20 floors (or maybe I just don't like elevators). There, John and I would attempt to put together a radio show.

I was terrible. I stumbled over my words, had no idea how to structure a microphone break (explaining what songs I'd just played or that the listener was about to hear) or how to distil what I knew into short punchy sentences. It was a frustrating stop, start, stumble kind of show that lasted about six months, and I'm glad that as far as I'm aware no recordings of these shows remain. On the upside, I did get to play The Ramones, Patti Smith, The Ronettes, The Shangri-Las, James Brown, Talking Heads and so forth.

I liked the concept of being on the radio, but found it stressful and unnatural, so once again radio was filed in the 'not for me' category. That was until the mid-1980s, when Charlie Fox, program director at 2MMM, suggested that I might be interested in co-hosting the Sunday-night album show with their resident presenter, Bruce Stalder. Why not give it another go? 2MMM was a big deal. And hell, there might be payment involved. I had bills to pay, drugs to buy.

So, on Sunday nights I wandered into MMM in Bondi Junction with a pile of vinyl. Once the show started, I chatted with Bruce, who did all the heavy verbal and panelling lifting.

Since my 2SER days, I'd added a particular element to my on-air presence – a fondness for speed and cocaine. My delivery on radio often reflected a heightened – or at least accelerated – state of being. Added to that state of mind was hesitation. Ideas were cascading around in my brain, valiantly in search of a form of coherent verbal articulation.

I'd pause, searching for the right word or expression: things I took my time over when writing. My experienced and supportive co-host let it slide for a few weeks – until, clearly, it not only bugged him, but I think he assumed it would be having the same effect on the listener.

'Have you ever noticed how much you say "um" and "err" on the radio?' Bruce said one day, when we met up at the station to talk about the music for the upcoming show.

'No – because I don't do that,' I retorted.

'Well, here's a recording of last Sunday night's show,' he said. 'You take a listen.'

I took the tape home, pressed 'play', and was horrified: every third or fourth word was 'umm' or 'err'. I made Molly Meldrum seem artic-ulate. In the weeks that followed, I tried to improve, but I was nervous, overthinking, and didn't really get much better.

Soon, the album show changed format. There was less emphasis on two guys chatting about an album or two; it moved to a wider selection of songs from new albums and with less talk (or maybe it was that I was still umming and erring too much). My time was up. Once more, I'd lasted about six months.

Charlie Fox was good about it, though, and gave me the opportunity to practise in a studio and hopefully improve and broaden my skills. During that time, I recorded one interview. It was a disastrous monosyllabic chat with an unforthcoming Tracy Chapman, then in Japan and on her way to Australia – which I don't think ever went to air. Yet again, I decided that radio wasn't for me. I was okay as a guest talking about things for quick grabs, but I *definitely* wasn't cut out to present radio shows.

And that's how it stayed for almost two decades. Then, in 2003 FBi radio went to air as a fully-fledged station, after years of test broadcasts, endless fundraising and license struggles. By pure chance I was at the station the day it first broadcast.

Ben Roper, a young guy who was doing work experience at Laughing Outlaw Records, as well as volunteering in the music library at FBi, wanted to go to the celebrations. I tagged along, having no idea that I was a month away from one of my life-defining experiences.

FBi was a breath of fresh air in Sydney. Sure, there were a bunch of other community stations in the city, but this was new, vibrant, contemporary, edgy, and very supportive of local music. It was in their charter that at least 25 per cent of what was played on air had to be new music from this city.

Along with the longstanding 2SER, Radio Skid Row and Koori Radio, it resulted in what Sydney had lacked since Double J went national at the end of the 1980s – a strong community radio culture, of the kind Melbourne had enjoyed for decades, with 3RRR, 3PBS, 3CR etc. I loved it and in those early weeks I listened constantly in the Laughing Outlaw offices.

The phone rang one day. It was Meagan Loader, the program director at FBi. I didn't know Meagan so I was a little surprised to get the call. She wanted to know if I was interested in presenting a show on the station – a roots/country/blues/songwriters show? I was. Very interested. But could I do it? My previous radio experiences suggested absolutely no way.

I agreed, though, partly because I'd get some training sessions on how to operate a studio (what do all those buttons do?). Someone else had always done this for me when I'd been on air, and I figured it was a good life skill to have. And maybe I'd be a bit better at it than in the past?

The training was, I recall, pretty rudimentary and basic. One thing you quickly learn about radio is that the essentials of operating a studio are rather simple. Once you've mastered them, you only find out how good you are when something goes catastrophically wrong. And with radio, it helps if you can talk underwater: by this stage I'd gotten pretty good at that. I still ummed and erred a bit more than I liked, but I worked on eradicating that from my vocab, and relaxing and enjoying the experience. And maybe not taking drugs helped with that.

I'd stopped taking drugs that made my heart beat faster and my thoughts cascade, just before moving to the Blue Mountains in 1990. So I was a different beast than during my previous radio stints in Sydney.

Everyone at FBi was required to do at least one midnight-till-dawn show with a more experienced presenter. If you fucked up, the chances were that not too many people would hear. I went in one Saturday night to inner-suburban Alexandria just before midnight to be confronted by a pretty crazy scene.

A crew of dudes, seemingly connected with the presenters on air, were hanging out on a ratty couch in the car park outside the back door, and people were wandering around the station in what looked like various states of heightened consciousness. It felt like party central more than a radio station.

The presenter who was meant to be teaching me the ropes appeared to be friends with everyone else there. He was seemingly more engaged with the party happening in his head, but he was nice enough. I have very little recollection of the night, beyond playing a few CDs and introducing and back-announcing those songs. By 6 am, I was apparently ready for my first solo shift the next week.

My show was named *Lyricism*. It was a concept which – somewhat cheekily – I swung pretty free and easy with. The name had been suggested by Meagan and I think it was meant to have a playlist oriented towards alternative country and roots music. I played a lot of that – and then some. And if anyone asked what I played, I quipped, 'Anything with lyrics' – which explained why the Ramones and the Shangri-Las found themselves in the mix for a roots music show.

Naturally I was super-nervous the first Wednesday night. FBi had only been broadcasting for about a month and here I was. What if things went horribly wrong? How would I manage my first-ever solo radio show? Would I fall apart and it'd turn into a debacle?

The show was scheduled to run from 10 pm till 1 am, and usually at that time of night only the presenter was in the building. In what was a lovely gesture, Meagan and board member Julia Thomas turned up as I was about to go to air, allegedly to vacuum and clean up. It wasn't until a few weeks later that it dawned on me that there was no carpet at the station, we had cleaners, and none of this needed attending to at 10 pm. Of course, they were there to check that I was OK.

To my huge relief, that first show went fine. There were no major technical meltdowns. Hey, maybe I wasn't as terrible at this radio lark as I'd thought I was. Gradually, I became comfortable with talking into a microphone in an empty room and operating the desk and started to love it. I'd usually take a sixpack of beer with me, but I was careful not to get slurry and for the most part I was successful.

I started to invite guests in for interviews – a mixture of local and interstate artists, plus visiting internationals such as Steve Poltz and Gregory Page – and have regular themed or guest-programmer segments. Fellow music lover Paul Howell used to come in every six weeks and we'd do a vinyl show, with him operating the turntables. Our love of noisy rock'n'roll and beer often resulted in these weeks totally pushing the *Lyricism* concept.

Once I played a Norwegian country band and my friend Vince Simonetti sent me a note about how he collected Norwegian alt-country artists. I invited him onto the show and it worked so well that it became a semi-regular segment, with Vince guesting every four or five weeks.

Another regular participant in the show didn't actually come inside. One night I walked out of the station a few minutes after 1 am, and there was a taxi parked directly outside. I always took a cab home – as I didn't drive and public transport was well and truly shut down for the night. The driver handed me a CD and explained that it was a demo of some stuff he was working on. From then on, I played things from him from time to time – and it was a mutually beneficial relationship. For close to a year his cab was parked outside at 1 am. I always paid the fare. No cash for comment here.

In fact, I'd learnt about that very early on in my tenure at FBi. I've always been conflicted over what to do with artists I'm associated with, when it comes to journalism or radio. Of course, I totally understand conflict of interest, but even back in my days with *The Sun-Herald* and *Dolly*, I found myself having a dilemma, particularly when I was working with high-profile artists.

If I wasn't the music writer, the Hoodoo Gurus and Paul Kelly would definitely be written about, so should they miss out on the exposure? And, given that I often gave coverage to other Australian independent artists, like Pel Mel, Machinations, Laughing Clowns and so forth, was it wrong to slip Tactics or the Lime Spiders – who I was involved with – into the mix?

When I started at FBi, they only had one show that would play roots/Americana/singer-songwriter stuff – and that was my show. Was it fair on the artists who'd had the good sense to do a deal with Laughing Outlaw that they missed out on the exposure on the station? So, one night around midnight, I bit the proverbial bullet and played a song by Jason Walker and his band The Last Drinks.

The phone rang in the studio within minutes. I picked it up. A male voice on the other end.

'*Fucking conflict of interest.*'

Then the line went dead. I must admit I was shaken. At the speed of the call. The vitriol. And that someone clearly gave a shit. Big-time.

Community radio stations seem to have a vague rule that present-ers can mention or play something they're connected with each show without causing too much ire. But I still don't do it often. A large percentage of people I work with never get played on my radio shows, and I let them know that straight up – so if I do it's an unexpected surprise, and not me fulfilling an obligation or promise.

But back to the interaction with listeners. Radio is by its very nature a very personal, intimate experience. I can't stand the sound of my voice – seriously, I'll sprint in the opposite direction from any situation where I need to listen to myself. I dread air checks as well. This horrible (but necessary) process involves sitting with the station program manager and going through a recent show to work out things that could be improved or changed.

We're taught on radio to speak to just one person: the way Phillip Adams says, 'Hello, listener.' There was one guy, whose show on FBi was after mine, who, after napping for an hour on the floor in the CD library, would come in and put a big stuffed toy – a sort of doll, I think – in a chair across the desk, where a guest would traditionally sit. And he'd present his show talking to this stuffed object. It was his way of focusing on the listener and not saying, 'Thanks to you all for listening tonight.' It was 'Thank *you* for listening tonight.' You and the listener having a conversation.

*Lyricism* finished in about 2006 when the station decided they needed a show more specifically playing country, roots and folk music – and not veering into punk rock and '60s girl groups, along with whatever else I felt inclined to play.

But FBi wanted me to continue broadcasting, so I suggested I take over presenting *Out Of The Box*, as the existing host was moving on. This was a show in which an interesting, usually non-music person came in to talk about their life and work, and play songs from their collection to illustrate and inform that. I did *Out Of The Box* for about a year, but became frustrated, because, whilst I enjoyed interviewing people, I had no input into the musical content of the show.

There was also the occasional issue of navigating around the guests' musical selections and the feel and sound of FBi. On one show, the guest was a highly intelligent woman talking about her battles with mental health and, in particular, bipolar issues. She was fascinating and insightful, but with rather un-FBi musical selections.

At one stage, in the producer's booth, as I was playing George Michael's 'Careless Whisper', I could see the program director grimacing and offering other pained facial expressions that said, 'Get this shit off!'

It was a tough one. George and FBi were uneasy bedfellows at the best of times, but the guest's rationale for playing the song and her interaction with it were powerful and poignant.

I had no desire to finish up at the station, but I desired a show where I chose the music, so I suggested that someone else take the reins of *Out Of The Box*. In time-honoured FBi tradition, I was the guest when the new presenter took over. I was tempted to select a George Michael song (maybe 'Wake Me Up Before You Go-Go' or 'Wham! Rap'), but decided against it.

One thing I loved about FBi was that we'd have very serious discussions at station meetings over the difference between a 'soft' fuck and a 'hard' fuck. You may now be wondering what the fuck I'm talking about.

By way of edification, a soft use of the word 'fuck' (where it's not loud or pronounced) in a song doesn't usually require a language warning before it's played on air. However, a hard 'fuck' or 'fuck's does (one that's loud and very clear). I was reminded one day after I'd forgotten to give a warning that the Nick Cave song I'd played during the show had a number of hard 'fuck's in it.

Next at FBi, I suggested to the programmers an hour of radio devoted to cover versions. Someone at the meeting asked, in all seriousness, 'Do you think you'll have enough material to do the show for six months?' I replied that I could play nothing but covers of Bob Dylan songs and, without repeating a version, do the show for 10 years.

*Tune Up* went to air for the first time in 2007, in a Tuesday timeslot, starting at midday. For many FBi programs, the audience was noticeably older than the 18–25 demographic – and that was certainly the case here. Older listeners wanted to keep abreast of contemporary music, but didn't mind the odd diversion back to the good old days.

With *Tune Up*, the audience usually knew the original, as well as the cover version. FBi loved these people because, being a bit older, typically they were more financially secure. When it came time for the annual supporter drive, they voted with their wallets.

So, the show was going well. But after about 12 months, for reasons I find hard to explain, I began to struggle psychologically. This time, it wasn't in the form of agoraphobia – it was crippling anxiety. In the days prior to the show, I felt it building. From the Friday before, I'd start to get a churning stomach whenever I thought about it.

Nerves are okay. They're part of the natural lead-up to any performance. One day I had the late Damien Lovelock from The Celibate Rifles on as a guest. I told him how anxious I got before a show.

'That's good,' he said. 'If you ever come in here and you're not nervous, maybe it's time to wonder why you're doing it.'

That was OK in theory, but on the Tuesday, from when I woke up, I was vomiting constantly until I somehow made it to the studio. I'm not sure how I made it through the show.

Over the next couple of years, it got worse. I progressed from just vomiting to full-on panic attacks. It became so bad that I couldn't face the train journey of a few stops from my home to Redfern, and the quick walk down to FBi.

I knew I had to keep doing the show, though. I needed it, I loved it and it got me out of the house. So, for those couple of years, I'd catch a taxi over to FBi and back, or Vicki would collect me. It was tough.

I'd developed all the classic symptoms – jelly legs, feelings of being about to faint, an inability to even walk 20 feet to the corner shop. I related to the saying I'd read: 'How do you recognise a panic-attack sufferer? They're the ones in the supermarket pushing an empty trolley around.' I did that. It was security. Something to hold onto.

That was when I did actually make it to the shops. More often than not, I'd go to the supermarket with Vicki, as I needed to feel involved – but then I'd sit in the car, whilst she did the shopping. Then, frustrated that I couldn't cope with the actual retail process, I'd help load and unload the purchases.

During that time, I couldn't go to gigs unless I could sit down. I was terrified to go anywhere by myself. I tried seeing a therapist about it, but when there wasn't any noticeable improvement, I began to panic even more about how much it was costing me. Then the therapist's building burned down. That wasn't a good sign.

I was struggling, completely frustrated, scared and desperate to find a way out. One day, finally, there was a chink of light. It came courtesy of a colleague at FBi.

It was 2011, I think, when my colleague sensed what was going on. He suggested we have lunch, so we went to the White Cockatoo in Petersham and chatted. He knew all about panic attacks, because he'd suffered with them for a long time too. He knew how debilitating they could be.

He told me about an online course for anxiety sufferers, run by St Vincent's Hospital. I was cynical, but I enrolled, and it was the best thing I could possibly have done. I worked through the course over a few months, looking at patterns of anxiety, learning not to be afraid of the physical manifestations. I did the assignments, and occasionally talked on the phone with the course supervisor. It shouldn't have succeeded – as I did most of the work at home alone – but it did.

I gradually noticed some improvements – and then great improvements. Suddenly, I was able to go to the supermarket, and actually enjoying it. It was fantastic not being totally freaked out at crowded gigs. I mean, I'm still not great at that.

The other thing that coincided with the course was a dramatic reduction in my drinking. It took me a long time to realise that I was a hell of a lot better as a radio presenter when I was clear-headed. Addressing my drinking problem began in earnest around 2013. I decided I needed to write my next book – on Michael Gudinski – sober. But I'll get to that.

It was quite a journey during those years on *Tune Up*. I loved presenting it, though, despite everything. One of my favourite aspects of it was that, if I was doing a show and played Roy Harper or Jethro Tull, the text line would light up – not with young listeners wanting more information, but from older folk who were delighted and surprised to be hearing this music on FBi. Recently, I received a text from a listener: 'I turned on FBi and heard the Allman Brothers – I knew it must be your show.'

*Tune Up* would often feature guests, and the deal was that they had to talk about, and sing, covers. One guest was American alt-country singer-songwriter Justin Townes Earle. He arrived for the show (which started at midday) smelling like he'd inhaled all the available pot in Sydney. He was still remarkably coherent and sang with such power that, even with all the microphone faders flattened (so they weren't picking up anything from him through the mixing desk), the signals were still bouncing into the red.

For his cover he sang a remarkable version of 'Dreams' by Fleetwood Mac. A few days later, his Australian record company rang, asking if they could include the song on Earle's forthcoming release. That live performance became the final track on his *Absent Fathers* album.

Then there was the time the semi-legendary Rodriguez arrived at 11 am. We shook hands and his opening words were: 'Is it too early for a drink?' Yes it was, even for me, who was drinking in those days.

*Tune Up* was also responsible for an unlikely reunion with Steve Kilbey. By 2011, he and I hadn't spoken for around 30 years. The anger from Kilbey seemed to have burned bright. In Robert Dean Lurie's 2009 book, *No Certainty Attached: Steve Kilbey And The Church*, Kilbey continued the vitriol, telling Robert I'd invited him on my radio show and saying he'd refused. (Actually, not that it matters, but I hadn't invited him on the show.)

Also, around that time, I was having coffee with Marty Willson-Piper from the band at a café near the town hall in the city. He was expecting Kilbey to collect him for a rehearsal, and the singer/bass player rang to say he was approaching. Willson-Piper told him who he was with: Kilbey said he'd wait for him two blocks down the road.

So we jump forward to 2011. When a mutual friend, Sue Campbell, proposed Kilbey as a guest on *Tune Up*, I said that I didn't have an issue – but I thought he might. Actually, there'd been an indication that he was finally softening a bit. The previous year, I'd woken up to a 'friend' request from Kilbey on Facebook. I assumed my account had been hacked, or someone was trying to mess with me. But I accepted and, yes, it was the real Kilbey.

Then the call came that he'd do the FBi chat. I was beyond nervous – and I imagine he was the same – but he came in with drummer Tim Powles. I decided to take the initiative and – trying to hide my concerns that he may be less than friendly – bounded from the desk where I was sitting with a 'Hi, Steve, good to see you'. He looked at me slowly, smiled, and said a guarded, but warm 'Hi, Stuart'. Then the show got underway and he and Tim chatted and sang. It was cordial, professional and, at times, lighthearted and engaging. Afterwards, we had our photos taken together. All was fine.

A little later, we appeared together on James Valentine's ABC arts and entertainment TV show *The Mix*. Still friendly. More photos. Then, in 2020, Kilbey came to my house to record a radio interview. I sent him some copies of his memoir, *Something Quite Peculiar*, to sign for my daughter. He did.

But the tension and memory of the past still lingers, albeit with a smile. Recently, Kilbey rang to check my address to send a copy of a new CD. He left a voice message: 'Stuart, this is the greatest songwriter who ever lived. Can you bell me back when you get this?' It took me a minute or two to realise it wasn't Bob Dylan who'd called.

And in early 2022, I heard that I was the fodder for a couple of not really malicious gags during a tour in which he was playing all The Church's singles.

I mentioned this to Kilbey in a Facebook message. He replied, saying that maybe I should become part of the show, coming onstage with my old *RAM* stories in a scrapbook, and reading extracts from them. I wrote back, saying I was totally up for that, but to date it hasn't been mentioned again.

Long may the banter continue.


Incidentally, in about 2011 – or maybe later – I was asked to do a brief stint on Radio National, filling in for Lucky Oceans on his late-night roots music show, whilst he was on holidays. Aside from loving the opportunity to present this highly regarded and popular program, it was a rare treat – the ABC asked for an invoice at the end of every broadcast.

Getting $250 to do a two-hour radio show. That was a novelty. More please.

During that time – sadly for me, a mere five weeks – I learnt something important about the voice and radio. I was pre-recording the programs in the afternoon and they sounded fine – but when I listened back, I sounded too chirpy and jaunty. I had my afternoon/daytime radio voice going on, which didn't translate so well at 11 pm. I had to work at sounding 'late night' in the afternoon for the subsequent shows.

After a decade of *Tune Up*, a period in which it had become one of the most popular shows on the station, across roughly 6500 cover versions, Dan Ahern, the new program director at FBi, felt that maybe the show had run its course. When he told me that in a program review meeting in 2020, he could see my look of concern. He hastily reassured me that this wasn't the end of my time at the station.

He said that my musical knowledge wasn't being utilised enough with *Tune Up* and that a new show was called for – one that allowed me to range far and wide with what I played. He had an idea for a new program: that's how *Wild Card* was born. That very day.

It would be the same timeslot, but I'd start with a contemporary Australian song or artist, and riff off that for an hour. So, from something that was released the previous week, I could jump back to 1973, and forwards and backwards and around – just as long as there was some (even very tangential) connection between each song.

The idea sprang from something former FBi presenter Paul Gough and I would do from time to time, when he was hosting the excellent *Inside Sleeve* on Radio National and had me on as a guest. He called it musical tennis.

This was around 2016 and 2017, and we'd go into the studio with a huge pile of music – CDs, laptops – and at the start of the show, we'd toss a coin. The winner would play a track (hitting a song across the net, if you will), and the other person would have to counter with a related song ('That was Patti Smith with "Gloria",' says Paul, and

Stuart counters, '"Gloria" was originally by Van Morrison and Them – speaking of Morrison, let's listen to "Light My Fire" by The Doors.'). That sort of thing. Because it was a live show, it was a bit hectic, but we loved it.

That's how *Wild Card* would work – except I'd be banging musical tennis balls against a wall. I hoped it'd be fun, pacy and unpredictable. The challenge was to create an hour of radio that would entertain and intrigue the listener.

Three years later, *Wild Card* is still going strong. I love doing the show and the audience reaction has been great. I hope I'll be banging those tennis balls against that wall at FBi for a while yet.

# 48
# WOKE UP THIS MORNING

For years, I'd had periods of massively excessive drinking. I drank pretty much every day from my early 20s until around 2011 – and then some. At the end of the '90s I was drinking constantly, all day and night. I was in an apartment in the city that was high enough from the ground that – well, let's just say that I Blu-Tacked photos of my children on all the opening windows, in case things took a turn for the worst. There were visits from Lifeline and times in hospital.

Apart from going to see the Swans play with Neil Rankin, a lovely smart guy who played drums in the Australian Doors Show, I rarely left the apartment. Neil's companionship was a bright light in my very dark world. How had my drinking reached that level? And believe me, it got worse. It had been a slow escalation over the years. When I snorted speed in the early 1980s, I could drink more – so I drank more. Usually beer. Sometimes wine. Cocaine was the same. Do lines, drink, do more lines, drink more, continue until comatose.

And I drank the most when I was unhappy. A friend once said after my life had taken a turn for the better, 'I thought you were an alcoholic – but I realised you were just sad.' The reality was that I was both.

In the 2000s I discovered vodka. Slowly at first – a hipflask here, a hipflask there, combined with beer – then half-bottles, then full bottles secreted around the house and under my desk at Laughing Outlaw.

I was like the guy in the film *The Lost Weekend* – the one who attaches a string to a bottle of booze and tries to hide it outside his apartment window. That guy.

I told myself that I really liked drinking – and there was some truth in that. I liked to climb to a certain plateau and then listen to music or read. That I couldn't remember much about either the next day was neither here nor there. Let's do it again. And I became nervous if the alcohol in the house started to run low. Very nervous.

I was (for the most part) a functioning alcoholic. My tolerance was high. I could, and often did, drink in the mornings. I'd never go to meetings without a flask of vodka in my bag. I could be temperamental – often grumpy, verbally cutting – but often jovial and, at least as far as I was aware, fun to be around. Maybe that was just my perspective.

At various times I'd tried to stop drinking – a few half-hearted attempts at AA, a week in rehab, a day in detox. I don't really think I wanted to stop. I would kid myself that things were improving by trying to make sure that I didn't have my first drink during a weekday until 6 pm. But was it Bob Hawke who said that, after a while, all you think about is how long it is till 6 pm? And all bets were off on weekends – champagne and orange juice first thing.

I wasn't – in hindsight – nearly as productive as I could have been. I thought I was doing OK, but it's only as I've looked at my post-drinking world that I realise how little I was really achieving, how much potential was being wasted, and how I fooled myself about friendships and relationships that weren't nourished or really didn't exist.

In 2011 a woman named Susan walked into Laughing Outlaw Records. For reasons I just don't know, she made me open up and really start thinking about what I was doing. It wasn't a fast process, and it wasn't easy, especially on her. But without that chance meeting, I'm not sure I could talk about a post-drinking world or a book about Michael Gudinski.

Back in 2003 or 2004, when I became aware of how many copies of *The Promoters* Gudinski had bought and his enthusiasm for the project, I began thinking about writing a book about him. Just him. It struck me that he was the most powerful and influential figure in the history of Australian rock'n'roll – by a fairly long shot. OK, 'Molly' Meldrum had wielded a lot of power over a long period of time, but Gudinski had done it in more diverse areas of the industry – records, publishing, promoting, management – and over a longer period of time. Meldrum worked with the talent that had been nurtured and developed by people like Gudinski.

Speaking of Meldrum, as I've mentioned I liked him a lot and always enjoyed talking with him. Apart from interviewing him for an early *Roadrunner* magazine, we had a number of encounters via *Dolly*. Around 1987, I remember going to his house in Richmond for an early-morning interview. Molly greeted me at the door in his dressing-gown and with a Scotch and Coke in his hand. It was 9 am.

Later in the morning, I was hanging around as a succession of visitors dropped by, many of them from record companies with new releases. At one point I was sitting with Molly and a publicity rep from EMI in his listening room. Out of the blue, Molly turned to the guy from EMI, and said, 'Have you actually met my boyfriend – this is Stuart.' Molly thought it was hysterical. So did I. The rep was speechless.

Molly is smart, super-smart. While he might sometimes have been nervous on television, and his umms and ahhs might have conveyed the image of a bumbling idiot, anyone who took him for a fool did so at their peril.

And he has a wicked sense of humour. Many years later, in 1996, I was at a party at his house with a companion. I have no idea why we were there – I'm pretty sure I wasn't invited. I'd explained to my companion – who I was trying to impress – that, yes, I knew Molly and we went back many years.

There were people everywhere around the swimming pool, and we were talking to Sue McAuley from Mushroom when Molly came over. She said to him, 'You've met Stuart Coupe.' Molly looked at me, affected drawing a complete blank, and replied, 'No, we've never met. What do you do?'

I felt like a complete idiot. I was being shown up as a total fraud – a big noter with nothing to back it up.

Then, after what seemed like forever – but was probably 10 seconds – Molly burst out laughing. 'Of course, I know Stuart – how are you, darling?' he asked, and threw his arms around me. Embarrassment to the max avoided.

But much as I loved Molly, he'd had a book about him published recently – and the Gudinski story interested me more. So around 2004 I started enquiring about his interest in me writing about him. I thought he'd jump at the opportunity – but it was the opposite. In fact, he said it would never happen. *Ever.* And this was despite my assurances that I didn't want to write a book driven by sex and drugs, and that I wasn't remotely interested in something full of innuendo. (Incidentally, I never did find out why he was so opposed to his story being told.)

For years, every six months or so I'd shoot an email to Gudinski's assistant, reminding her – and him – that I was still keen. Usually, there wasn't a response. When there was, it was *No*.

Then, in September 2011 Gudinski came on my FBi show to talk about Australian music in general, but specifically about a new hard-cover book, which told – largely through posters – the 30-year history of his Frontier Touring Company. I was worried about how I was going to keep the notoriously frenetic Gudinski amused, as he'd have to sit in the studio whilst the music was being played. But when he arrived at the station, he was frail and subdued. Only later did I realise that he'd been very sick with what he'd thought was pancreatic cancer.

Gudinski sat quietly in the studio, spoke calmly about the music and, whilst songs were playing, scribbled on an A4 piece of paper. When the interview was finished, he pulled out the Frontier book and copied what he'd drafted out into the front of it:

Stuart, I know this will rekindle lots of great memories. This is the closest you'll ever get to a book from yours truly. Thanks for being there (on) this amazing journey. Never let your incredible passion for music ever die. Thanks (for) The Promoters. Stick Em Up! Enjoy it Stuart. Michael Gudinski.

Undeterred, I kept pestering – politely. Still no dice. Then one day in 2013 I was talking with my publisher Matthew Kelly at Hachette, and we decided to just start working on a Gudinski book and see what happened. We agreed – somewhat naively – that we could do a book on him without his direct participation.

I think I'd called just one person about this before the phone rang. It was Gudinski. 'I hear you're writing a book about me,' he barked down the line. 'I don't want a book.'

Of course, everyone I called asked if the biography was authorised. When I said it wasn't, they said they'd get back to me. And then didn't. Clearly, they were all checking with Gudinski, who I found out was telling them not to talk to me – at the moment. *At the moment.* That was a slight movement. At least, I convinced myself it was.

What Gudinski didn't realise – and it's not uncommon – is that when it comes to books, you don't actually own your life. You can tell people not to talk, but if someone uses other sources and doesn't defame you and gets the facts pretty much right, there's not much you can do, beyond telling people you didn't participate in the book and not to buy it.

At one point, I explained to Gudinski that I was a big fan of most – not all – of what he'd done, and therefore was well placed to write a book about him. Semi-jokingly, I offered to send him a list of people who liked him a lot less than me who could all string a sentence together.

For six months, though, there was stonewalling. I kept researching and calling people. No-one was prepared to talk without confirmation that it was an authorised book and that Gudinski was onside. The project was moving very slowly and I wasn't sure if it would ever seriously get off the ground.

Then, one day I made contact with Michelle Higgins – the legendary figure in the signing Paul Kelly story. She'd left Mushroom late that decade, moved to New York and was living upstate there. I explained to her what I was doing and how it was being thwarted by everyone checking with Gudinski.

'Well, I'm not checking with him,' she said. 'It's too important a story not to be told. I'll talk to you.'

I called Gudinski to tell him. At this point I think he started to realise that this book was going to happen and that he may as well co-operate. Ironically, given that it was well known that I liked Gudinski and that he had a few dollars in the bank, it was widely assumed – especially on social media – that he was paying me to write a whitewashed book about him. (I didn't hear much from any of these people when the book came out.)

It might sound as if I'd done the hard part – getting Gudinski to agree to co-operate with the book. But was it *actually* going to happen? Very early in the proceedings, I'd gone on a drinking binge. I ended up hospitalised when I couldn't stop vomiting. The book deal was almost cancelled. My publishers weren't convinced I could deliver.

So, I decided to write the book sober. And I stuck to it. Seriously stuck to it. How did I do it? No meetings, no hypnosis. I'm pretty sure it's because of the way I am wired and the way I have always done things – I just stopped. With hindsight, I am sorta lucky I could still make that call. And although this period of sobriety served me well, it didn't last. Wanting to meet my obligations to my publishers was a good reason to stop drinking, sure, but it wasn't enough to make me want to give up completely. At that time I was still struggling to face the years of emotional carnage, broken relationships and sadness, and didn't think I had the will to do it.

Gudinski was drinking heavily when I was hanging out with him and it amazes me I didn't succumb. Pretty much whenever we met up, within a few minutes he'd say 'You still not drinking?' He'd look incredulous and kept asking how I did it – to which I replied the same way every time.

'Michael, I'll tell you how to stop drinking. You just don't drink.'

Oh yeah . . . right. It's actually not that easy. Who was I kidding?

I remember distinctly the first gig I saw sober. It was Iggy Pop and the Stooges on 2 April 2013 at the Hordern Pavilion. Support was the Beasts Of Bourbon. I was physically pretty weak and, to be honest, not convinced yet that sobriety was a great idea.

And Iggy and the Stooges and the Beasts? Surely that was a gig that required a certain degree of mood enhancement to really embrace and enjoy? What a surprise – I totally loved it and remembered everything about it the next day. Especially how fucking loud it was. But if I could do a Stooges gig sober, well, I could probably do any gig sober.

Slowly, I was given access to members of Gudinski's inner sanctum. However, his family were off-limits to me, which was disappointing – but that's the way he wanted it. I've often wondered if he told them that this was his call and not mine, and if they've ever wondered why I didn't approach them for an interview. Sue, Matt and Kate, I'd have loved to talk to you.

As the process went on, Gudinski gave reasonably freely of his time. On one occasion, he suggested I come to the Hunter Valley for a Rod Stewart show. He had his driver collect me from my home and then drive me to Newcastle, where we collected him from the airport and drove to the concert site. I have to admit, there was something very cool about driving through every security checkpoint at the venue and pulling up backstage in a chauffeur-driven car with Michael Gudinski.

At various times during the afternoon and early evening, I sat in his room backstage and interviewed him again, asking him about aspects of his story that weren't clear to me. In between he'd wander out and up on the stage to watch whoever was playing. At one point he said, 'I'd better go and say hello to Rod.'

Gudinski loved the thrill of the show and being on the road more than just about anything. But there was a pragmatic reason, as well, for him being at the gig. Frontier was under siege from the global deals and massive financial resources of the American company Live Nation, and he really needed his key artists to feel totally loved and cared for. If they didn't, they'd jump ship – and quickly.

Many were jumping, though, no matter how well the tours were run and how much Gudinski love they were showered with. But one of his secret tactics had always been to turn up when he was least expected. This was one of those occasions.

It was raining intermittently during the day, and the grassed areas, which made up most of the site, were slippery. At one point, Stewart started kicking dozens and dozens of soccer balls into the crowd. Gudinski and I were standing near the mixing desk. He was beyond nervous.

'If someone jumps for one of those balls and flips and hurts themselves, we're fucked,' he said, before reminding me that we'd be leaving two songs before the end of the show to beat the traffic.

And that's how it was. His bag was already in the car. We jumped in for the two-hour trip back to Sydney, Gudinski sipping on a bottle of red wine and answering questions whilst I ran my tape recorder. At his upmarket hotel, he staggered in, clutching the almost-empty bottle, before the chauffeur deposited me home. What the rest of the night involved for Michael was anyone's guess. I had the feeling he wasn't going straight to bed.

Another night, Gudinski and I had dinner at his favourite restaurant, Vlado's in Richmond. It was just the two of us upstairs, whilst his driver waited in the car. We chatted for three hours, ate a little bit, which was typical of a man who seemed to like the idea of food more than the reality of it – as the latter meant curtailing his talking. Amidst the conversation, Gudinski drank a few beers and a bottle of red that I later discovered was priced at $400. Then he had his driver take us past various landmarks from Mushroom's history – the first office and so forth.

Most of the conversation that evening was borderline unintelligible and, when it wasn't, Gudinski was trotting out the party line. He rarely deviated from it. And particularly when he was drinking, his words were largely jumbled together. I sensed that the years of drug and – in later years – alcohol abuse were starting to impact on him.

At one stage I mentioned this to Stephen Cummings, who, in a masterful reference to Colonel Kurtz in Joseph Conrad's *Heart of Darkness*, quipped, 'Michael went up the river a while ago – and he's not coming back.'

Matthew Kelly and I had given Gudinski an undertaking that he could read the manuscript for factual accuracy, but that he couldn't change my interpretation. There was a protracted period involving a number of sometimes-tense conversations over a period of weeks explaining to him the difference between these two concepts.

For the most part Gudinski seemed happy with the manuscript. As I've said, he wasn't known for his attention span, so I'll never be any the wiser as to whether he read it all or had someone do it for him. I suspect he spent a fair amount of time with it. He seemed particularly concerned what his wife might think, but I assured him there was nothing in there that would trouble him or her – and there isn't.

The chapter on Kylie Minogue really upset him as, well, it told the truth. He constantly asked me to change it, particularly to omit his lack of enthusiasm for signing Minogue in the early days. The conversation always went like this:

> Gudinski: 'Can you change that fucking Kylie chapter?'
> Stuart: 'Is there anything inaccurate? If so, tell me what and I'll have it changed.'
> Gudinski: 'Look, can you just change it?'
> Stuart: 'Is there anything that I've got wrong?'
> Gudinski: 'Well, no, but can you change it?'

The other sensitive issue was that he thought I'd relied far too much on the telling of events by his former financial manager Simon Young and the former (and now late) managing director Gary Ashley, who kept the record-label side of the empire humming along for decades. It was also Ashley who almost had Gudinski usurped as the head of the company, via an audacious power play with Rupert Murdoch.

I genuinely think that, until he read my book, Gudinski had no idea of how close he came to being removed. He had spectacular and explosive confrontations with both men in the mid-1990s and neither spoke to him again – or he to them. Until the book came out, Gudinski had never heard their side of the story and this was fairly confrontational for him.

There were other things he was surprised by. He wanted to know how I knew where his parents were married and how I'd found his father's arrival papers from when the family came to Australia. I explained to him about Google, which became a running joke between us as his son increasingly introduced him to basic technology. Over the years, if I asked a question Gudinski would smile. 'You ever heard of Google?' he'd say.

The funniest issue regarding fact-checking and corrections came literally the day the book was due to go to the printer. Both Matthew Kelly and I were at our wits' end with requests for changes and other bits and pieces. Matthew had put his foot down and said that the absolute deadline was this particular day.

I was at home in bed with an illness when my phone rang. It was Gudinski's lawyer, explaining that Michael was beside himself. He had been in London and up all night stressing about the book, and he really had to talk to me. The issue was that he was now on a flight home, due to land in Dubai for a stopover at 2.30 pm my time. He'd assured his lawyer that he'd call me the moment he landed and could ring. I begged Matthew to wait and he agreed. 'But that's it,' he said.

At 2.40 pm my phone rang.

This conversation went like this:

Stuart: 'What is it this time?'

Gudinski: 'Look, I've been up all night. Page 17, you say that the yellow car, the E-Type Jaguar, was new. It wasn't fucking new – I didn't have that much money.'

Stuart: 'OK, what else?'

Gudinski: 'You know when you came to the Rod Stewart show and Molly rang and you heard me say some things about St Kilda? Look, Nicky Riewoldt and some of the players will read this book. They're actually playing better than I thought – and that was early in the season – can you soften that a bit?'

Stuart: 'Easy. Anything else?'

Gudinski: 'No, that's great – I'm good. See ya.'

Yes, you've read that right. All that carry-on over the yellow car and an off-hand comment to Molly Meldrum about their beloved St Kilda football team.

The book came out in 2015 and was well received. Gudinski was still bitching about the Kylie chapter and would tell everyone, 'It's not authorised,' but I believe he was secretly delighted by it. He approached my publisher and bought 100 copies. He said that although he was never going to sign a copy for anyone else, he'd inscribe one for me. Sadly, I never took him up on the offer. There was always next time. Until there wasn't.

After the book was published, one unusual social-media thing that took off was that people would take their copies of the book to the most out-of-the-way location, photograph it and send it to me, and I'd post it on Facebook. The book on a Qantas plane, at a resort in Fiji, the Colosseum – dozens and dozens of locations. Gudinski was clearly watching all this and rang one night.

'I love that photo today,' he said, 'I've got a real thing about the Colosseum.'

Gudinski was beautifully empathetic and caring. I remember two occasions in particular. Soon after the book came out, I crashed. I started drinking again. After a particularly nasty phone call from someone close to me, I snapped and put an emotional post on Facebook.

It was the sort of oversharing that I can't stand others doing, but I did it. A cry for help. I was inundated with really caring responses, including from Gudinski, who called that night. What did I need? Did I want to go to his place in Port Douglas and rest? Whatever I needed, just ask.

Gudinski was compassionate, and a lot of fun to be around, but it was rare for him to drop his guard. Only once did I really see that, in 2019 – during a conversation at his Toorak home about Paul Kelly.

Between watching horse races on the TV and him answering three different phones – hey, this was Saturday afternoon – we spoke for a few hours. At one stage I asked him if he regretted giving Paul Kelly back the rights to his first two albums, which Kelly had subsequently withdrawn from sale.

Gudinski's voice lowered. At one point, I thought he was going to cry. 'If I'd known what he was going to do with them, I don't think I would have,' he said softly.

With me that day was my partner, Susan. Gudinski loved Susan and it was reciprocated. She was extremely ill from breast cancer and prolonged chemotherapy. As we were leaving, he went into his garden, found her a rose and gave it to her. She pressed it and still has it.

'She's good for you, really good – you hang on to Suz,' he told me more than once.

On a lighter note, just before Christmas a couple of years earlier, he rang me. 'Look, I'm a Jew. We don't do Christmas, but I've got something for you – what's your address?'

A few days later, a big box arrived with a vertical turntable in it, something that was new in Australia. It was accompanied by a nice note from him.

Gudinski didn't do any promotion for the biography. However, we did make an appearance together, at a Mumbrella conference in Sydney in 2016. It was a few days after a horse he part-owned had won the Melbourne Cup and the celebrations were still in full swing. Drinks were spilt over his shirt and he proudly showed the audience a miniature replica of the cup. He was in great form, the star of the show. I loved it, he loved it, and I loved being around him.

During COVID, he'd occasionally call me. It was usually to talk about *The Sound*, the music television program he'd created, and how proud he was of it. Then there was the day, late in 2020, when I was doing a supporter drive broadcast on FBi. I'd heard that he'd made a generous donation to 3RRR during their recent radiothon, so a week before the FBi one I'd emailed his assistant, suggesting that maybe Gudinski would like to make a donation to us.

I was doing the show and I saw my mobile vibrate. It was Gudinski. 'Put me on the air,' he said. 'I have something for you.'

After some stuffing around, we got him live on the radio. He made a very generous donation, and then – never missing a chance – he was in my ear whilst I was chatting to him on the show about a new signing of his, and telling me I should play her on FBi. Of course, I cued up the new song from Mia Wray.

That was the last time I spoke to him. I was in the audience for the Midnight Oil show at the Enmore Theatre in February 2021, and subsequently heard he'd made it to the gig, after over a year of not being able to travel due to COVID lockdowns. A few days later, he died. I was stunned, but managed to pull myself together to do what seemed like dozens of radio and television interviews.

I miss Michael enormously and still wrestle with the notion that I'll never see or speak to him again. He represented something very important in my life, although I'm still not exactly sure what it was. But I know it's profound – which is why I haven't figured it out yet. These things take time.

## 49
# EVERY DAY I WRITE THE BOOK

After I'd completed the Gudinski book, I continued to modify my lifestyle. The periods of sobriety allowed space for real self-reflection and change, which would eventually lead to a seismic shift in my behaviour. More than anything, it was torturous having to confront the damaged relationships with my children. They had been safety blotted out by the bottle.

I had to accept that getting sober and staying sober wouldn't automatically guarantee that those relationships would get better, but I knew that not being sober was a 100 per cent guarantee that they never would. Slowly, I had committed to stopping, really stopping. I took good advice, listened, and acted on that advice. I went to counselling and had cognitive behaviour therapy.

I was walking more and ate better. Increasingly, I found I had more energy than I'd expected. Lots more. I was waking at 5.30 am without a dullness in the brain or feeling nauseous. I was feeling like I wanted to write more and more.

What could I tackle after Michael Gudinski? What other stories were there to tell? Whilst I was mulling this over, my phone rang. It was a publisher at Pan Macmillan who wanted to chat about Tex Perkins.

I'd known Tex since he first travelled to Sydney in the early 1980s and knocked on the door of the Woolloomooloo place I shared with

Roger Grierson. He knew Roger and thought that coming to our house was a good way to begin his contacts with the indie music world here.

Over the years we didn't see a real lot of each other, although of course he'd been central to the Beasts Of Bourbon's debut album on G.R.E.E.N., *The Axeman's Jazz*. I followed his career as a fan, though, and when the Pan Macmillan publisher called me up in 2015 and asked what I thought about approaching Tex to collaborate on a book, I figured it was a good idea.

I arranged to meet Tex at FBi on a Sunday afternoon. He was in Sydney and I thought we could have a chat on the radio and then a meeting about the book proposal.

I was scheduled to do a fill-in show. Unbeknown to me, though, the station had approached two broadcasters to present the program that afternoon, and we both arrived at the station just before 3 pm. Normally, I would have shrugged and gone home, letting the much-younger presenter get the on-air experience. But I couldn't today.

'I really need to do the show as I have Tex Perkins coming in,' I explained.

He looked at me with a blank stare.

'I don't know who that is,' he replied.

Welcome to the latest version of the generation gap.

Anyway, Tex was agreeable to the idea of a memoir, a contract was signed, and we set about doing interviews. Frequently, it was tough going – Tex's moods are notoriously unpredictable. Sometimes he was a bundle of laughs as we played table tennis on my balcony and recorded his reminiscences. Other times I found him prickly, defensive and confrontational, especially if it was a bad day and he felt I was going into territory he was uncomfortable with.

Slowly we eked out a draft manuscript but as the deadline approached we were a long way short of a finished book. I flew to Byron Bay, Tex living on a property just outside town. He drove in each day for our interview sessions, but never invited me to his place.

After five days he was driving me and my partner to the Gold Coast airport to fly back to Sydney, and we started chatting about the animals on his property. I was recording this animated chat and as we pulled into the carpark I told Tex I thought there was a chapter in the conversation.

'You're kidding, right?' he said.

'Nope,' I replied.

The book contains a chapter called 'Animal Farm'.

Eventually, it was finished, and at the launch Tex and I played table tennis on a stage, recreating how many of the chats for the book had taken place.

A few months after *Tex* was published, a friend called me up and said, 'Stuart, what exactly did you do for the book? It reads just like Tex sitting in a pub, chatting and telling stories.'

That was the best possible compliment for a collaborator. My work was done.

In 2017, writing a book about Australian roadies was even further from my mind than doing one on concert promoters had been when Matthew Kelly suggested that idea back in 2001. Who'd buy a book on the people who haul musical equipment and PAs around the country, set it all up, dismantle it, and then move it to the next gig?

Then one day I was contacted by Adrian Anderson from the Australian Road Crew Association. It had been set up largely to provide emotional and financial support for roadies who'd fallen on hard times. Amongst other things Adrian told me that road crew in Australia had four or five times the national suicide rate, a staggering and alarming statistic. Of course, I wondered why.

One Friday afternoon, I mentioned my interest in roadies and possibly looking at their stories to Matthew. He is a measured, calm individual not prone to outbursts of intense excitement. This time he broke tradition. His antenna was raised.

'Don't tell me you've offered this book to another publisher,' he said. 'I'll see you on Monday morning – early.'

I wasn't convinced there was a book in this, but Matthew was. So I had a new project. It was one that I can honestly say was the most enjoyable of writing experiences.

I interviewed around 70 road crew – from those working in the early 1960s to the present day. I started with the godfather of Australian roadies, the great character Howard Freeman. If, as I approached other roadies, I found them reluctant to speak, as soon as I mentioned that Howard was on board they went, 'OK, I'll talk to you.'

I laughed, I cried, I was in awe. And I learnt an incredible amount about these people who I'd been guilty almost of taking for granted in my band-management days.

*Roadies* was published in 2018. It sold extremely well, largely because I had the best publicists that money couldn't buy. The road-crew community responded strongly to having their stories told.

One roadie called and, almost in tears, said, 'Thank you – now I can explain to my kids what I was doing when I was away from them all those years.'

Another rang to say that he and a roadie mate had been discussing the book. They wished so much that their parents had been alive to read it and understand their world.

I was fortunate to have had the opportunity to chronicle the lives of these hard-working, smart and resourceful individuals. Halfway through the writing process, I decided roadies are wired differently to most people. They don't wonder if something is possible – their only thought is *how* to do it.

It's a book I'm very proud of having written. And I get treated very well at gigs if I'm spotted by any road crew.

COVID and the pandemic had a surprising upside with regard to my book-writing pursuits. In 1999 I was taken on a three-week trip around Australia for the 'Virtual Elvis' tour. This extravaganza involved footage of Elvis Presley in concert shown on a big (and I mean big) screen, whilst Elvis' 1970s backing musicians – the TCB Band, along with musical conductor Joe Guercio and vocal group The Sweet Inspirations – performed live to accompany the images.

My gig was to spend a large part of every day interviewing all the participants for a projected book in which they'd tell stories of their time with Elvis in great detail, and for the first time.

After the tour was over I wrote a draft of the book, sent it to Stig Edgren, the co-creator and producer of this Elvis in concert experience. I heard nothing more and assumed the project had fallen in a heap. I'd been paid, so life moved on. Until one day in 2020.

More than two decades after I'd written the draft, I was walking to FBi to do a show when my phone began ringing. It was a Los Angeles number I didn't recognise. I was going to ignore it, thinking it might be one of the endless spam calls we get these days, but decided to answer.

It was Stig. He explained that COVID had curtailed a lot of his business activities, that he was looking around for projects to keep him busy, and he'd remembered the Elvis book. Was I interested in tidying it up for publication?

Thankfully I had the manuscript on a disc, so I set about revisiting the manuscript and my interview transcripts. A few months later, towards the end of the year and just in time for the Christmas market for the Elvis fan who thinks they have everything, *On Stage With Elvis Presley: The Backstage Stories Of Elvis' Legendary TCB Band*, as told to Stuart Coupe, appeared. It's done rather nicely and I've since been the recipient of regular royalty payments.

Lesson learnt: never assume a project is completely dead in the water.

When Paul Kelly and I stopped working together in the late '80s, we'd ended things on good terms. So, I guess it was rather strange that, except for one brief phone call and a quick hello at a gold record presentation around 1996 at the State Theatre, I wouldn't see him for 22 years. Even when I attended the premiere of the *Stories Of Me* documentary about Paul in Melbourne in 2012, we didn't run into each other at the party afterwards. I spoke to his son Declan, but not Declan's father.

It was mainly that we lived in different cities, and when Paul played in Sydney, I didn't feel the need to go backstage and say, 'Hey, I'm here.' So when I had the idea for a biography of Kelly in 2015, after I'd finished the book on Gudinski, all my correspondence and phone calls went through his manager. Nothing happened for ages, but every six months or so I'd email him explaining that, sooner or later, someone would write a book about Kelly, and that I was the person best placed to do it.

After what seemed like a couple of years, and much to the surprise of his manager, Kelly expressed some interest and asked for an outline of the book. I sent a page of notes and a message came back that Kelly wouldn't get in the way of the project. In fact, he said he'd sit for some interviews towards the end of the research.

Away I went. And I'd done maybe 50 interviews, and written 85 per cent of a draft of the book, when Kelly entered my life in person once again. And this was not for the book. He was out doing interviews to promote a new record, the second volume of the compilation *Songs From The South*, covering the years from 1985 to 2019, and his label EMI asked if I was interested in a chat. I explained that I was writing a book about Kelly, but sure – let's do an interview.

So, more than two decades after we'd stopped working together as manager/artist, Paul walked through the door at 2SER. I suspect we were both nervous, but within 10 minutes I was half-expecting him to ask me what time soundcheck was that night.

We then met at the Domain in Sydney before a 'How To Make Gravy' show, part of his by then annual run of pre-Christmas concerts. We spent a couple of hours talking backstage. I knew Kelly liked literature and tennis, so I took him a gift: a copy of John McPhee's masterful *Levels Of The Game*, about the tennis match in 1968 between Arthur Ashe and Clark Graebner. We used to play tennis against each other – he usually won.

One interview swung into another, and he suggested I travel to Tamworth, as he'd have more time during his appearances at the Country Music Festival. So we lunched at my hotel and hung out where he and his partner and Kev Carmody and his wife were staying.

I had the chance to see him perform on a bill with Cold Chisel, sing Hank Williams songs at a Lucky Oceans CD release gig, and do a cameo singing with Joy McKean. There was another long session at the Continental Hotel in Sydney.

Soon afterwards, I completed the manuscript. As it wasn't an authorised book, I was under no obligation to let Kelly read it prior to publication. However, I was inclined to find out whether I had a supportive, antagonistic or ambivalent subject on my hands. I offered Paul the chance to read it, and he wrote back thanking me and saying that he didn't expect to like it all – because if he did, I hadn't done my work thoroughly.

Still, with a high degree of nervousness, I sent him the book on a Tuesday afternoon. Four days passed – silence. By this time I was convinced Kelly hated it and was working out how to tell me. Or maybe I just wouldn't hear. On a Sunday afternoon my phone started vibrating. The letters 'PK' showed up. My stomach started to resemble a washing machine in spin mode.

Kelly then came on the line. He told me he'd read 196 pages – a little more than half the book – and while he found the first 180 particularly confronting, he didn't have 'a beef' with what I'd said. He told me he'd read the remainder and get back to me.

That was a massive relief. Paul contacted me about a week later and seemed happy with the rest of the manuscript. He suggested we have another chat, so he could expand on and clarify certain things. The plan was I'd meet him in Melbourne at his place; after we'd talked, we'd go to a training session with the group of friends he'd played footy with for a number of years.

Unfortunately, COVID put paid to that, so instead we spent three-and-a-half hours on Zoom. Paul had clearly read every word of the manuscript and gave invaluable feedback. To his credit, he didn't ask for one thing to be removed. I self-censor well before the final stages, but there were a couple of things that I wouldn't have fought Kelly too hard over if he'd requested that I delete them. He didn't, so they're in there.

There was one overall indication that he was good with the book. Towards the end, he sent me some photographs that I hadn't seen published before. One was a photo of most of his brothers and sisters and the family dog. A note from Kelly said that I should credit the dog. 'It's Whisky – without an e.'

# 50
# DIRT MUSIC

**O**ften things in my life begin slowly and with the suggestion that longevity is not a big factor. And then they take on a life of their own. My tenure at FBi was like that – 'no more than six months' turned into '20 years and still going'.

It was the same in about 2011, when Andrew Khedoori and Anthony Dockrill contacted me. They had this idea of me doing a short stint of a roots music-oriented show at their station, 2SER. The idea was that it would run from February through till the upcoming Bluesfest in April.

That sounded like fun, as it was the chance to play things that I didn't usually get to air on FBi. And it was only for three months. There was the small matter of me having a long-running commitment to the city's other major community radio station. I mean, community radio is one big happy family, but as a friend from Melbourne said, 'That's like having a show on 3RRR *and* 3PBS – it would never happen down here.'

FBi were good with it, though, so I started presenting weekly shows on both stations. Three months and a Bluesfest came and went, and Andrew and Anthony asked me to stay on. Then it just rolled along until, as far as I was aware, no-one even thought about it. And so it remains.

The name *Dirt Music* was a nod to Tim Winton's novel and Hugo Race's European band. It fitted the brief for the show – earthy, authentic, unpretentious independent music – and for the most part that's what it is. It's a cool show to do. I get to interview a lot of artists who I love and admire – hey, it's not every day a shortish guy walks in and says 'Hi, I'm Graham Nash.' And the show is syndicated by the Community Radio Association, so it goes out each week to about 75 other community stations around the country. That's a good reach – from Broome to Hobart to Cairns. *Dirt Music* gets around.

I love the idea that, these days, radio shows can be pretty much accessed any time and from anywhere. For a few decades now, whenever I've been in New York I've visited writer and radio presenter David Fricke. He'll open a cupboard containing all his spare and duplicate CDs and records. I usually depart feeling like several Christmases have come at once – and then my mind wanders to excess baggage. But I've always figured that if your excess doesn't hurt to carry through customs, you're really not trying.

Anyway, on one occasion after I'd done a Fricke raid, a few weeks later I was back in Sydney and playing some of the things he'd given me on the radio. Next thing I knew, there was an email from David, saying he was glad I'd got back safely and that the new acquisitions had come in handy. Yep, he was sitting in his apartment in New York City, listening to community radio in Sydney – in pretty much the same way I regularly tune in to stations like WFMU from New York. Then there's the guy who says he never misses a *Dirt Music* show. He lives in Bangkok. It's a wonderful world.

Having a radio show is – I've always thought – an incredible privilege. Anyone who has the opportunity to sit behind a microphone and share music and chat is very, very fortunate. People say that the golden days of radio have gone, but I'm not convinced of that. Sure, there's a lot of terrible radio around – but that's nothing new. There are still great shows being presented by caring and passionate people.

People might say that, courtesy of the Devil's Streaming Service (OK, I just don't like saying Spotify), everything is accessible, but I think that's not the real issue. Yes, pretty much anything (but not *everything*) is available to stream. What's missing, though, is the personal touch, the human curation, and the voice giving you information about songs and artists and explaining why you might dig this particular tune. During the two years of the pandemic, I realised once again how important that human touch is. Not everyone is good with being by themselves, and there are a lot of lonely people out there. Radio is one of their main connections to the outside world. It's a voice chatting to them. Just them.

And when you have a caring and knowledgeable radio presenter, even the most connected of us can learn something. I regularly put on a wide range of stations from Australia and overseas. Chances are that within a few minutes I'll be scribbling notes, sending myself text-message reminders, or Shazam-ing to find out new things I'm hearing.

Anyone can assemble a great Spotify playlist. That's fine, but please don't carry on that radio doesn't have a place anymore. Hell, the next thing you'll be telling me is that vinyl is all over. How did that work out for you?

# 51
# SHAKE SOME ACTION

And the musical love affair continues. It evolves, whilst also remaining constant. New bands. Old bands. New records. Old records. The same me, looking for exhilarating, life-changing moments and feelings, as I continue to dive headfirst into this aural forest.

After finishing the first draft of this book, I headed to Bluesfest. I hadn't been for years – in fact, since I worked for a couple of years as the festival's publicist, which was over two decades ago.

This was a largely Australian line-up and held after a number of cancellations and postponements. On one heartbreaking occasion, it was called off the day before the first artists were due to perform – simply because there was one COVID case in the (sorta) vicinity of the festival site.

Massive flooding around Lismore and northern NSW had occurred only weeks before, and the Bluesfest site had copped a drenching. It was slippery, muddy and overcast, but with an overall sense of exhilaration and relief that finally there was a large music festival happening.

Backstage, it was extremely emotional. Artists reuniting, many for the first time in a couple of years, and relishing doing that thing they do – performing to large crowds. Just the simple stuff: playing music together, playing in public.

I slid around in the mud and meandered around the five tents, watching bits of Jimmy Barnes, Tex Perkins, Missy Higgins, Baker Boy,

Crowded House, Briggs, FOOLS, Jeff Lang, The Wailers (there were a handful of international artists) and many others – including some talented buskers in an area designated for them.

The next day, I was getting ready to head to the site. On the bed were two t-shirts. Which to wear? A purple Sun Ra shirt I'd bought a few years earlier, whilst watching the Arkestra perform at the Lincoln Center in New York? Or a reproduction 'It's Time' shirt, the same image I'd worn around Launceston in 1972? I chose the latter.

As I walked backstage, promoter Peter Noble did a double take. 'How did you know?' he asked. 'It's meant to be a surprise.'

I had no idea what he was talking about. He explained that prime minister-in-waiting Anthony Albanese would be arriving at the festival in half an hour.

I sort of knew Albo, in the way that pretty much everyone in the inner west of Sydney sort of knows Albo. He frequently DJ'd at pubs in the area, was a Record Store Day ambassador, and sometimes turned up at his local record shop RPM Records to buy *vinyl*. He wore Celibate Rifles and Radio Birdman t-shirts and knew who TISM was. This was the prime minister I wanted. The prime minister music fans wanted.

And he loved footy – his beloved Souths in the NRL, as well as my code of Australian Rules. He'd played for the Western Walers in the Community Cup AFL game one year, when I was pretending to coach the Sydney Sailors.

One time that I'd met Albo, he said he'd been reading my music writing for years. He'd also been a guest at my 60th-birthday bash at the Marrickville Bowling Club. And this afternoon he jumped out of the car and saw the shirt – I was a photo op in the making.

He was followed by Shadow Minister for the Arts, Tony Burke. He took me aside and apologised for only just finishing reading my *Roadies* book. I'd met Burke earlier in the year at the inaugural Roadies4Roadies fundraiser in Sydney when we'd both spoken. I joked that it must be a good perk of the campaign to get to come to Bluesfest.

He said, 'Stuart, I've come every year for the last decade as a fan.' He was the guy I wanted as arts minister.

And I wanted live music back. Big time. Whether it was being squashed in the crowd watching Baker Boy, perched side-stage on a viewing platform and looking out at 12,000 delirious fans as Jimmy Barnes roared through his set, or literally looking up at Crowded House from the front of the stage after accidentally being pushed into the photography pit. I wanted live music – badly.

A few weeks later, I was in Melbourne, a city I love, but which I hadn't been able to visit very often during the COVID years. Over the course of that trip, I was able to indulge in a few of my passions – chatting on 3RRR with my friend Brian Wise, and getting a guided tour of the new 3PBS studios in Collingwood.

Community radio is part of the fabric of Melbourne and it resonates there in a way that is so powerful and embracing. It's a city in which two things are essential – having an AFL team and listening to these hugely influential stations. Why is live music such a force in Melbourne? Community radio.

And then there are the record shops. No other Australian city has as many great places to fossick for vinyl – new and old. They are *everywhere*. In the space of a few days, I made around 65 new black-vinyl friends, who had no choice but to accompany me back to Sydney. Some were new, the majority old; some battered, others in great nick. Soul records. Nigerian funk records. Old acoustic blues records. New Melbourne groove/funk/jazz outfits. Wigged-out psychedelia. Records I knew, records where I just thought, 'What the heck – give me one of those.'

(A friend asked how that trip to Melbourne had been. I watched his jaw drop when I said, 'Great – but have you ever tried carrying 65 albums onto a plane as part of your hand luggage?' I was back in Melbourne a few months later, and sent him a message: 'You'll be stunned but I'm being calm – current count is only 27 albums and only another day till I come home.')

My last record-shop stop during that first trip back involved grabbing the new Tyler, The Creator album for Hugh, the 15-year-old in my life. I'm loving being able to observe his musical evolution. It moves seamlessly – as did my listening at his age – between songs, artists and styles. So our home resonates to Tyler, The Creator, The Beatles (*lots of Beatles*), to Queen, Boney M, Paul Kelly, James Brown, AC/DC, The Clash (there's something thrilling about a youngster cranking 'London Calling' on the car stereo), and all manner of other artists – many of whom he's picked up on from film or television series soundtracks.

His listening is as eclectic and passion-driven as mine was at his age. He's a good piano player, not a bad trumpeter, and I recently bought him his first electric bass and a small amplifier. He doesn't like my comments about him and Paul McCartney now having something in common as bass players (he knows how much I love McCartney) – but he and three friends are about to form their first band, with the same headful of dreams that a young Liverpudlian would have had and no sense of what the future might hold.

I'm still the same crazy fan that I was all those years ago. And I frequently think about the incredible array of experiences that have been part of this caper. Notice I'm not calling it a journey. I'm not a big fan of the band with that name either.

But, going to Paris to hang out with Bruce Springsteen, spending a night in Mick Jagger's hotel room, being sketched by Leonard Cohen, managing Paul Kelly *and* the Hoodoo Gurus, writing millions of words; and hell – after being so tentative at it in the beginning, I've now clocked up 20 years presenting radio on FBi. I've worked with The Clash, The Cramps and the Gun Club – three bands that were life-changing for me. And that's just for starters.

I've worked really hard, but I've been so very lucky. I smiled recently when one of my favourite music writers, Nick Kent, was asked to sum up his life. 'I was in the right place at the right time, on the wrong drugs,' he said.

I think I was also totally in the right place at the right time. As for the drugs and other addictions – I'm glad they're behind me.

I do think that, at some point, I should be eligible for an Honorary Jugglers Award – for keeping so many balls in the air for so long. I'm really not sure how I managed it, but here we are in 2023 with another book, and a couple more on the go, two ongoing radio shows, a crazy amount of freelance publicity work, and a mooted music-documentary project. And I still find time to go to see the Sydney Swans play footy, and edge into any record shop that crosses my path. It's pretty good really, this juggling business.

Being and staying sober does get easier, but still requires constant vigilance. I don't celebrate sober birthdays. All I know is that I haven't drunk alcohol for many years now. I like that, I don't miss it, and I don't get concerned being around people who are drinking. I'm in and out of bars and pubs all the time.

I get up early, I feel great, I sleep well, and I've achieved a lot sober – much more than I would have if I'd continued. But I don't moralise or lecture others. There's no point. One thing I know is that doing that will never help. Everyone has to reach their own conclusion about this stuff. But I do know that you're more likely to be successful when you do decide to give up if you're completely honest with yourself, as hard as that might be, and have someone who really supports you.

And I'm still listening to, and loving music, like the fan I've always been. On a daily basis, I'm saying, 'How fucking great is that?' as I hear something new on FBi, or via an online music blog, or a tip from a friend. I still spend *much* more money on it than I should, and still listen to music at least 16 hours a day.

Recently, I was back in the Bruce Springsteen zone and listening again to him and the E Street Band in Sydney in February 2014. (You can see and hear it on YouTube.)

The venue is dark; then there's that roar. Springsteen is standing onstage at what was then known as Allphones Arena and, as he becomes visible, he sings, 'Monday morning feels so bad . . .'

Miami Steve Van Zandt, Tom Morello and Nils Lofgren play the guitars. Maybe the chords are still beyond Springsteen, but he sings it with all the intensity you'd expect. He's feeling it. I'm feeling it. You're feeling it. It's in our blood. In our hearts. May it always be so.

# ACKNOWLEDGEMENTS

A couple of years ago, I'd had an early-morning coffee with Penguin Random House publishing director Justin Ractliffe to catch up and chat about mutual music loves (The Flaming Lips, The War On Drugs, and Steely Dan are always three starting points) and book ideas – of which I had a few. As I ran though my 'Great books that haven't been written, but that I can write' list, Justin nodded and then gave good and succinct reasons why he didn't think they'd get up at Penguin Random House.

At the end of the chat, he said, 'Have you ever thought of writing a memoir?'

I chuckled and said that I hadn't.

'You should,' he replied.

I didn't think too much about this, but every few months Justin sent an email reminding me that he thought it was a good idea. Eventually I wrote an outline, then a couple of chapters – and here we are.

The sealer was Justin saying that I should use Donald Fagen (he of Steely Dan) and his book *Eminent Hipsters* as a guide/inspiration. I loved that memoir. It ranged far and wide and is short – as it turns out, much shorter than this one.

I won't pretend that writing *Shake Some Action* hasn't, for the most part, been a lot of fun. And unlike my previous books I didn't need to interview anyone – just from time to time call friends and associates to check on recollections, and see if theirs were different to, or better than, mine.

The passing of time and the circumstances surrounding various events makes it inevitable that some things are a little hazy. I've done my best and if there's the occasional oversight, embellishment or mistake, well, that's all down to me and my memory.

After Justin moved on from Penguin Random House, this book passed to the very fine and caring hands of Brandon VanOver. He has superbly, and with great care and insight, nurtured the project, and offered great suggestions and reassuring words when I began to panic and stress – two things I'm an expert at.

My editor – Patrick Mangan – did an amazing job and I remain totally in awe of his abilities. Early on I was chatting with fellow music nerd/author/friend Murray Engleheart, who has previously worked with Patrick. When I told him who was editing this book, he said, 'Some advice, Stuart. When Patrick makes a suggestion, don't even think about it – just say yes. I gave him a pretty OK car, but he sent me back a Ferrari.'

It's probably not surprising to say that the process of writing this book has at times been cathartic. By their very nature, memoirs require reflection and examination of one's past. What would I have done differently? Maybe not tried to be a concert promoter. Certainly not drink and take as many drugs as I did. What should I have done differently? Most certainly, prioritise my children and worked much harder at being a good father to them.

And I should definitely have told my parents – Patricia Irene Craw and David Reginald Coupe – more often how much I loved them.

In that process of examination, I've learnt a lot about who I am and hopefully grown as a person and become less likely to repeat the mistakes of the past. I've also gained the insight and – yes – courage to try to make amends for some of those failings.

Equally naturally, the writing of this book caused me to reflect on the (sadly) ever-increasing number of friends and associates who have passed away. I wish these fine people were around to read these pages:

Colin Talbot, Bronwyn Stephenson, Basia Bonkowski, Doc Neeson, Martin Armiger, Pam Swain, Andrew Penhallow, John Pinder, Tom Zelinka, Jim Paton, Annie Burton, Justin Cosby, Ian Smith, Richard Neville, Martin Sharp, Shelley Roye, Gary Rabin, Sarah Longhurst, Genevieve Farmer, Bob Ellis, Broderick Smith, Michael 'Snapper' Knapp, Michael Carson, Peter Walker, Marla Smith, Peter Corris, Renee Geyer, Stephen 'Goose' Grey, Chris Plimmer, David Jarrett, Colleen Ironside, Ron Blake, Buck Emberg, Bob McMahon, Annie Greig, Jonathan Coleman, Karl Broadie, Robert Adamson, Damien Lovelock, Stuart Matchett, Chris Winter, Bones Hillman, Andy Glitre, Peter 'Speedy' Dick, Greedy Smith, David Brearley, Adrian Rawlins, Pete Steadman, Craig McGregor, Sarah Dease, Tim Thorne, Tony Cohen, Adele Horin, Simon Holmes, Oana Gilbert, Sylvia Lynch, James Freud, Ian Rilen, Janine Hall, Rowland S. Howard, Steve Connolly, Greg Sawyers, Andrew McMillan, Cath Synnerdahl, Spencer P. Jones, Anthony O'Grady, Paul Comrie Thompson, Paul Gardiner, Neil Bradbury, Michael Gudinski, Warren Costello, David Day, Iain Shedden, Ken West, Marc Hunter, Eric Robinson, Chris Bailey.

Of the gloriously living, I would especially like to thank Susan Lynch, my partner in love, reflection, growth and good times. Susan read every word of this book many, many times, and made endless and valuable suggestions, asked the right questions, and reminded me of some of the core tenets of our world together – respect, understanding and nuance.

Susan – I can't begin to imagine a world without you. Thank you.

# THE OFFCUTS
## THINGS THAT DIDN'T FIT, BUT ARE FUN TO YARN ABOUT

# TICKET TO RIDE

I never asked my parents whether it was a burning desire to introduce me to the world of live music – or that they were too cheap to pay for a babysitter for me and my brother – which led to the Coupe family attending its first and only live musical performance together.

It must have been 1967 after the Seekers returned from the UK – even though it feels like it was earlier – because I can't imagine that, prior to then, they would have had the drawing power to fill the Albert Hall in Launceston.

Certainly, my parents owned the 1966 album *Come The Day* and 1968's *Live At The Talk Of The Town*. I was 11 years old and I don't remember a real lot about the concert. I have a recollection that I was in my school uniform. I didn't go with any real sense of excitement – not the same delight that had me heading to the State Theatre in Sydney in 2012 to see one of their 50th-anniversary gigs. Boy, was that a show to make you feel young . . . even if you were a long way from being exactly that.

But that was the beginning of my live concert experiences. A few years later, I'd start seeing local folk gigs and visiting interstate artists, such as Jeannie Lewis and Graham Lowndes, along with local rock'n'roll bands – all of whom seemed to draw from the Hendrix/Cream/British blues school and end their shows with a version of 'Gloria'.

There weren't a lot of international artists visiting Tasmania – and certainly not Launceston. An exception was Donovan: again, an artist I'm more excited about knowing I saw, than I was when I actually saw him. Maybe he was a bit too hippy-drippy for me.

I mean, it wasn't bad and kinda cute, Donovan sitting cross-legged on a box surrounded by flowers. It was late 1975, the only time he toured this country until 1982, so I was on the cusp of leaving Launceston, no doubt smoking pot amongst the throngs of groovers at the Princess Theatre. These days I'm much more of a Donovan fan and would relish the chance to time travel back to those days.

By this stage I'd already travelled to the mainland to see Fairport Convention, the English folk/rock band that I adored. My parents had asked me what I wanted for my 18th birthday and my request was for a ticket to Melbourne to see Fairport. I was probably hoping I'd run into Rob Smyth in the foyer – even though I had no idea what he looked like. He was probably there.

As it turned out, I managed to see two shows at Dallas Brooks Hall – an afternoon matinee and the evening performance. I travelled with a friend from Launceston who I don't recall coming to the show – he being more interested in hanging with a new Melbourne-based girlfriend. I slept on the couch which saved considerable money.

Fairport were magnificent. I was mesmerised by fiddle player Dave Swarbrick and totally stunned to be seeing Sandy Denny singing with the band. This was beyond thrilling. Songs I knew backwards performed live and in front of me as I sat and then stood with the assembled masses of devotees. This was the live music experience I'd waited for. What I'd watched on television, listened to on record and was now being part of.

(I'm thinking particularly of The Who's *Live At Leeds* album. How many times had I sat in front of my parents' stereo with my cheap headphones on, dreaming of being either Roger Daltrey or Pete Townshend – hundreds of times is how many). I was hooked.

For the second show I found myself sitting next to some 'old' people, who seemed out of sync with the rest of the audience. I asked them what they were doing there, and they said they were the parents (maybe even grandparents?) of Trevor Lucas, the Australian-born member of the band.

In between Fairport and Donovan, I'd had my first Lou Reed experience. I was in Adelaide as part of the Tasmania squash team for the 1974 Australian championships. The evening before the tournament began, there was a reception for all the teams, so, along with my teammates, I attended dressed in my uniform, complete with a blazer with the emblem of Tasmania sewn on it.

This was all fine – except for the fact that my friend David Woodhall had 10th-row centre tickets for Lou Reed's concert that night, and I had no time to dash to my hotel and change. So there I was – feeling like a complete dork – amidst the coolest of the cool of Adelaide, assembled before – gulp – Lou fucking Reed.

The show itself blew my mind on every level blowable. Reed was sooooo coool, soooo wasted, soooo magnificent. The best band. Everything was making my head lift off. At one point, he started teasing an audience member, winking at him and seemingly inviting him to come towards the stage and dance with him. Which the guy did. As he clambered onstage Reed turned his back and walked away, as security descended on the hapless individual and – I think – threw him out of the theatre.

The concert ended, and as Reed went to walk off, he miscued and walked straight into the wall next to the door. It was just *so* perfect.

Soon afterwards, when I moved to Adelaide, I was in heaven. The Sports, The Angels, Jo Jo Zep And The Falcons, The Dingoes, Richard Clapton, etc. Band after band after band came to Adelaide. There was hardly a weekend when someone wasn't in town.

This is where I first saw Radio Birdman and once again my mind was blown. This incredible sonic onslaught. It was punk, it was rock, it was intense and I was so there.

And so many international artists came to town – Blondie, Little Feat, Frank Zappa, The Eagles, Ike and Tina Turner, Bob Dylan, The Beach Boys – I saw them all.

When I moved to Sydney, as I've mentioned, my first assignment for *RAM* was going on tour with Graham Parker & The Rumour, supported by Sports. This was heaven. I was getting paid to see live music, hang out and write about it.

I almost lived at the Sydney venues of the day, particularly the Civic Hotel in Goulburn Street, where I'd see Midnight Oil, The Saints, the Boys Next Door and countless others. Sydney city was alive in those days: Chequers, The Governor's Pleasure, The Basement, The Stage Door Tavern.

The latter was this heaving sweatbox under an office block. As far as I could see, there'd only be one way out if there was a fire – the front door. And with 1000 or so people crammed inside for The Stranglers, Midnight Oil, Australian Crawl or whoever it was, well, the thought was terrifying.

I was there on the venue's last night (headlined by Midnight Oil) when a riot ensued after the uncalled-for arrival of the cops – one of whom took a dislike to my speed and beer-induced taunts and chased me down the street. I still had the remnant of the stamina of a squash player, which is why I wasn't arrested that night.

I was out almost every night. The Flaming Hands, Laughing Clowns, Tactics, Sacred Cowboys (if they were up from Melbourne), Amazing Woolloomooloosers, The Johnnys, The Passengers. These were the days when it was possible for bands in Sydney to play seven nights a week without leaving the city.

Tuesday night at the San Miguel Inn in Cammeray – the Sunnyboys playing to 500 ecstatic fans, and finishing at midnight. Not a problem. We were young. Invincible. Midnight? Time to head to the Cross and see who was playing at the Manzil Room – or just play backgammon and do drugs till dawn in one of its dark corners.

Speaking of the Sunnyboys, I loved them. Would go and see them constantly – pretty much anywhere. One of their earliest gigs was at my 25th-birthday party. On a whim I decided to throw a bash at the Rock Garden, a venue in William Street just below Kings Cross. I asked every attendee for a $1 donation to cover beer for the bands and paying the sound person. (The bill included the Surfside 6, The Introverts, The Clones and The Proteens as well.)

The next time I decided to throw a gig as part of a birthday celebra-tion was when I turned 45, and I organised for an array of Laughing

Outlaw artists to perform. Because of that night in 2001, pretty much no-one ever forgets my birthday. The party finished, most heading home just as planes started flying into the World Trade Center.

Over the decades I've seen thousands of live performances. I love them. My favourite moment is always just before the show starts. The lights start to go down, the roar begins and grows and grows. *Bang*. There they are. It's never less than spine chilling for me.

And what I love most – if I'm lucky enough to be backstage – is to watch this all unfold. A tour manager will announce 'showtime' and the artists will move towards the stage. Torches will light their way up the darkened stage area as the roar builds. They'll pause, walk onto the stage, the noise will be thunderous. Then an explosion of light and sound as the performance begins. I'm getting chills just writing this.

Shows that stick in my mind? Wow. Where do I start? Bruce Springsteen with the E Street Band on each of the 50 or so occasions I've seen them around the globe. Maybe best of all was in New Jersey. It was like the Pope had hit the Vatican stage with an electric guitar.

Then there was the time Neil Young and Crazy Horse were here for the tour to promote *Greendale*, a sort of weirded-out concept album that was performed like a musical theatre piece. I'd bought tickets for the Entertainment Centre with about 12 friends, but through the promoter so I had no idea where they were until we filed in – and the usher moved closer and closer to the stage. Five rows from the front.

*Greendale* itself was indulgent. It was like Young's Rock Eisteddfod. Silly story, sort of acted, not great songs. Totally dull, except for some of my music-writing friends onstage as extras.

There was a break and then 45 minutes of the loudest and most exhilarating rock'n'roll I've still ever seen. Young and the Horse clustered together on the massive Entertainment Centre stage, using up the space of the average kitchen table. Loud? It was L.O.U.D.

At the end I remarked to one of my friends who was down the end of the row that, if it had got any louder, I'd have had to leave as I couldn't physically take it. But it was thrilling. And clean white noise. I thought I wouldn't be able to hear for weeks, but there wasn't even a hum in my ears the next morning.

Little venues. Large venues. Dr Feelgood at the Tivoli in Adelaide from decades ago still resonates. So does going to every night of The Clash's stand in Sydney.

And I was there the night of the riot at the Regent Theatre in 1978 after Elvis Costello & The Attractions' supposedly short, no-encore performance. It clocked in at 58 minutes. People weren't happy. They took the venue apart. Seats rained down on those of us downstairs. It was mayhem. I didn't get it. What do you want – a truly great 58 minutes or two hours of ordinary. Wasn't get on, make your statement and get off the essence of punk rock?

For some strange reason I remember being mesmerised by Adam & The Ants at the Ritz in New York in 1981. Ian Dury & The Blockheads at the State Theatre was celebratory. There was Bob Marley and The Wailers, just visible through the clouds of pot smoke at the Hordern Pavilion. Leonard Cohen's first tour with his big band was beyond emotionally engaging. And around the same time Hall & Oates gave the best blue-eyed soul performance I've ever seen and made a believer out of a non-believer.

Of course, I loved the hundreds of shows I saw by the Hoodoo Gurus and Paul Kelly and The Messengers. I revelled in every show I promoted, even if, as I was watching, I knew I was dropping lots of money I didn't have.

I'd go and see Bob Dylan any time. Just because he's Bob Dylan and there's something about just being in the same space as him. And Bob does what Bob does. Anyone who doesn't get that simply hasn't been paying attention over the past four decades.

He probably won't sing 'Blowin' In The Wind', and if he does the chances are you won't recognise it. He can be really bad – I walked out of the first 1992 show in Sydney and gave away the tickets I had for the other nights. But Bob and I are on good terms these days. Very good terms.

More recently, David Byrne's 'American Utopia' show was unlike anything I've ever seen, with its incredible choreography, and left me delirious and speechless. I was enthralled watching Courtney Barnett – whose songs and records I love very much – own the stage at the

Domain in Sydney, when she was one of the openers for Paul Kelly. And at the 2022 Bluesfest I was moved by Baker Boy and Briggs' sets.

The Flaming Lips set out to blow minds and they've done it every time I've seen them. I've seen Iggy Pop when I've arguably been more out of it than he was – and a few times completely sober – and he's always astonishing, intense and ferocious.

I could tell you about watching John Sebastian singing 'Summer In The City', the Lovin' Spoonful classic – in Central Park in New York in 2019, and Jesse Colin Young from the Youngbloods doing 'Darkness Darkness' at the same show. Or The Blasters tearing up a small club in New York the day after I'd seen the Springsteen on Broadway show, and a night before the glorious magnificence of ELO at Madison Square Garden.

I'd travel great distances to see The Dirty Three and will carry with me forever the memory of Warren Ellis dancing onto the stage of the Opera House to the sounds of Boz Scaggs singing 'Lido Shuffle'. Wilco, Calexico anytime. The first time the Old Crow Medicine show did a three-hour marathon at the Metro in Sydney. The first time Kamasi Washington toured and lifted the roof of the same venue.

William Crighton has lifted my spirits every time I've seen him. I remember The Go-Betweens at the Ritz in New York doing 'Apology Accepted' with Grant McLennan singing it on his knees and looking up at partner and band member Amanda Brown. Gillian Welch and David Rawlings at the Enmore was passionate, beautiful and soulful – and only the second time I've been in the front row at a seated venue – for both their concerts. The other was a last-minute ticket for Dylan at the Opera House. Note: never buy a front-row side ticket at the Opera House – my neck hurt for days, but I was looking up at Bob.

And that reminds me of Nile Rodgers and Chic, and Bobby Womack at the Opera House, and did I mention James Brown at the Lone Star Café in New York in the mid-1980s? And every show Patti Smith gave in Sydney on her last visit. And Keith Jarrett at the Opera House in the early '80s, grunting and groaning and transporting me beyond heaven to places far, far away.

Then there were a number of Drive By Truckers shows – with and without Jason Isbell – in Austin at SXSW, and finally getting to see Alejandro Escovedo live one evening on a big stage down by the lake, and being in tears as he played 'Beast Of Burden' one sultry night at an outdoor show, in front of shops and bars just back from the South Congress roadway.

Or queuing for what seemed like hours trying to get into a Stax Records tribute at Antone's. It was so crowded the fire marshals were watching like hawks – one person left, another could go in. My turn arrived just as Booker T and The MGs played 'Green Onions', one of my favourite-ever instrumentals and by a band I sometimes think are my favourite-ever band.

Did I mention Joni Mitchell at the State Theatre on her first visit to this country in the early 1980s? Or Steely Dan at the Opera House, Donald Fagen and Walter Becker playing with a big band that just oozed 'We are the finest musicians that money can buy'.

What's it all about? It was distilled for me watching the Counting Crows at the Hordern Pavilion. Their show was OK – not great – but there was one moment that will stick with me forever.

Towards the end of the night, singer Adam Duritz stood on a foldback speaker and sang 'We are not alone' repeatedly as the house lights went on. In 10 seconds the entire live-music experience was there in front of me.

'We are not alone,' continued Duritz, gradually joined by the voices of the audience who could now see each other clearly. All 5000 of us who'd paid our money to be there.

Ten minutes later the show is over and we all spill out of the Hordern and head off in our different directions. We don't know each other, but we've shared a little of the magic that rock'n'roll can and often does present. And we've been reminded that we are not alone. We come together to worship this intangible thing that is music and emotion and heart and soul. We are not alone.

# LOOK OUT
# (HERE COMES TOMORROW)

I'm sitting at my desk on the first day of January 2022, listening to Roxy Music's *Siren* album. The one with the future (and now ex) Mrs Murdoch on the cover. Jerry Hall is a mermaid with a strange, half-seductive, half-frightening and intimidating look on her face. Maybe that's an image for these times. Let's ignore the fact that the album came out in 1975. That's just splitting hairs.

It's a vinyl copy I'm spinning, on my office turntable. That's not a particularly political choice, even though the old chestnut of vinyl versus everything else still rages. My vinyl copy just happened to be easier to find. If the CD had been nearby, I'd have played that. And if I was in a hurry I may have gone to a digital file on a hard disc or – heaven forbid – the Devil's Streaming Service.

I don't have a lot of time for the debates about which format for preserving recorded music is best. Vinyl snobs drive me crazy – but so, from time to time, do people who only stream, and, in effect, give very little back to the artists who created the music in the first place. But in the end it's about the experience of listening to music. That's all. It doesn't really matter how you travel from A to B – it's the destination that matters.

I certainly don't buy into the argument: 'Everything sounds better on vinyl, maaan.' It doesn't. Some CD reproduction is vastly superior to the vinyl equivalent – especially in the era of CDs, when music was recorded digitally.

I've heard far too many albums from the past 20 or 30 years that were recorded digitally and, more recently, released on vinyl. In too many cases there's been no thought to the difference in formats, no allowance for remastering for vinyl, and, as a result, the vinyl sounds pretty terrible. And the equipment used to press vinyl isn't what it used to be. Most of it is old and seemingly in need of a good overhaul.

I've lost count of the number of new vinyl albums I've bought that on first listen have sounded noisy and scratchy. When I fork out $50 or more for a new vinyl record, there is a reasonable expectation that I will not hear scratches on the first play through. Am I asking too much? I don't think so.

For some music, CDs are just perfect. I'm a total and unashamed Deadhead. I love – and then love again – the Grateful Dead and, in various formats, own many hundreds of their recordings, particularly live concerts. The Grateful Dead made studio albums which they openly admit they didn't care too much about, and which didn't really reflect what they were all about. The live performance was central to the band and in that respect vinyl records are a complete pain. A Grateful Dead show is all about the elongated jams, escaping into the experience. And jumping up every 20 or so minutes to turn over a record just kills the engagement.

Classical music – with its often long, long pieces – is also much better suited to the CD or digital format. Same goes for quite a bit of jazz. Like a Grateful Dead performance, it's all about the ebb, flow, build and engagement between the musicians over an extended period.

Mind you, I love old jazz records and collect them semi-obsessively. I'm now listening to an LP by Herbie Mann called *Latin Jazz*. I buy any album I see by the jazz flautist, so long as the asking price isn't crazy. I'm guessing I have well over 100 and I listen to them a lot.

I'm not really a completist and, in fact, don't think I own absolutely everything by anyone. That includes Bob Dylan and Bruce Springsteen – but I do own a *lot* of music by both.

There are – according to a record-dealer mate – at least several hundred Herbie Mann records, so there's still a lot more out there for me to find. If I ever amass a complete collection, I almost certainly won't know, as I'm also not big on keeping lists.

There are degrees of obsessive behaviour in my life. I'm obsessive about *buying* any Herbie Mann album I have, but not obsessive about actually *knowing* which ones I have. Often my dealer mate will send me a message after I've asked to buy one: 'Stuart – I think you bought a copy of this from me last month.'

Part of the reason I don't really know what I have is that I don't keep things in any order. Digital files are easy. You just do a search and it tells you what you have. I'm guessing I have around 15,000 CDs – maybe more; certainly not less. Most of them line the passageway of my home and (thanks to a work-experience kid some years ago) are sort of in alphabetical order: well, by letter at least. All the 'A's are kinda together; ditto for 'B's, and so forth.

They're in precarious piles from the ground up, and I must say that, increasingly, if I need a particular song or album for a radio show it becomes easier to rebuy it on iTunes than scour through the piles to find it. Inevitably, it'll be near the bottom of a pile and the rearranging to get it is just *toooo* hard. I have a torch for such searches as, especially in winter, the passageway can get rather dark and CD spines are hard to read.

Before you ask, the system is by artist surname or first name of band. The Beatles and The Rolling Stones are 'B' and 'R' respectively. What about Alice Cooper's progression from band name to artist name in the mid-'70s? *Welcome To My Nightmare*? Welcome to Stuart's nightmare.

Compilations are all together. Same for film soundtracks. *MOJO* and *Uncut* sampler CDs have their own piles, unless the particular CD is artist specific. Reggae compilations (of which it seems I have a ridiculous number) also have their own pile. Then there are piles and piles of seemingly unrelated and homeless CDs everywhere around the place. Just ask my partner. She will tell you about this.

Vinyl, on the other hand, is completely random in this house. This means that there are piles and piles of records all over the place too – but there's no pretence at them being in alphabetical piles. They used to fit in the shelves and as we found more discarded shelves on the streets – we must have a chat about how we've furnished our home – they, too, filled quickly and now they just spill out everywhere.

'I swear they're breeding,' Susan smiles from time to time. I point out that, whilst she's not as obsessive as I am, her own buying and enthusiasm for music does contribute to the vinyl growth.

The randomness works for me and the way my brain works. It's incredibly frustrating when I actually want to find something quickly – like Television's *Marquee Moon* the other night, as I had a total need to hear it *now* – but I get a kick out of flicking through piles of records (or CDs) and settling randomly on something to listen to. I also have the sort of memory that's pretty good at filing where a particular album is.

It's not perfect but it functions, so that if someone walks in and asks, 'Do you have any Jimmy Buffett albums?', I can say, 'OK, the CD box-set is over there with the other box-sets, individual albums under 'B', but if you want to hear my favourite, *Living And Dying In 3/4 Time*, there's a vinyl copy over there. It should be towards the back of the third pile from the left.'

At its most extreme, I remember walking back into my home after being overseas for a month. A neighbour had been checking in on the house. Almost surreally, I noticed some changes in the Sinatra section of my CDs. On closer examination I realised there were a couple missing. This is in a wall of CDs, remember.

I gently asked the house minder if they'd listened to anything whilst I'd been away. 'Yes, I played a few Sinatra CDs. There's a couple I still have at home – I'll drop them up later today.'

That's what I mean.

But, as I say, the randomness works. It means I'm constantly finding different and unexpected things to listen to and discovering records I haven't played for a long time. And OK, I don't want to get into what format is superior, but when it comes to random flicking, vinyl wins out absolutely every time.

Like so many people, I parted company with a large percentage of my records during the height of the CD boom. I hung on to my then-current collection of about 8000 records until 1998. By this stage I was largely in the world of CDs, the vinyl had been moved from Blackheath to Balmain, and whilst I still listened to it, often I was mainly playing CDs. And I needed money.

So I sold maybe 4000 records – in most cases copies of things I now owned on CD. The price wasn't great – but neither was the demand for vinyl in those days. As far as most people were concerned, its days were over. Some hard-core vinyl obsessives were hanging on – and probably always going to. But most people were off-loading their vinyl, or putting it in boxes in the garage.

I really don't think anyone can honestly look you in the eye and say they knew vinyl would make a return. And don't start me on the so-called cassette revival. Recently I've started noticing things coming out digitally, on vinyl, CD, cassette . . . and eight-track. That used to be my gag: what's next, the eight-track revival? And it's sort of happening.

Did I regret selling any of my records back then? Not really. Well, occasionally. Maybe I should have hung onto the first two Big Star albums on the Ardent label. And selling the Sandy Denny box-set was plain stoopid – but for the most part the sales didn't bug me. Most things are out there if you really want them. And as I said, just so long as I can hear the music I'm pretty OK.

One thing I find endlessly fascinating looking through my current collection is what records have travelled with me through the whole journey. Since I began buying records in the early 1970s, tens of thousands of them have passed through my hands. I've culled my collection for all the usual reasons – most often to pay bills. Other times, it's been out of my hands. Once, I left a bunch of records and books in what I thought was safe storage in Adelaide. When I returned to collect them, they'd all gone – to where, I've never found out.

But through all the culls some records have stayed with me constantly, attached like superglue to my psyche. They've been the soundtrack to every house move, every relationship. I know them all because they have white dots in the top right-hand corner of the cover. They're the lifers.

Then there are the very, very early records, which have impossible-to-remove stickers in the same corner, identifying what number record they were in my buying life and my address at the time: always 19 Walden Street, Newstead 7250. And the date of purchase.

Some of those have gone – others have stayed. I still have my copy of David Bowie's *Ziggy Stardust & The Spiders From Mars*, but I've sold my copy of Dylan's *John Wesley Harding* – which is kinda weird, as it's one of my two or three favourite Dylan albums. I guess I figured I had it on CD – but I also have *Ziggy Stardust* on CD. So what was going on there?

I just found that copy of *Ziggy Stardust* – purchased October 1972 – and whilst doing so I realised I have two copies of Roxy Music's *Siren*. I only need one. Email me with a persuasive reason why you need the extra copy and it could be yours: coupe@laughingoutlaw.com.au.

I'm reminded of a book I read a few years ago about a guy who sold all his records and then, years later, decided he wanted to own them again. Not just any copies of these albums but *his* copies – so he set about tracking them down. The book's called *Old Records Never Die: One Man's Quest For His Vinyl And His Past* by Eric Spitznagel, if you want to search for it.

Here's a story, not about searching for a particular record but having it come back to find me. So when, in 1998, I had my last big vinyl sell-off, one of the records I decided to part with was the first Crosby, Stills & Nash album. I also had it on CD and was in an interim period with listening to it. By that, I mean that I listened to it obsessively as a kid, but grew to know it so well that I didn't feel the need to revisit it that often, plus I'd developed much more of an affection for the next album the trio made – which came with the arrival of Neil Young.

I loved early Neil Young – still do – and his guitar playing added an edge to the first CS&N album. On the debut album they looked like genial hippies. With the addition of Young, as well as Dallas Taylor and Greg Reeves, they looked menacing. They had attitude.

But I digress. I sold my vinyl copy of the first album. And, in all honestly, I didn't think too much about it. Another copy came into my world a few years back. A superior American pressing with a gatefold sleeve that I hadn't even known was part of the deal when I bought the Australian version.

Two brothers-in-law had bought all those records from me – Barry and Ric had a shop in Newtown in Sydney called Egg Records. Ric has since moved back to Brisbane and now runs Rocking Horse Records.

I don't go to Newtown all that often. It's not like it's that far away (it's only three train stops from my place) and Egg Records is right by the railway station, but I tend to go through Newtown rather than to it. And on the few occasions I'd dropped into Egg Records, Baz (as everyone knows him) hadn't been there.

So to cut a potentially long story short I hadn't actually set foot in Egg Records when Baz had been behind the counter since – well – 1998. But that had to change one day – and in fact it did when I was called in for a meeting about a publicity campaign for Jeff Lang, an artist I admire very much. His manager's office was a couple of doors from Egg Records, so after we'd finished, I put my head in for a quick browse before heading to the train.

I'm not sure Baz even knew I was there until I went up to pay for the couple of second-hand records I'd found.

'Stuart,' he exclaimed when he clocked who I was. 'Hang on, I have something for you.'

With that, he left me at the counter and headed to the office at the back of the shop, returning a few minutes later with a copy of the first Crosby, Stills & Nash album. And not just any copy. My copy.

'Here – take this back,' said Baz. 'This was among all the records we bought from you in the '90s, and it's got a sticker on the cover, saying it was one of the first records you bought. We figured we couldn't sell it and that you should have it, so I hung onto it for you.'

That was one of the nicest gestures and unbelievably poignant. I hadn't actually missed the record until I had it in my hands again. And at that point I missed all the records I'd ever sold, because, whilst I'd need a separate house to hold them all, each one had been bought at a particular time and in a particular place. They all had a physical and emotional connection to who I was, and where I'd been in my life.

Most of who I was in 1972 has vanished, along with so many other memories. But there are moments when I hold that record that I can be transported to a time and place – me at that time and place. That CS&N album can conjure up not too many specifics about Stuart Coupe circa 1972/73, but I can sense who I was at that time, in the same way as I can sense who I was when I hold the first Television or Sex Pistols or Clash albums from a few years later.

Is it the object, is it the stickers and handwriting? Is it the music and words? Maybe a bit of them all. But I'll tell you one thing – that's the last time I let go of that CS&N album – and for the life of me, I'd love to remember the first album that I put a sticker on.

Whilst I was writing this book I went back and rebought cheap vinyl copies of some albums I had as a kid. They're all pretty easy to find on eBay – although some are ridiculously expensive, especially the first pressings, which, in many cases, are what I would have had. But I don't care too much about that. The Jimi Hendrix album *Smash Hits* sounds pretty much the same (i.e. very, very great), no matter which version you have.

But the best way I've found to reacquaint myself with those old records combines my home town and a good old-fashioned record shop. Avenue Records in the main drag of Launceston is a fine institution. It has a lot of CDs, but a large array of vinyl, and it's here I often find copies of the records I grew up with.

Of course, I wasn't the only person buying records in Launceston and there were a lot of wonderful collections around. Now, with the passing of time the owners of such collections are either rationalising space in the garage, realising there is cash in those old records, or sadly have passed away and their kids and/or relatives (if they're not afflicted with the love of vinyl and music) are moving those dusty boxes on.

I'm in Launceston two or three times a year, and Callum Nobbes who runs Avenue Records sends out a regular listing of new arrivals. It's amazing how many classics from the 1970s turn up, and usually at a price that's a fraction of what they'd go for in mainland record shops.

When I was running the Laughing Outlaw shop, I didn't really grab too much of what came through the door – and continued from time to time to sell things I'd cull from my own collection and tired of. CDs ruled my life and I was good with that. Less so, as my eyesight deteriorated, and I found the booklets harder and harder to read.

Then – and I can't really pinpoint why – I started buying records again. Maybe it's just that aspergian need to constantly be on the lookout for things – searching and acquiring. I began buying a few vinyl albums. Then more. And more. I started hanging in record shops again – particularly when I was in Melbourne, as that city has always had *the* best record shops. And they started cropping up everywhere. And eBay was always there – and suddenly Facebook Marketplace – and some friends started selling online. Then COVID hit and it seemed a good way to support independent artists – buy their vinyl online.

I also started buying a lot of jazz from the 1950s, '60s and '70s. I'd loved jazz since the mid-1970s but it really fitted by COVID mood – or maybe I'm just using that as an excuse. My friend David Messer travels to Japan frequently and ships back boxes and boxes of amazing jazz from that era, of which it seems there is an endless supply in that country. He sells online to a group of vinyl nerds every Thursday and Sunday night, and rarely does a week go by without me picking up a few items. I realise I get more enjoyment from this than I did from drinking away the money, which is what I did until seven or eight years ago. Often transcendent music and no hangovers.

One thing about jazz is that there is no shortage of things to look for. These cats made a *lot* of records. Four a year was nothing out of the ordinary. If – like me – your taste swings to Sonny Rollins, Albert Ayler, Sonny Clark, Lester Young, John Coltrane, Miles Davis and so forth, there's no shortage of albums to find. Even the ones who died young seem to have made a ridiculous number of records.

And there's still the discovery. My eyes will always go to the interesting cover by an artist I've ever heard of and, more often than not, that or those records will leave the shop with me. Describe something as a ''60s free jazz gem' and I'm sold – even if it's actually a German death-metal album from that era. I'll find that out later when I ask myself, 'What was I thinking?'

# HOUSES OF THE HOLY

I mentioned earlier how, when I was a teenager, I loved a particular furniture and white goods shop in Charles Street, Launceston. Not so much because I was an aficionado of Kelvinator and Frigidaire, but mainly I liked it because it also sold records.

A little later, the town got its own (almost) dedicated record shop – Wills & Co. It also sold radios and other stereo devices, but it was principally a record shop. It had *lots* of records and I wanted pretty much all of them, or at least that's what it felt like. I used to put records on layby – I remember one of them in 1973 being the first Bryan Ferry solo album, *These Foolish Things*. Those were the days.

So, I'd slowly pay off the record. Then I got my first bank card but quickly realised that credit cards and me didn't go together. It wasn't long before my parents were bailing me out after I'd spent a couple of hundred dollars on records. I'd convinced myself that what I earnt at the squash centre would cover it. Of course, it never would, particularly if I continued buying more records.

Towards the end of 1973, I found myself with a part-time Christmas holiday job in the record department at one of the local department stores. I'd never really done much in the way of work experience before. Sure, there'd been a paper run and working at the squash courts – and a day in a hot dusty factory. That induced such a hay fever attack, I had to retire hurt.

A record-selling caper should have been a heap of fun. It wasn't. For starters, the record bar was in the middle of a massive shopping centre. Think Target or Kmart. It therefore attracted those sorts of customers who wanted chart hits, cheapo greatest hits or TV-advertised compilations – and not much else.

It was noisy and I quickly learnt that standing on your feet all day on a hard floor isn't all that much fun – even when you're young. But what hurt the most was the constant – and I mean constant – playing of 'Tie A Yellow Ribbon' by Tony Orlando and Dawn. The single had been a big hit earlier in the year and the album must have been out for Christmas, as the woman who ran the record bar played it non-stop on the record player.

When I'd first heard that song on the radio, I'd hated it with a passion, and by the end of my stint at the record bar – which I recall was starting to feel like a decade, but was in fact just a week – I despised it with an intensity that hasn't dissipated all these years later. I. Hate. That. Song.

As well, I was lucky in that Launceston had a travelling record shop in the form of a large, domineering, supremely opinionated figure by the name of Stefan Markovitch. I mentioned him earlier (don't tell me you've forgotten). He brought the latest hip'n'groovy discs to your school yard, or if you were in Hobart, to the markets at Salamanca Place.

Stefan played an enormous role in my musical education, and I still regularly listen to so many of the albums I bought from him back then. If there is a holy trio of influences on my life in this area, it's John Woodroffe, Rob Smyth and Stefan.

Then there was mail order, which I didn't do much of, but Martin's Records in Sydney offered: bootlegs, illegal concert and studio record-ings that came usually on coloured vinyl and with screen-printed covers. That's how I ended up with some live Rolling Stones, Bob Dylan and Rod Stewart albums. Others came from a company called Bullfrog Records (Toad Hall).

How did I find out about these outlets? Small ads in *Nation Review* and other magazines like *Revolution*, the fledgling *Rolling Stone*, and later in *RAM* and *Juke* most likely. How did I pay? Without a credit card, I'm guessing I sent cash. Would you do such a thing? Probably. (Or maybe a money order, which was kind of like a cheque.)

In 1973, when I went to Perth as part of the Tasmanian team for the Australian squash championships, I came home with second-hand copies of every Lovin' Spoonful album – on Karma Sutra – and the triple album recorded at the last days of the Fillmore in San Francisco and featuring The Grateful Dead, Santana, Quicksilver, It's A Beautiful Day and New Riders Of The Purple Sage. I parted ways with the album at some stage but rebought a copy a few years ago.

My favourite of the Lovin' Spoonful records was – no real surprises here – *Do You Believe In Magic*. So, here's a story involving this particular album. Whilst writing this book I've been listening a lot to records that I had as a kid – and working out which ones went by the wayside, and which ones I kept. This is one of the keepers.

My very first records have stickers with my home address on them; the second wave white dots in the top right-hand corner. So recently I was listening to this Lovin' Spoonful album which was second hand. It had the owner's name printed in pen on the back cover. It was a slightly unusual name, so I looked it up on Facebook. There was one guy with that name. I sent him a message, asking if he lived in Perth in the early 1970s.

A week later, I got a message from him, asking why I wanted to know. I explained. And, lo and behold, it was his. It turned out he'd sold all his records in the early '70s to fund an extended period living in Europe (and then he re-bought all the key items as soon as he had more money).

But the kicker was that, like me, this guy had a lifelong love for The Lovin' Spoonful. I almost fell off my chair when he messaged saying he'd written to John Sebastian – once when he was 15, again in his 30s, and again in his 60s. And each time JB had written back. Like, how cool is that? I told my new buddy about seeing JB in Central Park in NYC a few years ago. He opened his short set, as part of a multi-artist bill celebrating the Woodstock generation, by singing the goosebumps-inducing 'Summer In The City'. It's all about the journey.

These things run deep. Despite selling thousands of records over the years, I've always hung on to those Lovin' Spoonful albums.

# AND KIEDIS, GINSBERG, H. G. NELSON...

As the internet's tentacles crept everywhere, in the mid-1990s I was involved in an early attempt to monetise the cyber world. A group of cashed-up people decided to start what became known as VELVET. It was a music news service/magazine portal that would only be accessible to those who subscribed. Great idea in theory.

The reality was that we were asking people to pay when most of the internet was free and paywalls weren't even a concept. It was way ahead of its time. I was paid really well to contribute to a few issues and go to endless meetings with advertising types. A couple of editions appeared online, and then it disappeared. I still have the t-shirt that was given away at a media launch that virtually no-one came to.

With my freelance work, I made it very clear that I didn't want to interview artists I had no interest in – and if record companies and publicists insisted, I was going to write the piece the way I wanted it. Music writing was increasingly turning into paid advertorial, and I had no interest in being part of that process.

That one came home to roost in the mid-'90s. The Red Hot Chili Peppers were touring on the back of their *One Hot Minute* album. The record label were on my case to do an interview with the band.

At the time I didn't like or appreciate the Peppers nearly as much as I do now. I'm still not a massive fan, but I'm better with them – especially the *Stadium Arcadium* album, which I listened to a lot before going to see them with my daughter Jay, as they were her favourite band at the time. I went thinking I'd suffer through the show, but ended up loving it.

But with *One Hot Minute*, I wasn't into it and told the record company guy the same. He insisted, so I did a telephone interview with Dave Navarro from the band. He was far from forthcoming and I wrote a less than complimentary piece which ran in *The Age*. I think the headline was something like 'One Dull Minute'. The record label hit the roof. The band saw it and were furious. I told the label I'd given them full warning, but they seemed to have forgotten that part.

Then came the invitation from the band to come to their show and go backstage afterwards. Are you fucking kidding? Did they seriously think I'd go for that? What could possibly go wrong? I declined. They insisted. I declined – and kept declining. These days, I'd actually love to meet Flea. And my daughter considers Anthony Kiedis' memoir, *Scar Tissue*, the best book she's ever read, so I'd be pretty happy for 15 minutes in a room with her and Kiedis.

There are many interviews that I'm very fond of, none more so than chatting with one of my Beat Generation heroes. Back in the early 1980s when I was in San Francisco with the Hoodoo Gurus, I made the obligatory homage to City Lights bookshop. One of the central locations for the Beat Generation as it is, and I was downstairs wandering around when I spotted Allen Ginsberg doing the same.

I was too nervous to approach him – plus I was reminded that 'Hello, you don't know me but . . .' encounters often drove me crazy and I was a nobody compared to Ginsberg. So I just followed him around, hoping to see what he saw.

Twenty years later Ginsberg had an unlikely number one on the Triple J Hottest 100, with his long song/piece 'Ballad Of The Skeletons', and I was offered a phone interview with the great poet. We talked for ages in what was one of the last interviews he ever did. At one point, Ginsberg asked me how my love life was. I told him it was pretty good and asked about his. He responded that his was fine too and that he had a couple of younger chaps who helped him get it up. Moments like those in interviews stay with you. I had some amazing opportunities and made the most of them in freelance land.

Over the years, I've done a lot of radio and television appearances, and along the way I've established a reputation as what they call a 'music commentator'. This means that when a big event in the music industry happens, the phone starts ringing. If my phone rings at 5.30 am with a series of blocked-number calls (that's ABC radio policy), I can usually assume someone famous in the music world has died overnight.

I'm often at the ABC in Sydney as a guest on Richard Glover's 'Critics' segment or on the *Book Show*. One day, though, I was walking through the foyer there when I spotted H. G. Nelson, who I've known for years. He didn't initially say hello, just yelled out, 'Who's died?'

There was a time when the going rate for freelance journalism was a dollar a word. And 'a' was a word just as worthy of a dollar as 'extravaganza' or 'sesquipedalian'. You'd score a gig writing a 1500-word piece for a magazine or newspaper and, hells bells, there was a cheque for $1500 waiting at the end.

Newsagents were full of magazines, and newspapers were big and contained more than a few stories and 20 pages of Harvey Norman ads. The weekend editions of *The Age*, *Sydney Morning Herald*, *The Australian* and so forth were huge. As well, during the week there were supplements in the papers every day. I once earnt $1200 for a piece on crime-themed computer games back when the *Herald* had a computer liftout once a week.

But in the same way as video apparently killed the radio star, so the internet largely killed the freelance writing caper. Sure, there are lots of outlets – maybe too many. But they pay peanuts if they pay at all. For publications, it's a buyer's market and the pay rates have shrunk. Remember the dollar a word days? It went to 60 cents, then 30 . . .

These days – for those reasons – I don't do much freelance writing. I'm a Senior Editor at *Rhythms* magazine. I enjoy writing for them and there's the occasional request to contribute to a magazine or paper from time to time, but I don't actively pursue it.

I love many, many things about the internet – who doesn't? But I sure miss poring over big newspapers and getting ink all over my fingers. And I miss big piles of magazines everywhere. Maybe I'm just getting (a little) older.